PRAISE FOR *KARMA GONE BAD*

"A wonderful adventure of self-discovery. I could not put this book down. It is a delight and awakens your senses while sweeping you away. I could almost taste the chai and smell the spices of India."

—Soleil Moon Frye, author of *Happy Chaos*
and *Let's Get This Party Started*

"I LOVED it. I would never, ever have the courage (or stomach) to live in India for two years, and now I don't have to because I lived vicariously through Jenny in the pages of her book. I couldn't put it down for days, completely addicted to the experience of her lifetime. Plus? No malaria pills for me!"

—Jill Smokler, *New York Times* bestselling
author of *Confessions of a Scary Mommy*

"Warm, funny, evocative, endowed with a winning voice and a moving conclusion."

—Vivian Gornick, critic, essayist, and author of
The End of the Novel of Love, *Fierce
Attachments: A Memoir*, and *The Men in My Life*

"I'm incredibly tempted to put Jenny on a plane to another exotic locale just so I can read another compelling, hilarious take on the city gal gone native. *Karma Gone Bad* is just that good."

—April Peveteaux, author of *Gluten Is My Bitch:
Rants, Recipes, and Ridiculousness for the Gluten-Free*

"Jenny Feldon's generously told and absolutely addictive memoir is about learning to embrace the unexpected, not just in our environment, but within ourselves. This well-crafted story is a perfect reminder that we often emerge from life's biggest challenges with gratitude that they arose in the first place."

—Claire Bidwell Smith, author of *The Rules of Inheritance*

KARMA GONE BAD

HOW I LEARNED TO LOVE MANGOS, BOLLYWOOD, AND WATER BUFFALO

JENNY FELDON

Sourcebooks and the colophon are registered trademarks of Sourcebooks, Inc.

This book is a memoir. It reflects the author's present recollections of her experiences over a period of years. Some names and characteristics have been changed, some events have been compressed, and some dialogue has been re-created.

Published by Sourcebooks, Inc.

P.O. Box 4410, Naperville, Illinois 60567-4410

(630) 961-3900

Fax: (630) 961-2168

www.sourcebooks.com

Library of Congress Cataloging-in-Publication data is on file with the publisher.

Printed and bound in the United States of America..

VP 10 9 8 7 6 5 4 3 2 1

for Jay

AUTHOR'S NOTE

Karma Gone Bad is a true story. Most names have been changed to protect the privacy of the individuals who shared this journey with me. For the sake of storytelling, the timeline has been altered in places and a few characters have been combined.

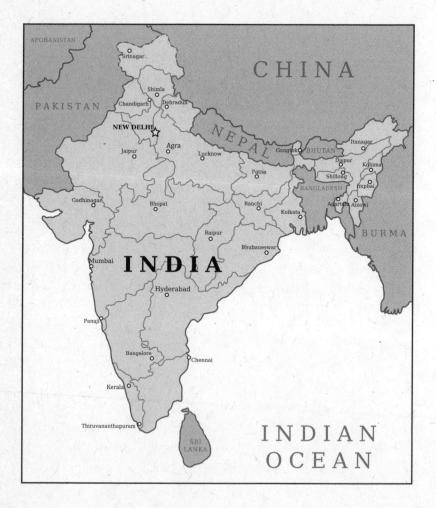

PROLOGUE

I just need another minute."

The cab driver grunted and spit out the window. I stood on Ninth Avenue in the pouring rain, huddled over the taxi's trunk. Inside was a mountain of rainbow-colored fabric, designer dresses I'd spent years coveting, collecting, and paying off on my MasterCard. Once, they'd hung proudly in the closet of our Upper West Side one bedroom. Now they were crushed in a sad, wrinkled heap next to an ancient bottle of window washer fluid, a case of Yoo-hoo, and half a dozen water-logged emergency flares. And they, like me, were about to be shipped off to the third world.

Double parked next to us, unfazed by the angry slur of horns whizzing by, was another cab. My husband Jay sat in the back, his foot propping the door open just enough to communicate but not enough to let the rain soak his Armani suit. He was on his way to work. I was on my way to brunch at Pastis. We'd met halfway so he could confiscate my entire dress collection, which I'd planned to pack in my carry-on luggage.

"Pick ONE," Jay said, gritting his teeth. "One for the party. That's it."

"But…"

"It'll be fine, Jen. I promise. You'll have them back in a couple of days." He picked up his BlackBerry and scrolled through his messages, the technological equivalent of an exasperated eye roll.

In forty-eight hours, we were moving to India.

India, the country.

Jay had decided, at half-past the eleventh hour, that we were bringing too much stuff on the airplane. By "we," of course, he meant me. Our apartment was already packed into a shipping container the size of an eighteen-wheeler. The apartment looked desolate and empty now, inexplicably smaller without our four-year collection of belongings cluttering its hardwood floors.

The *Moving Guide for Expatriates* Jay's company sent in the mail recommended taking our essentials as carry-on luggage to safeguard against accidental losses. He and I had different definitions for "essentials." For Jay, that meant his laptop, his BlackBerry, and his red fleece sleeping hat. For me, that meant four pairs of designer shoes, two hundred manuscript pages of my novel-in-progress, the dog's teddy bear, and an assortment of cocktail dresses. Plus the dog himself, a small white Maltese named Tucker.

Preparing for Tucker's move had been even more complicated than preparing for ours. First, there was the stockpiling. Two years' worth of training pads, dehydrated chicken breasts, and chew toys. A velvety blanket for inside his carrier so he wouldn't get cold or insecure on the plane. A travel-sized stuffed animal, because his favorite was too big to fit in my carry-on bag. His favorite stuffed animal was a brown Gund teddy bear named Bear. I'd never seen Tucker look as sad as he did the day Bear got wrapped in plastic and tossed into a cardboard box, sentenced to a journey by sea. I took one last look at the dresses in my arms and understood exactly how he'd felt.

I rescued a white strapless Diane von Furstenberg as Jay leapt from his cab and snatched the rest away.

"See you tonight," Jay called as he dove back into his cab and slammed the door. The cab darted back into traffic. Through the rear window, I watched him brush off his lapels, the rest of his body swallowed by a mass of chiffon and lace-edged satin. The gold-embroidered hem of the Cynthia Steffe I'd worn to our rehearsal dinner was trapped in the door jam, trailing in the muddy street. I shouted after him, but the rain was too loud and by the time I got the words out, he was already gone.

"Come on, lady," my cab driver bellowed, his "meter's-running" complacency abruptly disappearing into the mid-city fog. "Get in or walk. It's like a monsoon out here. I can't wait all day."

We sloshed downtown. Traffic, as always, was oppressive. The day stretched before me, my swan song in the big city. First there were farewell burgers and mimosas at Pastis with my best friend Kate. Then a visit to the salon for blow-outs and manicures, and then the going-away party Kate and her husband were throwing for us tonight. I'd wear the white strapless DVF with gold stiletto sandals and drink too much champagne. Laugh at our friends' jokes about curry and call centers and holy cows. Make a speech about big dreams and big adventures, not making eye contact with anyone so the tears would stay put. Wear waterproof mascara, just in case.

"Seventeen-twenty, lady," the cab driver barked. I handed him a twenty and climbed out into the rain, the yellow warmth behind Pastis's windows beckoning like a lighthouse. Before I could even close the door properly, he made a U-turn and screeched off, spraying my legs with gray water that lurched up from the overflowing gutter.

Was I going to miss this? The rude taxi drivers, the claustrophobic subways, the grit and the rush and the perpetual sneer of the Big Apple? More than I could say. From the minute I had moved to Manhattan from the Boston suburb where I'd grown up, my soul felt at home in a way I'd never known before. I loved the lights and the skyscrapers, the crowded streets. The exhilarating feeling of humanity—fervent, focused—scrambling over each other with a single collective purpose: *GO*.

I loved Central Park and hot dog vendors, walks along the Hudson River, and the bodega on the corner of Seventy-Second and Broadway where I bought my coffee every morning. I loved the underground vibrations of the subway, the collective pulsing energy of 1.6 million people trying to make their dreams come true.

I thought we'd live in New York forever. I'd just finished my master's degree in creative writing; Jay worked in computer forensics at a Big Four accounting firm. First there would be my debut novel, then his partnership, then one day a red Bugaboo stroller parked in the lobby of the Upper West Side brownstone we'd rent—a two-bedroom with a tiny sliver of park view. In the meantime, there would be art museums and yoga classes and dog parks and late-night drinks with friends. There would be vacations in the Hamptons or St. Barth's.

Then Jay came home one night, a night that should have been a typical Tuesday spent curled up on our worn blue couch with pad thai from Siam Inn. But instead of asking me to order extra spring rolls, Jay walked in, dropped his briefcase in the doorway, and looked around our apartment like he'd never seen it before.

"BKC wants me to move to India," he said. "To start up the new practice."

Berkeley, King & Coolidge, BKC for short, was the global accounting firm Jay worked for. Bill Gates had been the first American to stick his corporate flag in the crumbling Hyderabadi soil, instantly transforming the barely developed Indian city into the newest stomping ground for dozens of international companies. BKC was an early adopter of the overseas model, tapping into the talent of India's rising technology stars to create a U.S.-owned, Indian-run outpost—nicknamed Region 10—that could process investigations at twice the speed and half the cost of its American counterpart. With the Region 10 office running a full nine and a half hours ahead of Eastern Standard Time, BKC would be able to serve their clients' needs twenty-four hours a day. Jay had been talking about the India project for months. Now, it seemed he'd been chosen to get the entire operation up and running.

I stared up at him with Tucker on my lap. It was like he'd just said something in Mandarin. Or Urdu. I couldn't wrap my mind around the words.

"India?" I repeated. "India, like the country?"

"For two years. They said we could think about it, but I don't know if we really have a choice. I think we have to go."

℘

It's karma! That's what everyone said when we broke the news. I'd been studying yoga for ages. I was the manager of a busy Upper West Side Bikram studio. What better adventure for a dedicated yogini like me than a pilgrimage to India: the birthplace of yoga, the spiritual homeland of the Far East? And for a writer, a life abroad was the holy grail. *Think of Hemingway! Think of Gertrude Stein!* People said these things, and I smiled and nodded and agreed. Because, just like with the move itself, I didn't really have a choice. Fate—and a multinational corporation—had chosen this path for me.

Sure, OK. It was a dream come true, right? I'd visit ashrams and study with real live yoga masters. My blog, *Karma in the City*—formerly a journal about Manhattan living—would become a travelogue, full of photographs and anecdotes about my exotic new life. My literary dreams could still come true—I'd just have to chase them from the Far East instead of the Upper West Side. Instead of living the New York writer's life, I'd become the best Indian housewife anyone had ever seen. Jay and I would become citizens of the world. I would make an "Indian bucket list" for all the amazing things we would do, like ride elephants and visit the Taj Mahal. Maybe we'd like it so much we'd stay expats forever, roaming from one exotic country to the next. Moving to India was the opportunity of a lifetime. A gift from the universe. Karma at its very best.

Except…not really. The truth was, I'd never had the urge to travel farther outside U.S. borders than Cabo San Lucas, where we'd gone for our honeymoon. My wanderlust was satisfied with a ride on the R train to Brooklyn. Ashrams weren't really my style; I was perfectly happy practicing my asanas on Seventy-Second Street overlooking the M-13 bus stop. I loved our life. I loved New York. Everything we'd ever wanted or needed was right here in front of us—our family, our friends, our happily ever after.

Jay and I were both twenty-seven years old. We'd been married less than a year. Our lives were mapped out in a way that did not include international visas or typhoid vaccinations or pamphlets on common Hindi phrases. I lived by Zagat, not Lonely Planet. Yet here I was, soaking wet in Jimmy Choo sling backs on the side of Ninth Avenue, clutching a lone cocktail dress that I'd soon realize was as useless and ill-suited to life in India as I was.

INDIAN SUMMER

CHAPTER 1

There were no lights.

The seat-belt sign was on, our carry-on luggage was stowed, and a dull ache in my ears confirmed the changing pressure of descent. But out the window, over the massive wing of the Airbus A340 that was delivering us to our new life, everything was dark. Beneath us, I could feel the grind and clank of the plane's landing gear. I pressed my forehead against the window and rubbed at my contacts, which were shriveled in my eyes like plastic wrap from twenty-four straight hours of wear. There must be a control tower, an airport terminal, a runway down there. My worst neurotic-flier fears kicked in: *the pilot made a terrible mistake, the plane ran out of fuel, our adventure was over before it even began.*

Tucker growled softly in my lap. I stroked the fur behind his ears, but he saw right through my fake reassurance to the anxiety beneath. Dogs are good like that. He growled again, deeper. I reached over and grabbed Jay's hand. He squeezed back, still slumped in his seat, his red fleece ski hat pulled down over his ears so his head wouldn't touch the germy back of the airplane seat. In New York, he'd brought the hat with him every time he traveled on business, too much of a germaphobe to sleep without a layer of protection between his skin and the hotel sheets. He called it his "sleeping hat."

"Ladies and gentlemen, we are making our final descent into Hyderabad. Please ensure your seat belts are fastened and your seats are in the upright position. *Dhanyavad*, and thank you."

I stared out the window again, and now I could see them…faint, orange dots of dusty light that formed a narrow strip below us, an almost-invisible pathway in the vast darkness. Located in the southern state of Andhra Pradesh, Hyderabad was supposed to be a *city*, an up-and-coming metropolis in the "cone" part of India's ice-cream shape on the map. Shouldn't there be lights? Buildings? No city I'd ever seen looked so dark from the sky. I closed my eyes. The plane bumped and jerked, touched down.

"Welcome to India," said the voice over the loudspeaker. "You are here."

This was really happening.

I grabbed my carry-on bag, a white monogrammed Yves Saint Laurent I'd gotten for graduation. It was the first designer handbag I'd ever owned.

"Don't you think you should take something a little more practical?" Jay had asked, watching me arrange and rearrange its contents for the hundredth time, carefully wiping my fingerprints off the bag's shiny leather. "Something less expensive, less…white?"

I'd ignored him and packed the YSL with essentials: sunglasses, lip gloss, fuzzy pink socks so my feet wouldn't get cold on the plane. A bottle of malaria pills. Dog treats for Tucker. A copy of *Lonely Planet: India*. I tried to read it on the plane, but I couldn't concentrate. I was still reliving everything that had come *before*: before I worked my last shift at the yoga studio; before we said champagne-soaked, sentimental good-byes to our friends; before we turned in our apartment keys to Eddie, the doorman, who took off his crimson-and-gold cap and saluted like we were going off to war. I was waiting for that moment when it would all sink in, when it would become our reality instead of something we talked about in foggy hypotheticals. Like the moment in a dark theater just before the movie begins, India had been something that was *about to happen* for so long I kept forgetting that, one day, it was going to be real.

In the shuffle of passengers getting ready to disembark, I looked for Jay, expecting him to take the first step off the plane with me. It would be symbolic, like the groom carrying the bride over the threshold. Except on *our* wedding day, Jay had raced me to the bathroom so he could brush his teeth first, then passed out in the hotel bed before I'd finished unpinning my veil. As if to prove our new life would still have the comfortingly familiar elements of our old one, Jay had already disappeared down the Jetway, determined to be first in the customs line.

At least I had Tucker to help me savor the moment. I patted the side of his carrier bag. He growled in reply, scratching at the zipper. "Just a few more minutes, buddy," I whispered. I thanked the pilot and stepped off the plane with my right foot, a superstitious gesture of gratitude for a safe arrival. Then I walked straight into a wall.

That's what it felt like, anyway. Never before had an atmosphere felt so physical, so oppressive. I rocked back on my heels, disoriented by the onslaught of heat and smells. The air felt like it was boiling around me, damp and thick, scented with a combination of spices and mold and camphor and trash. The ceiling of the airport was low and uneven, lit with naked bulbs that threw shadows across mildew stains creeping along the walls. Beneath my feet were beautiful mosaics, works of art being trampled and forgotten as three hundred people shoved their way into the customs lines, clutching cases of— were those chocolate bars?—with determined expressions.

"Do you have anything to declare?" asked the customs agent, his brow furrowed as he studied our packet of travel documents. "Weapons, alcohol, chocolate, meats?"

"No, but we have a dog," I said, pushing a pile of paperwork toward him. Tucker had needed almost as much entry paperwork as we did: an international health exam, full medical records and vaccination reports, a special visa from the embassy in New York. Even a U.S. pet passport I'd custom-ordered online, complete with a government-standard photo of his furry, bewildered face.

The customs agent ignored me. He stamped our passports so hard he tore the paper. "Step through x-ray over there and then claim your belongings."

"But what about the dog?" I asked. People at home told me horror stories about pets being quarantined. I'd chain myself to the customs desk before I'd let them take Tucker away. I planted my feet, ready to fight. No one was taking my dog anywhere. He was American. He had rights.

The agent looked right through me to a woman in a sari holding a twenty-four-pack of Reese's peanut butter cups.

"Next in queue."

"I can't put the dog through the *x-ray*," I whispered to Jay, hurrying to keep up with him.

"Just take him out of the bag; it'll be fine." He reached in and patted Tucker on the head. "We could have brought a dragon here, and as long as it wasn't holding a Hershey bar or a rib-eye steak, we'd have been all set."

The baggage claim area was packed. Children ran everywhere,

pushing metal luggage carts around, climbing onto the ancient, creaking luggage carousel and riding it like a surfboard until their hassled parents grabbed them away. We waited.

An hour later, an ear-splitting siren announced the arrival of the luggage. One bag at a time made its way around the dilapidated circle, each one more dust-covered and exhausted-looking than the last, like they'd made the passage from Germany on the back of a camel. Some of the bags were marked with giant chalk Xs.

"What do you think those mean?" I asked. Jay was prowling the edges of the carousel, looking for the black set of Samsonites we'd bought for our new world-traveler lifestyle. Another chalk-marked bag, an old-school plaid suitcase with a metal frame, moved toward us. Just before its owner could reach it, a security guard snatched it away, barking orders over his shoulder as he hauled it toward a metal door near the exit.

"I'm guessing something bad," Jay said as the appalled-looking owner chased after the guard, his distressed pleadings swallowed in the noise of the crowd.

Bags collected, more papers stamped, and we were finally ready to leave the airport. It was four o'clock in the morning in Hyderabad; I expected it to be quiet and tranquil outside. The solemn dawn of a new day, a new life. Wheeling our suitcases behind us, we stepped out of the airport and into absolute chaos.

A thousand eyes stared back at us from behind a chain-link fence. The drone of chatter came to a halt as we appeared—two pale, stunned Westerners before an endless sea of brown skin and bright fabric. Their sudden silence felt accusatory. Entire families were camped outside the airport, waiting to welcome their loved ones home. Jay and I weren't the brothers or nephews they'd been hoping to see, but pale-skinned interlopers wearing the wrong clothes and unable to keep the shock from showing on our faces.

My skin crawled as those eyes raked over me. I felt like an exotic zoo animal on display, but with no cage to protect me from the tidal wave of aggressive curiosity. A dark-haired child ran forward to touch my arm, giggling as her mother pulled her back into the crowd. Her siblings huddled around her, whispering.

Staring back into the ocean of bodies, I made eye contact with a woman, her wrinkled face the only skin visible inside the orange and gold fabric swathed around her like a cocoon. She hissed and pointed at me. I glanced down at my bare shoulders, my naked collar bone, the swathe of skin visible between my tank top and the waistband of my low-rise jeans. I should have read the *Lonely Planet*. I'd been in Hyderabad less than two hours—hadn't even made it out of the airport—and already I had the distinct impression I was getting it all wrong.

Auto rickshaws were idling in disorganized rows. These rickshaws, called "autos" in Hyderabad and "tuk-tuks" or "tempos" in other parts of India, were essentially tricycles with motorcycle engines and horns that sounded like shrieking ducks. They were made of tin, without doors or windows. Painted yellow with black checkered plastic awnings, the rickshaws looked like puttering, miniaturized New York taxi cabs. Looking at them made me homesick.

Jay scanned the crowd, looking for a sign with our name on it. I huddled behind him, shielding myself from the onslaught of stares. My New York bravado had inexplicably gone missing. Tucker trembled in his bag. I set my purse down so I could reach my hand in and soothe him. Instantly, a man wearing only a white *dhoti*—the Indian menswear equivalent of a giant cloth diaper—appeared out of nowhere, grabbed my bag, and ran.

I opened my mouth to scream.

"Is OK, Madam! I having!" someone yelled. A teenager—black

T-shirt, black knit beanie, wide-leg acid-washed hip-hop jeans—hurtled past me. He dodged stray dogs and sleeping humans, leaping over suitcases in pursuit of the would-be thief.

"*Apandi*! *Donga Ni*!" he cried in Telugu. He caught up with the *dhoti* man just as he tossed my YSL bag into the back of a brightly painted auto rickshaw, its tiny lawn-mower-like engine still running. A scuffle ensued. The beanie-wearing teenager won, hurling one last rude gesture over his shoulder before he came bounding back to my side with the sly, graceful energy of a fox. He placed the bag at my feet.

"I am Venkat Reddy," he said, holding out his hand and removing the beanie to reveal a rumpled pompadour of glossy black hair. "I am your driver. Welcome Hyderabad. You are being here."

Jay and I stared at him. He waited, hand extended, the other tucked deep into a pocket decorated with a thick metal chain. Finally Jay shook hands with him. Venkat pumped his arm up and down enthusiastically.

"Thanks for saving my bag," I said, my heart still racing.

"You are having more of suitcase? The car I am parking over there. I bringing."

"You're our driver? I thought we were just taking a taxi. My company sent a form." Jay fumbled through the manila file of documents he'd been clutching since JFK.

"You are Jay Sir, yes? BKC is sending me. Being part of Team Assist for American workers. I am working BKC six months now. Much good record. Now my leaving, be personal driver for you and Madam." Venkat looked down after his speech, suddenly shy. He stirred up a cloud of dust with the toe of a newly polished shoe.

"Well, OK. Thanks," Jay said, looking at me, his eyebrows raised in confused submission. We followed Venkat through the crowd. He stopped in front of a battered tan Hyundai.

"Foreign car, Sir and Madam. Much good," Venkat said with pride. "Company car. For borrow until you are having your own." He opened the doors and waited for us to climb inside.

Jay and I were among BKC's first expats on long-term assignment in India. Most of the other U.S. employees were in Hyderabad on temporary, three-month rotations, which meant BKC handled all the details for them. They were given per diem food allowances, assigned to corporate housing (often with roommates), and shared drivers from a pool that served the entire company. Being long-term residents, plus my status as an accompanying spouse, meant Jay and I would need to make different arrangements for our stay than the short-term expats. We had to take care of things such as opening a bank account, leasing our own house, and purchasing a car. Team Assist would help us get started, but for the majority of our stay in Hyderabad, we'd be on our own. Looking around at the airport madness, I shuddered a little at the thought.

"Jay! Jenny! Wait!" I whipped around, convinced I was hearing things. We didn't know a soul in Hyderabad. No one was expecting us. Yet there they were—a tall guy with glasses, a petite brunette—jumping up and down and waving from twenty yards away. Their white faces peering out over the crowd of Indian people looked like a scene from *Where's Waldo*.

Jay and I looked at each other, perplexed, as the couple came rushing over. He was wearing a navy blue polka-dotted bow tie and held a jar of peanut butter and a giant bottle of water. Her arm was in a sling.

"We heard you two were coming in tonight," the guy said, extending his hand to Jay. "I'm Peter. This is my girlfriend, Alexis. You're gonna need this." He handed me the water, a squashed plastic liter labeled "Himalaya" with a pink drawing of mountains on the side.

"We're expats with BKC too. I'm in tax. Welcome to 'Bad. Don't drink the water."

Alexis smiled. "I'm not in tax, just the plus one on his work visa. I'd shake your hand, but…" She gestured to the sling, which was actually a batik-print scarf tied over one shoulder. "I'm a little out of sorts at the moment."

"What happened?"

"Bug bite. We're not sure what kind. It swelled up like crazy overnight, and we had to call the doctor. He gave me this ointment and a couple of pills and told me to wear a sling. The scarf was the best I could do."

"Whole thing cost two hundred rupees," Peter said proudly.

"Is that a lot?" I asked.

"Like four dollars," Jay replied. "What are you guys doing here? Isn't it like four o'clock in the morning?"

"Meeting you," Peter said with a grin. "We figured you'd need some help finding your way around."

It was the nicest thing anyone had ever done for us. My eyes stung, a combination of the dust in the air and the kindness of these strangers who'd waited for us in a crowded airport in the dead of night.

"We should get out of here before the traffic gets worse," Alexis said. She spoke to a uniformed man behind her. "Younus, they'll follow us." She jumped into a tiny white car with the engine idling. "Meet you at Matwala Shayar!" Peter winked at us and climbed in next to her, his legs folding comically in the cramped backseat.

Venkat and Younus conferred in Telugu, then did a complicated hand sign/backslap combination before taking their respective places behind the wheel. The steering wheels were on the right-hand side. It made the car seem cartoonish, like I was on a ride at Disneyland.

"My friend," Venkat said by way of explanation. "Younus. Driving Peter Sir and Sir Madam. Also living Matwala Shayar."

"Sir Ma'am?" I whispered to Jay.

"I think he means Alexis," he answered. Tucker sneezed. Venkat startled at the noise. "Madam?" Venkat asked, gesturing to the carrier bag. "Bag making…sounds?"

I unzipped the top and Tucker's head sprang free like a furry, white jack-in-the-box. Venkat yelped and folded himself flat against the dashboard. Tucker yawned, stretched, and sniffed the air around him furiously, trying to get a read on his new surroundings.

"Madam, is ANIMAL," Venkat said, braving another look. "Is your animal? Is coming on plane?"

"This is Tucker. He's our dog," I said. "He came with us on the plane, yes."

"Is pet?" Venkat asked.

"Yes, pet." I picked up *Lonely Planet: India* and flipped to the phrase section in the back. "*Kuta?*" I tried. "Dog?"

Venkat shrugged and swerved onto the main road, peeling out into traffic faster than seemed advisable, even at this time of night. "Would you like mine giving Sir and Madam tour on way Matwala Shayar?"

"Sure," we said at the same time.

He grinned and hit the gas.

Venkat Reddy, we'd soon learn, was much more than just a name. "Reddy" was also Venkat's caste, setting him apart from legions of other drivers with less illustrious backgrounds. The Reddys in Hyderabad started out as rulers and warriors in ancient days. Later they became respected farmers and landowners, recognized through-out the state of Andhra Pradesh as village aristocrats. Being a Reddy accounted for the swagger in Venkat's walk—and, I suspected, the mischievous twinkle in his eye and cocky angle of his carefully coiffed head. In the months that followed, any question of his knowledge or authority on a subject was snuffed out by a single sentence: "I am Reddy, Madam and Sir. I knowing best."

Venkat's tour was definitely *not* approved by the Hyderabadi Board of Tourism, if there even was such a thing. I'd expected temples and monuments and landmarks. But Venkat was only interested in showing us things that made us gasp. Exposed power lines dangling over pools of stagnant water. *Dhoti*-clad men clinging to giant plungers while they washed the windows of four-story buildings in total darkness, no helmets or safety ropes in sight. A family of stray dogs huddled together inches from the road—panting in the heat, clearly starving. "Hyderabad, many things much danger," Venkat informed us.

The darkness was fading into a hazy orange dawn. There were fields of burnt grass and tent cities. Buildings alongside the road were half-demolished, their fronts literally sliced away, revealing dioramas of abandoned life: broken toilets, clotheslines with brightly colored squares of fabric still stirring in the breeze. A sign hanging askew from a rotting wooden post read "Welcome MADHAPUR." I used to be a New Yorker. Now, what was I? A Hyderabadi? A Madhapurite? Exhausted, I closed my eyes for a minute, trying to wrap my mind around it all.

When I opened them, we were surrounded by cows. Enormous cows with long white horns sticking out from their black, menacing heads. I leapt into Jay's lap. "Cows! Are cows much danger, Venkat?"

Venkat laughed. "No cows, Madam. Buffalo. Many buffalo. They looking food during nighttimes when no so much cars." He honked, but the buffalo ambled on, oblivious. One turned its massive head and stared into my window. We made eye contact. I looked away first. Yikes.

"Is better see buffalo at nighttimes," Venkat said sagely. "In daytimes buffalo much tired, sometimes sleeping at check posts. Traffic making for very bad." He slowed the car to a crawl. Ahead of us there was nothing—no lights, no buildings, no tents. Just as I convinced myself this strange Indian teenager was driving us straight off the ends of the earth, a giant white arch loomed out of the darkness: HITEC CITY.

"We are being here," Venkat said, pulling off the road into a cluster of buildings separated from the road by a circular driveway. The entrance was blocked with a rusted metal gate. A mustached security guard, stooped and gaunt in his worn tan uniform, asked Venkat a bunch of questions. Finally, shining his flashlight in our weary faces, he waved us through.

"This is it," Jay said. "Matwala Shayar. This is home. Until we find our own place, anyway."

Alexis and Peter pulled up behind us. A pounding techno bass streamed from an apartment on the second floor, reverberating across the concrete. Shouts of laughter, followed by the sound of clinking bottles, floated into the night.

"Isn't it pretty late for people to be up?" I asked, staring at the lit-up windows above us.

Alexis made a face. "There's a lot of late-night partying at Matwala Shayar," she said. "You get used to it. Or you can sleep with earplugs, like Peter does. Most of the expats work American hours, two in the afternoon to midnight or later. Once they're done with their shifts, a lot of them party all night and sleep until noon. It's kind of like a frat house. Only instead of keg stands, they light absinthe shots on fire."

"Really?" Jay looked impressed. I nudged him with an elbow. That was so not the kind of party scene I'd had in mind.

Out of the shadows, a small, thin Indian man appeared, shivering in a beige knit sweater. I was still sweating in my tank top.

"Jay Sir?" the man asked, looking us up and down.

"That's me," Jay said, stepping forward. Venkat began to empty the trunk. "This is my wife, Jenny."

"I am Subu," he said. "I am being the manager of Matwala Shayar luxury apartments. I am here for your comfort and convenience. When there is something needing, you will be finding me." He held a key ring in one hand and a loaf of sliced white bread in the other. "Are you ready to see your flat, Jay Sir?" He noticed the small crowd behind us—Venkat, Younus, Peter, and Alexis—and did an anxious double take.

"Peter Sir? Sir Ma'am?" Subu asked. "Is there being a problem in your flat?"

"No, we're just helping these guys get settled," Peter said, giving him a reassuring pat on the back. Subu staggered from the unexpected force. Peter, at six foot three, towered above him.

Subu managed a smile. "Very well, Sir, if you all will be following me. Jay Sir and Madam will be staying in Alpha block." He jingled the keys. We followed in a solemn, single-file procession through a dim parking garage into a narrow, stifling elevator that groaned under our weight, up one floor and then down a trash-filled hallway to a black metal door marked 112. Subu produced the key and opened the door with a flourish. "Your new home, Sir and Madam. I am hoping for your continued happiness here. May I be giving you the tour?"

I nodded, praying that this tour had fewer dangerous things.

"May I be presenting your elephant swing, Sir and Madam," Subu said, bowing his head and caressing the thick gold chains of a wooden swing suspended from the living room ceiling. I squinted at it with blurry eyes. It was, indeed, carved into the shape of an elephant. "It is being the perfect place for relaxing after your very long journey," Subu added.

After twenty-four straight hours of travel and the strange, livestock-filled ride home from the airport, all I wanted was to collapse in bed somewhere and sleep for a week. But Subu was intent on showing us each individual detail of our new Indian home. He was especially proud of the bathroom, where the toilet was inexplicably mounted smack in the middle of a green-tiled shower stall. (*"All the modern conveniences, Sir and Madam!"*) The kitchen window offered a view of a building site that bustled with activity despite the unusual hour. Women wearing cotton saris and construction hats balanced cement blocks on their heads in the predawn light.

"And this, Sir and Madam, will be your *puja* room," Subu said grandly, gesturing to the left.

"What's a *puja* room?" Jay asked. Subu beamed with joy and opened the latticed double doors to reveal the most perfect dog bedroom I'd ever seen.

"It's a room just for Tucker!" I exclaimed, overjoyed.

Inside the room were dozens of statues. The smallest, an elephant sitting cross-legged on top of some sort of rodent, was no bigger than my thumb. The largest, a blue man in a giant headdress playing the flute, was almost as tall as I was. The room had a low ceiling and a row of tiny windows with glossy wood-paneled walls. It was perfect for Tucker. I imagined where his bed and toys would go, once we got rid of all the clutter.

"This is the most important room in the flat, of course. You will be having all the idols you need to do prayers here, Sir," Subu said, beaming with pride.

"We can get rid of all this stuff, right?" I asked at the same time.

At that moment, Tucker's scratching finally broke through the zipper of his bag, which I'd left open a crack so he could have some air. He leapt to the floor and headed straight for the *puja* room, clearly recognizing it as his domain.

Subu screamed. Venkat looked appalled. Peter and Alexis laughed out loud. Even Younus couldn't keep the smirk off his face. Tucker sniffed at the feet of a statue of a woman with a lot of arms.

"Sir! Madam! Please! Get your wild animal away from Lakshmi!" Subu scooted toward Tucker, then darted away, waving his arms in frustration. "The *puja* room is sacred! No wild animals will be being allowed!"

"He's not a wild animal," I said, insulted. "He's a Maltese."

CHAPTER 2

I woke up to the sound of hammers. Next to me, Jay was sprawled on his back, his red fleece hat pulled low over his ears. Tucker was curled upside down near Jay's shoulder. The air conditioner had clanked to a halt sometime after we'd finally climbed into bed and now the room was sweltering. I stretched my arms over my head and winced. Our new Indian bed consisted of an inch-thick foam pad on top of a creaking wooden platform. My aching back already missed the Crown Jewel mattress that was floating somewhere in the Atlantic, packed into a container ship with the rest of our belongings.

Without an international SIM card, my cell had no service at all, which meant it was useless both as a clock and a phone. Not that I had anyone to call. Still set to New York time, the digital display said 3:00 a.m. I wasn't sure what time that made it in India; my brain was too foggy to tackle so much math. Daylight streamed through the curtainless windows. I stumbled toward the kitchen.

The refrigerator was empty. Subu's loaf of bread was still on the counter. Peter and Alexis had left the jar of Skippy and another of

Smucker's strawberry jam next to the bread, along with a Post-it where Alexis had scribbled her Indian cell phone number. "You're going to need these," the note said. I'd never been so overjoyed to see peanut butter in my life.

I made myself a sandwich and hunted around for a coffeemaker. There was none. My head throbbed, an early warning sign of the full-on, caffeine-addict migraine brewing behind my forehead. I looked out the window at the construction site. The women had ceased their steadfast, antlike movements and were squatting on their heels in a circle, digging rice out of metal cylinders with their hands. Between bites there was a flurry of conversation. Strewn on the ground around them were piles of discarded yellow hard hats. But instead of being smooth and round on top, the hats had open plastic tubes in the center. That must be how they balanced those giant dishes of concrete and water on top of their heads.

A peek back into the bedroom confirmed that my husband and my dog were still asleep. I found a pen in my bag and scribbled a note on the back of a boarding pass: *Looking for coffee. Back soon.* I looked around for a key to the apartment but found none. It felt weird to leave the house with nothing: no keys, no cell phone, no cash. Wherever the coffee was, I hoped they took AmEx.

I opened the front door slowly, trying not to wake Jay. As I pushed the door forward, it banged into something solid. A huddled form collapsed onto my ankles. I clapped a hand over my mouth to muffle my scream.

Venkat stood up quickly, shaking out his shoulders and rubbing his eyes with his fists. "Madam, something wrong?" He looked around, anxious.

"You almost gave me a heart attack! Why are you sleeping in front of the door?"

"I not sure what is 'heart attack,' Madam."

"You scared me, Venkat. To death practically. What are you DOING out here?"

"No dismissal. You and Sir no sending me home, Madam."

"It was five in the morning! Of course you should have gone home."

"I no leaving until dismissal. Is my duty." Venkat stood up tall, hiking his jeans a little higher around his narrow waist. He couldn't be more than seventeen or eighteen, I realized. In America, he'd be studying for the SATs. Here, he was pledging knightly driver-allegiance to an under-caffeinated American woman who just finished hitting him in the head with a door. Was it safe to get in the car with him? He'd barely slept and now he had a concussion, maybe. Could you drive a car with a head injury? My own head throbbed harder. I knew I should probably send him home, wherever that was, but this was an emergency.

"Um, Venkat, do you know where there's coffee?"

"Coffee, Madam?"

"Yes, coffee." I pantomimed drinking, curling my fingers around an imaginary mug. "Like Starbucks?"

"No knowing Starbucks, Madam. But coffee being one place only. Jubilee Hills. I taking."

Confession: I was enthusiastically, irreparably, entirely addicted to coffee. Coffee was not just a morning routine; it was more like a religion. Nothing revived my soul like that first whiff of freshly brewed beans or the warmth in my palm through the side of the mug. It wasn't just about the caffeine (though oh, how I loved the caffeine!). It was the ritual, those few moments of contemplation before the madness of the regular world set in. Any occasional worries I had about whether such an addiction was healthy were soothed by reminding myself how many other, worse things there were to be addicted to: doughnuts, tequila, crack cocaine.

Obtaining coffee on my morning commute was as integral to Manhattan life as Metrocards and knee-high rubber boots on rainy days. I knew the best bodegas, the snobbiest Intelligentsia coffee-houses, and the location of every Starbucks and Dunkin' Donuts within two miles of our apartment. There'd been other beverages I'd dallied with in my adult life: coconut water, wheatgrass smoothies, carrot juice. But those were the liquid equivalents of summer flings: flighty, insubstantial. Coffee and me were the real deal.

Nothing sustained me like coffee. With it, I could do anything. Without it?

I was pretty much a disaster.

Twenty minutes into the ride, I could feel myself unraveling. Traffic moved at a crawl. The road was crammed with cars, all of which seemed to be moving in multiple directions, like a giant game of bumper cars. Except the cars had no bumpers and the only way to avoid collisions seemed to be blasting the horn as loudly as possible. On the backs of trucks, motorcycles, and auto rickshaws were small, circular stickers that read "HORN OK PLEASE" or "STOP HORN PLEASE," both of which appeared to mean exactly the same thing: *Please give us warning before you run us over.* Honks erupted around us like a hailstorm. The racket upgraded the throbbing in my head to pounding. Even my eyeballs hurt.

"How much longer, do you think?" I asked.

"No much coffee Hyderabad, Madam," Venkat said. "Only Cafe Coffee Day. Jubilee Hills."

"Is Jubilee Hills nearby?"

"Yes, Madam."

I got the distinct impression his statement wasn't even a little bit true.

At this point, a cup of coffee wasn't going to cut it. I needed a whole gallon. Or an IV drip.

"Here, Madam," Venkat said after what surely had been hours, pulling up in front of a squat beige building with a red awning. Even from the side of the road (there were no curbs or sidewalks anywhere) I could see the familiar, reassuring silhouettes of a pastry case, an espresso machine, groups of young people huddled around paper cups. "I staying here or going?"

I wasn't sure what the driver/drivee etiquette was. Was he supposed to stay with the car? Would it look strange if he came in with me? Was I supposed to offer him a beverage? I had a flash of homesickness for the 1 train. Faster service, fewer decisions.

"I'll go. Do you want anything?"

"Madam?"

"To drink? Like a coffee or something?"

Venkat looked surprised, then ashamed. Maybe I wasn't supposed to bring him something after all. But who goes into a Starbucks—or a Cafe Coffee Day—and doesn't offer to bring back drinks for everyone?

"Maybe...*chai*?"

Oh. OK. Chai. They had those here too. "Got it. Be right back."

When I walked in, every single person in Cafe Coffee Day turned to stare. All five baristas behind the counter, which seemed like overkill for one espresso machine and no customers in line, and the handful of teenaged patrons hunched over low iron patio tables. In the center of each table was a blown-glass hookah with smoke spiraling from the top. A jean-clad kid with hipster glasses and a turban on his head stopped, mid-inhale, to look me up and down.

"Welcome to Coffee Day. What can I be of preparing for you?" asked one of the five baristas. She wore a red cap and a starched red polo shirt. Her nametag said "Rashmi."

"Hi. Thanks. Can I get...just a coffee, please?"

"A coffee?"

"Yes, a large. With milk? Nonfat if you have it."

Rashmi looked sad. "I'm sorry, Ma'am. We are having no coffee."

"But this is Cafe Coffee Day, right? How can you not have coffee?"

"We are having many beverages, Ma'am. *Chai*, chocolate, cafe mocha…"

The stares were now accompanied by a lull in conversation and a heightened feeling of tension, a shift in the room's barometric pressure. Everyone had turned to watch, hookahs and beverages forgotten as they watched my discomfort with growing interest.

"Are you sure? I don't want anything fancy. No espresso. Just drip…the kind that comes from a machine?"

"I am not knowing what is 'drip,' Ma'am," said Rashmi. Then she clasped her hands together. "But you are from U.S., correct? I have what is perfect for you. Cafe Americano!"

"OK. Sure. I'll try that," I said, trying to be agreeable. "And a chai too, please. For my driver." I looked into the display case, hoping for a muffin or a croissant. Instead, there was a plate of fried samosas and a couple of pieces of chocolate cake, their gluey frosting sweating with condensation behind the glass.

Twenty minutes later, according to an old-school, wall-mounted Felix the Cat clock that ticked off each minute with the flick of his plastic tail, Rashmi handed me two waxed paper cups. I sniffed at Venkat's. Instead of a creamy blend of milk and spices, Venkat's chai was just…tea. Black tea. Rashmi must have heard me wrong. I hoped he wouldn't be upset.

"One hundred fifty rupees, please, Ma'am."

Juggling both cups in the crook of my elbow, I reached into my back pocket and retrieved my credit card. Rashmi looked at it blankly.

"Sorry, Ma'am, but we are not taking cards. Rupees only."

I had no rupees. Coffee was *so close* and now I was stranded without a way to pay. I looked at her helplessly. "Can you hold these for a second?" I pushed them back across the counter and ran back to the car.

"Venkat, can I borrow some money?"

"Money, Madam?"

"They won't take my credit card and I don't have any cash. Rupees. She said it was a hundred and fifty. I can pay you back as soon as we get back to Matwala Shayar. Jay must have gotten some cash before we left."

Venkat shrugged and reached into his pocket for a battered nylon wallet, the kind my little brother used to carry his allowance in fourth grade. He ripped open the worn Velcro and removed two small, tan bills with a picture of an old man on them. So these were rupees. I had no idea if he was handing me pocket change or his monthly salary.

"I'll pay you back as soon as we get back, I promise. Is it a lot of money?"

Venkat looked uncomfortable.

"*Chai* in mine village costing ten rupees, Madam." He didn't quite meet my eyes.

Back in Cafe Coffee Day, I paid Rashmi, collected Venkat's fifty rupees in change, and took our drinks. I looked around for the little table where the condiments should be: sugar packets, mixing sticks, cardboard holders so my hands wouldn't suffer permanent nerve damage from what were surely the two hottest beverage containers I'd ever felt. There was none.

"Ma'am? Are you having everything you need?"

"I was just looking for milk, and some Sweet'N Low. And the holders for the coffee? The paper ones that go around the cup?"

Rashmi took a yellow, waxed cardboard box labeled *Nestlé Slim* off a shelf and tore off a foil tab. She pushed the carton and two white pellets across the counter. "This is what we are having, Ma'am. Milk is being here. And these are saccharin tablets. There are no holders that you speak of. My apologies."

Fingers blistering, I hurried back to the car, convinced my coffee was tainted with salmonella. Who'd ever heard of milk in a box? I'd need to find the refrigerated kind as soon as possible, but for today this would have to do. It was just a little bit—maybe harmful food-borne bacteria only worked in large doses.

Venkat opened his door to accept his cup. In the backseat, I popped a saccharin tablet through the hole in the lid. Was saccharin even safe to eat anymore? Wasn't that the one that caused cancer in lab rats, like M&Ms dyed with Red #3? Shaking the cup a little to stir, I closed my eyes and took a sip. Which I promptly spat out the window.

"Madam?" Venkat asked, clearly shocked. I'd seen drivers spitting out their windows all over the place on the ride here. Women passengers must be held to different standards. Oops.

"Sorry. The coffee…"

The coffee was awful. Worse, there was something chunky in it that definitely did *not* taste edible. I lifted the lid to investigate. It crumpled in my hand. Little bits of melted plastic floated at the top of the oily black liquid inside. The lid was *melting*. Into my Americano.

Venkat sipped at his chai and made a face. "No good, Madam. Chai better at stand. Road #2. Tomorrow we going. No good Cafe Coffee Day."

Jay was pacing the hallway outside the apartment when we got back.

"What took so long? I was worried about you."

I stood on tiptoe to give him a kiss. "Sorry. I went in search of coffee. Can I have some rupees? I owe Venkat money."

Jay pulled a couple of wrinkled bills from the pocket of his jeans and handed them to me. "Did you bring me any coffee?"

"Don't ask," I said, pitching the melted cup on top of the pile of trash outside our door. "I can make you a peanut butter sandwich, though."

I turned to go inside, but Jay grabbed my elbow and steered me back toward the car instead. "Let's go. I want to go to the car dealership before I need to be at the office."

I frowned. I'd hoped to spend the day settling in, unpacking a few things, maybe taking a tour of the city. Also, I was eager to get started on our search for a place to live. The corporate apartments at Matwala Shayar were just temporary accommodations while we waited for our sea shipment to arrive. And based on Alexis's description of the all-night parties, it seemed like we'd be better off moving sooner rather than later. But Jay was all business, ticking off things from his mental checklist.

"You're going to work already? We just got here," I said, climbing back into the Hyundai reluctantly. I handed Venkat his money and thanked him again for the loan. He looked relieved.

"I should have been in this morning. They've been waiting for me for weeks."

When we arrived at the car dealership, it looked like a car dealership...a fact that filled me with dread after my experience in the familiar-looking but shockingly foreign Coffee Day. But the giant Mahindra showroom was, in fact, filled with cars. The salesman on the floor ignored me totally, which also felt familiar. Apparently, buying a car in India was just like buying one in America. Smoke, mirrors, negotiations, gender discrimination.

"I should get behind the wheel too," I informed the salesman as he drooled all over Jay, who was perched behind the wheel of a massive SUV that looked like a combination of an Escalade and a toaster oven. "I'll be driving too."

The salesman ignored me. He waved his hand through the glass, demonstrating the superior opacity of the windows, which were tinted Mafia black.

"And I was hoping for something fuel efficient," I continued. "We like to reduce our carbon imprint whenever we can."

The salesman turned to me with disdain. "The Scorpio is not running on *carbon*, Ma'am. The Scorpio is only running on premium diesel."

Diesel? "Well, what about one with an automatic transmission?"

"No, Ma'am. You will only be finding automatic transmissions with costly imported vehicles. None are being available for purchase here at Mahindra."

I turned to Jay, who was kicking tires and looking all too pleased at the Scorpio's impressive height. "Can we look somewhere else?" I'd tried to learn how to drive a manual transmission just once, when I was seventeen, with a boyfriend who made the unfortunate decision to start me off on a hill. I panicked, closed my eyes, and drove his '94 Toyota Supra straight into a row of magnolia bushes. Sitting on the sidewalk while we waited for the tow truck, I vowed never to touch a stick shift ever again.

"Too expensive. We'd pay double what we would in the U.S. We need to buy Indian to make it worthwhile. We're only here for two years."

Venkat was in the corner, looking gleeful. His eyes positively glittered with anticipation.

"Venkat, can you drive this car?"

"Oh, YES, Madam," he said. "Scorpio MUCH good car. I driving very well, much better Hyundai." He took a tentative step forward to stroke the Scorpio's ebony paint. "Best car for Americans. Much strong and tall, black windows. Much safety."

"Can you teach ME to drive it?"

A flicker of horror crossed his face, but he recovered quickly. "Is more safety I driving. More skills. In India is better."

Jay laughed. I looked at him, suspicious. "Are you laughing at him, or at me?" I asked.

"You can't *drive* here, Jen," he said. "You can barely drive at home. It's the wrong side of the road *and* the wrong side of the car, and you saw how insane traffic was. That's why we have a driver. So you don't have to worry about it."

"Are you going to drive?"

"Sure, once in a while. On Venkat's day off."

"So why can't I? I can learn. Venkat can teach me."

Venkat made a muffled sound, like a sob.

"We'll see."

Jay turned back to the salesman. Venkat retreated to a corner, his feet practically clicking in the air at the prospect of being behind the wheel of the massive, diesel-sucking, environment-hating *thing* Jay seemed to be about to purchase with or without my approval. I sat down on a bench and took *Lonely Planet* out of my bag. Sulking, I pretended to read.

An hour later (why did everything take so *long*?), we got back into the Hyundai: Jay clutching a fistful of papers, Venkat beaming, me still in a sulk. Our new black Scorpio with Mafia black windows and a tankful of diesel would be delivered to our apartment in a week. Jay, the salesman, and Venkat were in agreement: I was forbidden to drive it.

After a stop at Airtel for new Indian cell phones (called "mobiles" in India, we were informed, with numbers so long and confusing I was sure I'd never memorize them), Jay told Venkat to bring us back to Matwala Shayar so he could change and go to work. I watched him put on his suit with a feeling of dread.

"What am I supposed to do if you have the car at work and I'm stuck at the house?" I asked.

"I'm sure you'll figure something out." He gave me an absent-minded kiss on the top of my head.

"Don't leave me yet," I begged, throwing my arms around him. "I'm not ready to be alone here."

"You'll do fine," Jay said, hugging me back before he gently untangled himself from my embrace. "Just don't leave the apartment. Take a shower, get settled. Call Alexis, if you get lonely. I'll be home in a couple of hours and we'll go somewhere for dinner."

The door slammed behind him. Tucker circled my ankles, sniffing uncertainly. I scooped him up and stood at the window, watching them drive away. Jay waved from the backseat.

"Looks like it's just you and me," I told the dog. "You want some peanut butter?"

CHAPTER 3

After another sandwich and a half-hearted attempt at fixing the broken air conditioner, I gave up and climbed back into the wooden bed, clutching *Lonely Planet* but too lonely to read. I stared at the ceiling with its one lilting fan, wondering how many hours were in two years, how many casseroles and roasted chickens and loads of laundry could possibly fill all those hours. Then the electricity shut off with an ominous click. The apartment went dark. The fan went still. And I—jet-lagged, uncertain, fighting off a wave of crushing homesickness—went to sleep.

I woke to the sound of a key in the lock. Tucker, curled around my elbow, jumped to attention and barked like crazy. I was sweaty and tangled in the stiff sheet. I'd meant to shower and make myself look decent, maybe open the suitcases and organize some things in the closets. But somehow Jay was already home again. It was dark outside, hours had passed, and I had nothing to show for it.

Oh well. It was only the first day. Jet lag was still making my head feel like it was stuffed full of Styrofoam peanuts. I'd be more efficient tomorrow. I hurried to the door to meet him, eager to be the encouraging wife after his first day on the job. Then I took one look at him—pale-faced, horror-stricken, tie loosened and hanging askew—and panicked.

"Oh my god. What happened? Was there an accident? Was it a buffalo?" Jay wavered in the doorway, his six-foot frame listing to one side like a capsizing ship. I grabbed his briefcase and steered him by the elbow to the living room sofa, an ancient looking red-and-gold brocade piece with those things that went over the arms. *Antimacassars*, my grandmother called them. He resisted.

"Germs," Jay wheezed. "Not sitting on the couch. Get a towel."

I raced to the bathroom and grabbed a towel, then hurried back to Jay, smoothing the worn scrap of cloth over the sofa. He collapsed, his head in his hands, his elbows on his knees.

"Jay!" I said urgently. "You're freaking me out. Please tell me what's wrong!"

"Sick," he muttered into his hands. "Everything hurts."

"How can you be sick? We just got here. You were fine this morning."

"Bed," Jay murmured weakly. I helped him up and we stumbled awkwardly toward the bedroom. He lay down and moved his arms and legs obligingly, a floppy puppet in a pinstriped suit, while I took off his shoes and socks and unbuttoned his shirt.

"Don't take my shirt off, I'm freezing to death. Can you get me a sweatshirt or something? And socks?"

I felt Jay's forehead. He was burning up. This was bad.

"Jay, you have a fever. You need medicine." The only pills I had in my bag were Malarone, a bottle ominously marked with a million warnings (*possible side effects: dizziness, back pain, diarrhea, nightmares, insomnia, hives*), intended to prevent malaria. I dug through every suitcase to be sure, but my worst fear was confirmed: we didn't have so much as a single Tylenol.

Jay was the strong one in our relationship. I needed an instruction manual for absolutely everything; he tackled every task like he'd been born knowing exactly what to do. I got colds; he brought me Kleenex and takeout chicken noodle soup and teased me about my weak immune system. I got food poisoning; he could eat from the shadiest hot dog vendor in Central Park without even a whisper of heartburn. When life got stressful, I got panicky. Jay got blasé. In our fledgling marriage, he was the one who took care of everything: set up auto-pays for the rent and the utility bills, monitored our credit scores, booked vacations on tropical islands. His lifelong super-independence made mine unnecessary.

Except it was the second night on our Great Adventure and he wasn't the strong one. He was sick, and I was scared, and he needed me. Jay was huddled under the covers, shivering in sweatpants, a giant Red Sox sweatshirt, and the fuzzy pink socks I'd brought on the airplane. I reached down and adjusted the socks. On his left ankle was a red, sore-looking welt. "Did you get a bug bite or something?"

"Don't know." Jay rolled to one side and whimpered.

"Where's Venkat?" I whispered, patting at his forehead with a damp towel.

"Sent him home," Jay said through chattering teeth. "He'd been working for twenty-four hours straight."

Shit.

I dug through the pile of paperwork Jay had left on the coffee table, looking for Subu's number. He was the apartment manager; he must deal with expats and their unusual requests all the time. He would know what to do.

Subu arrived in moments, bowing and carrying a box of tissues and several bottles of water.

"I am bringing cloths, Ma'am," he said, craning his neck around, looking for a glimpse of the patient.

"Thanks, Subu. I need a doctor. Or medicine. And a thermometer, something to take his temperature with. Is there a drugstore? A pharmacy?"

Subu looked confused. "If I may be asking, what are Sir's ailments, Ma'am?"

"His ailments? Well, he says he's freezing but he feels really hot. I think he's got a fever. And his body hurts."

Subu nodded sagely. "Is sounding like *chikungunya* fever, Ma'am. Very many peoples are having *chikungunya* right now. Almost two *lakh* in Hyderabad only. Is Jay Sir having any marks on himself from insects?"

"He does have a bite on his ankle, I think. Why? Is that what's making him sick?"

"*Chikungunya* is coming from mosquitoes, Ma'am. It is serious healthful epidemic."

A mosquito bite? Was chicken-whatever fever like malaria? I'd started taking the Malarone pills before we left; Jay had refused. Last night, there had been swarms of mosquitoes clustered around the airport terminal. I'd swatted them away religiously out of habit; I'd always been allergic. My bites would grow hard and scary-red, swelling to the size of a baseball within minutes. *You can't move to India; you're allergic to bugs!* Kate said, scandalized, when I first broke the news, as if that mere fact would be enough to sway the company's decision. If only. When our move became official, she gave me an industrial-sized spray canister of DEET as a going-away present.

Jay liked to joke that the bugs just didn't like his blood. There could be just one single mosquito in a room with a thousand people and I'd be the only one to get bitten. Jay, however, could sleep with a mosquito *in his bed* and wake up without a bite. Now, it seemed his lucky streak was over. Maybe Indian mosquitoes had a more sophisticated palate.

"Is chicken fever…deadly?" I asked Subu. My voice came out in a squeak.

"No, no. No death. Just fever, chills, pains. Sir will be feeling all right in a few short days." He inched toward the door. The medical consult was over.

"Where can I find medicine?" I called after him. The door slammed. Damn it.

"Subu says you have something called chicken fever," I informed Jay. He moaned. "I think we should call a doctor."

"No doctor," he said, pulling the covers over his head. "I just need aspirin or something. Where's my sleeping hat?"

He fell asleep a couple of minutes later. I stayed there and watched him breathe for a few minutes, reassuring myself with every rise and fall of his chest. His eyelashes, long and dark and utterly wasted on a male, flickered against his cheekbones. I crept out of the room and called Alexis from my new Indian mobile.

"Hey, it's Jenny. Are you busy? I need some help."

Younus's tiny hatchback hurtled over the dirt road at warp speed. Seeing his deft maneuvers in and out of traffic, his horn honks and mad swerves across lanes, I was beginning to understand the number-one rule of the road in Hyderabad: survive. Herds of buffalo weaved through traffic, belligerent and massive. Instead of yielding to oncoming traffic, cars just blared their horns and plowed forward, forcing less-confident drivers to dart out of the way. There were no lanes, no traffic lights, no turns indicated or slowing for pedestrians. People, animals, cars—it was a total, death-defying free-for-all.

It was almost 8:00 p.m. Alexis and Younus had pulled up outside the flat with true action-movie hero flair—engine running, doors flung open, techno music blaring from the car stereo, Alexis in the back shouting orders to Younus. I stared at the back of his head—smooth black hair beneath a woven cap. It was like the yarmulkes my brothers had been forced to wear to temple on High Holy days when we were young, only square-shaped and edged in black. Both the cap and Younus's uniform, which fit his lean body like a second skin, were worn but bleached to a pristine white.

"Muslim prayer cap," Alexis whispered as I climbed in beside her. "Most of the drivers around here are Muslim. Hyderabad wanted to separate and become part of Pakistan, did you know? Not so easy to do when you're smack in the middle of the country. Don't try to get anywhere on a Friday; the drivers are all at prayer and the streets are completely jammed."

"Excuse me, Ma'ams?" Younus turned to look at us. "Again what is it you finding?"

"Jay is sick," I said. "Fever." I put my hand against my forehead and lifted it off fast to indicate *hot*. "I need a thermometer to take his temperature. And medicine. Pills to make the fever go away."

We'd explained this to Younus several times already, but his English wasn't as accomplished as Venkat's; a fog of confusion passed across his handsome face each time Alexis tried to convey the exact nature of our mission. This time, though, I saw a flicker of recognition in his eyes.

"Tablets, Ma'ams?"

"YES. Tablets. Do you know where?" I cried.

"Yes, Ma'am." Younus stepped on the gas. The car jolted forward. I gripped the sides of the vinyl seat, patched together with electrical tape, and closed my eyes. This was not a good time to get carsick.

Around us, the city began to disappear. There were no buildings, no construction site, no stores. People were huddled over cooking fires. Wooden shanties and cement block stalls with sheet metal awnings lined either side of the road. Chickens darted everywhere. As we approached, people began to mull around, startled by the sudden appearance of headlights on the darkened street.

Younus slowed to a stop.

"Is village, Ma'ams. No more pass," he said. "Need walk."

We got out and looked around. Every person on the street stopped to stare. Younus was speaking sharply in Telugu, pushing back some of the more curious observers. He whistled at us and pointed to a stand with a red-painted sign. Then he leaned against the car with his arms folded.

"I guess he's not coming with us," I muttered. "We could use an interpreter."

"I think he's afraid to leave the car," Alexis replied.

We headed for the stand Younus had pointed to. Its red wooden sign had a cross in the center, drawn there in white chalk.

"Do you have medicine? Pills?" I asked a man behind the metal grate, trying to remember the word that had finally hit a note of recognition with Younus. "Tablets? And a thermometer?" Again, I put a hand on my own forehead and pantomimed *hot*. "My husband is sick. Fever. Chicken…*chikungunya*." The man behind the makeshift counter nodded vigorously. He dug around in the plastic bins on the counter and produced two slender, dusty cardboard boxes and a foil bubble pack of white pills.

"*Edi*?" He displayed the contents of the boxes. One was a regular mercury thermometer, like the one my mom used when I was a kid. The other was a digital version that was an exact duplicate of the one from our bathroom cabinet in New York. I looked in confusion at the tiny village around us: bins of grains and lentils, women in saris with giant baskets of laundry on their heads, naked children and chickens and a dirt road too narrow for a car to pass through. It looked like we'd stepped into a time warp, yet this man was offering me a twenty-first century thermometer and what definitely looked like aspirin.

I chose the digital version, fairly certain mercury was outlawed back in the seventies, and asked him, repeatedly, if the "tablets" really were aspirin. The last thing I needed was some crazy drug mix-up. Jay hated taking medicine in the first place. If I accidentally slipped him Xanax or antacids or cyanide, he'd never forgive me. Alexis slid some rupees across the counter. The man counted them and bowed in thanks. I squeezed her elbow, grateful. We'd come all this way and I didn't even have money with me. The useless AmEx was still in my pocket.

We got back in the car, giddy with victory.

"I hope these work. Jay never sees doctors," I said. "Not unless it's really bad." I paused. "I hope it doesn't get really bad." We were back on the main road. Everything was dark. The half-finished buildings loomed like shipwrecks, greenish and hazy in the dusty gloom.

"Peter said a bunch of the guys at work got *chikungunya* last week," Alexis said. "It's supposedly over in a couple of days, but sucks while it lasts. Did you eat dinner?"

"No, and I'm starving. I should probably bring something for Jay too. I don't think he's eaten all day."

"Younus, can you stop at Little Italy?"

Younus nodded and floored the engine, cutting across three lanes so he could pick up more speed. A man on a purple motorcycle shook his fist. Behind him, a woman and two children clung fiercely to each other's waists, struggling to stay upright as the bike rocked off balance in Younus's wake.

Back at Matwala Shayar, I brought Jay his aspirin and forced him to swallow them. I felt his forehead; he seemed less clammy but he was still shivering. The digital thermometer read 38.3. Celsius. Damn it. I had no idea what that meant. Feeling useless, I sat with him until he fell back into a restless sleep.

Alexis and I camped on the floor of the living room, leaning against the antique sofa as we ate soggy pasta straight from Styrofoam containers. "What's with the towels?" Alexis asked as one slid to the floor in front of her.

"Jay's got a germ thing. He doesn't like strange stuff touching him."

"He'd better get a hazmat suit if he's going to live in Hyderabad. Germs aren't even the half of it." She slurped a noodle into her mouth. "It's sad to admit because this stuff tastes like Chef Boyardee, but Little Italy is my favorite restaurant here. We eat it like three times a week."

I was so hungry I hadn't been paying much attention to the taste, but now that Alexis pointed it out...yes, my ravioli *did* taste distinctly familiar. It reminded me of electric can openers and nights when my parents went out and the babysitter let us eat carrots dipped in ketchup and watch TV hours past bedtime. The flavor was strangely comforting.

"Leave it to India to make us wax nostalgic about spaghetti that comes in a can," Alexis said with an exaggerated sigh.

"Do you like it? Living here, I mean."

A look crossed her face I couldn't quite read.

"It's the experience of a lifetime," Alexis said quietly, like she'd recited the line a thousand times before.

"But do you *like* it? Are you glad you came?"

"It may take me another lifetime to figure that out." She dipped a piece of bread in her sauce. "You could ask me every single morning and get a different answer by the afternoon." She glanced down at her phone, checking for a message from Peter. "It's your first night; let's get to the boring stuff later. Tell me about New York. I've always wanted to live there."

It was almost midnight when I finally climbed into bed next to Jay, brushing the damp dark hair out of his eyes. I lay down beside him and watched him breathe—the easy rise and fall of his chest beneath the sweatshirt, the occasional shudder as he huddled deeper in the sheets. Tucker stretched out between us, a furry horizontal line that made an H out of the three of us. This, at least, felt normal. I twirled the dog's floppy ears through my fingers, staring at the ceiling fan, trying to fall asleep.

CHAPTER 4

THURSDAY AFTERNOON

Pizza Corner: Chikunwa Hameda Mumeda Hameda, Vishnu speaking.

Me: Hello, is this Pizza Corner?

Vishnu: Yes, Madam.

Me: Great. I'd like to place an order for delivery.

Vishnu: Delivery, Madam?

Me: Don't you deliver? I'm looking at your menu and it says you deliver.

Vishnu: Certainly, Madam. What will you be having?

Me: I'd like a medium plain pizza.

Vishnu: Deep dish or original crust?

Me: Original, please.

Vishnu: Will you be having any meats or vegetables on your plain pizza?

Me: No, just plain pizza. Cheese pizza.

Vishnu: OK, Madam, we will be delivering your original crust meat and vegetable pizza to you within thirty-nine minutes. Thank you for calling Pizza Corner.

Me: No meat or vegetables. CHEESE PIZZA! And don't you need to know where I live?

Vishnu: Yes, Madam.

Me: I live at Matwala Shayar, on Madhapur Road. Flat number Alpha 112, first floor.

Vishnu: And what would be the flat number?

Me: 112. In Alpha block. Alpha 112.

Vishnu: And what floor is that on, Madam?

Me: The first floor.

Vishnu: Madam? I regret to inform you that we are being out of original crust pizzas today. There will be only deep dish.

Me: Well, why didn't you tell me that when I ordered it in the first place?

Vishnu: Pardon, Madam? I do not understand. What size pizza would be to your liking?

Me: Medium. Same as before.

Vishnu: You ordered another pizza before, Madam? Have you received that one yet?

Me: I meant before when I ordered the...forget it.

Vishnu: Very good. Your order comes to 140 rupees.

Me: Great, thanks. *(Finger poised on hang-up button.)*

Vishnu: Madam? It will be costing minimum of 150 rupees to deliver your order to Matwala Shayar. Would you like to order something additional?

Me: Do I have a choice?

Vishnu: I beg your pardon, Madam?

Me: Just give me a Coke or something.

Vishnu: OK, Madam, one of Coke. Your order comes to 185 rupees. Congratulations! When your order comes to greater than 175 rupees you get a free gift. It is a Coke. I'll be sending it with your order.

Me: Wait. I just ordered a Coke so you'd deliver to me. Now you're giving me a free one? I don't want another Coke. I don't even want the first one! How about you keep your free Coke and just deliver my pizza for 140 rupees?

Vishnu: I'm sorry, Madam, but that cannot be done. You must order 150 rupees to be receiving your delivery in Matwala Shayar.

Me: But you'd save the money on the free Coke if you'd just deliver without the first one. It's win-win!

Vishnu: Win-win, Madam? I am not understanding what is "win-win." Your order will arrive in thirty-nine minutes or it will be free of charge.

Me: Really? Free? Well, that's good, at least.

Vishnu: Madam, I must be informing you, however, that long distances or traffic may interfere with the driving time, in which case the thirty-nine-minute offering would be invalid. Thank you for calling Pizza Corner, Madam. We hope you will be having a good day.

FRIDAY MORNING, 7:00 A.M.

Me: Hello?

Pizza Corner: Good morning, Madam, this is Supriya calling from Pizza Corner. How are you today, Madam?

Me: What? Pizza Corner? Why are you calling me? It's SEVEN IN THE MORNING.

Supriya: Well, Madam, we are calling in regards to your order for pizza.

Me: But that was yesterday. I ordered a pizza yesterday. Not today. I didn't order anything today.

Supriya: Yes, Madam, this is a customer service call. We are calling to find out how you were liking your medium meat and vegetable deep dish pizza and the Coke which you were ordering from Pizza Corner yesterday?

꒰

I'd been ordering a lot of pizza.

At first it was just a practical decision: Jay was recovering from his fever; obviously I needed to stay close to him in case he needed me or relapsed or something. Then he got better and went back to work, and I went back to eating peanut butter and jelly sandwiches and staring out the kitchen window at the construction site. Alexis had stopped by to visit a few times, but her new Indian painting class occupied most of her waking hours. She tried to convince me to take the class with her, but I assured her anything more advanced than stick-figure drawing would be way out of my league.

I hadn't braved another trip to Coffee Day. Caffeine withdrawal was making me crabby. There was also the jet lag to overcome, the heat to contend with, the never-ending cycle of *electricity on, electricity off*. The Matwala Shayar apartment complex had a backup generator, but it was just as unpredictable as the power cuts themselves. I'd used my to-do list (*unpack, explore the town, buy groceries, meet the neighbors, write a blog post*) to kill a giant spider on the bathroom floor. When I tossed the list in the trash, crumpled and covered in spider guts, not a single item had been checked off.

Comments on my blog were pouring in, asking if we'd arrived safely and demanding details of our Indian journey so far. I'd developed a decent following in New York, writing about daily life as a writer and a yogini. My readers were eager to read about my new experiences in the third world. I scrolled through the comments (*"Where are you? What's happening? We miss your posts!"*) on my new Indian BlackBerry without responding to a single one.

The truth was, I was being lazy. Lazy and afraid. My clothes were wrong, my communication skills poor, my sense of direction unreliable. I hadn't even so much as glanced in the direction of my computer. We didn't have Internet yet, and besides that I was too overwhelmed to face the mocking tyranny of an empty page. Instead of fascinating stories to tell and exotic pictures to share, so far I'd collected nothing but a bunch of crushed expectations.

Venkat arrived each morning and waited outside, engine idling while he examined his slicked-back hair in the rearview mirror. Jay woke up, took a shower, put on his suit, kissed me good-bye, and went to the office. When we heard the Hyundai's engine grunt to life, Tucker and I got out of bed. I went to the bathroom, cursed Jay out loud for soaking the roll of toilet paper AGAIN ("It's not MY fault the toilet is in the shower," he'd say, indignant, when I complained), and took a shower of my own, relishing that fleeting moment of clean before the heat and dust of the day set in. I'd sit on the sofa with Tucker on my lap, flipping through the pages of *The Times of India* Subu left outside our door every morning, and wonder when our great adventure would begin.

I knew Jay was feeling stressed and insecure about his work in Region 10. He'd never admit it, to me or to anyone, but I could see it in the tilt of his shoulders and the stubborn way he clenched his jaw. Things didn't feel quite right between us. I missed the *old* us, the ones who laughed together and teased each other and kissed goodnight before rolling our separate ways to go to sleep. The past few nights, Jay had been so exhausted he'd passed out as soon as he pulled his sleeping hat down over his ears, turning and moaning to himself in fitful sleep. I watched his restless tossing and felt guilty for being the one with so little to accomplish.

I was chewing absently on a breakfast slice of leftover pizza and watching the construction site (today the women were climbing the scaffolding with bowls of water on top of their heads, a feat I found as fascinating as it was dangerous) when a chorus of honking horns came from outside, followed by knocking at the front door. I grabbed Tucker and opened the door a crack.

"Yes?"

"Jay Sir?" A man holding a clipboard and wearing an enormous garland of orange flowers looked over my shoulder, clearly disappointed I'd been the one to open the door.

"He's at work. Can I help you?"

"I am Vishnu, from Mahindra? Today is the most auspicious day we are delivering Jay Sir's brand new top of the line Scorpio, color black? We are here for celebration."

I peered over the top of the staircase, looking down into the parking lot. Sure enough, there was the Scorpio—dark, hulking, and inexplicably adorned with dozens of the same orange garlands Vishnu was wearing. The flowers were marigolds. Behind the Scorpio was a procession of similarly decorated cars, all bearing the Mahindra logo. It was a car delivery parade. If I'd known, I would have put on something more festive.

"Wow. This is pretty awesome, thanks. Jay will be sorry he missed it. Do you need me to sign or something?"

"My apologies, Ma'am, but you cannot sign," Vishnu said, clutching the clipboard. "Only Jay Sir. When will he be available?"

"He won't be back for another few hours. I'm happy to sign." I reached for the papers. Vishnu held them over his head.

"Might you be calling him to let him know of our arrival? Perhaps he will be coming with more haste if he knows his brand new Scorpio vehicle is waiting for him?"

I called Jay's mobile.

"Is everything OK? I'm sort of in the middle of something."

"Yeah. It's just the guys are here with the car and they won't let me sign for it. There's a lot of them and it's all wrapped up in these flower things? Can you come home?"

Jay sighed. "Not for at least another few hours. Do you want me to talk to them?"

I held the phone out to Vishnu. He bobbled his head back and forth, horizontal instead of up and down, a native gesture I couldn't figure out. It seemed to mean "yes" and "no" simultaneously, but whatever action followed the head bobble was usually the opposite of the one I'd expected. Vishnu's bobble seemed to indicate acknowledgment, maybe gratitude. I added these to my running mental list of possible bobble meanings.

Vishnu spoke to Jay for less than a minute before handing the phone back to me. "Jay Sir will be coming. Imminent. We will wait."

Jay showed up two hours later, hopping out of the back of Younus's hatchback and high-fiving Peter, who gave the Scorpio a thumbs-up before heading toward the Delta block flat he and Alexis shared.

Vishnu drew himself up off the ground outside our door, where he'd been camping with his clipboard in anticipation of Jay's "imminent" arrival. *So there*, I thought as he rubbed at an oily stain on his pants. *Should have let me sign the papers after all.*

After a few minutes, Jay came in whistling. He dangled the keys to the Scorpio like a giant trout he'd just caught. "Should we take it for a spin?"

I gaped at him in horror. "Right NOW? On these roads? With YOU driving? You've lost your mind. Where's Venkat, anyway? I saw you get out of Younus's car."

"He needed a couple days off. Something about going back to his village. A festival or something."

"But it's Friday! I was thinking we'd do some sightseeing or something. Go out to dinner. Maybe get groceries."

"We can still go. I can drive."

The only thing that scared me more than braving the city on my own was the thought of being a passenger in a moving vehicle, on Hyderabadi streets, with Jay behind the wheel. He was a terrible driver on a good day in a familiar country: reckless, impatient, a tad belligerent when things weren't going his way. The thought of him on the wrong side of the car, on the wrong side of the road, mixing it up with livestock and motorcycles, possibly plowing over small animals or sleeping humans in the massive Scorpio…I shuddered. Why didn't India have a decent system for mass transportation? When we made it back to New York, I was never taking the subway for granted again.

"No way. You're not qualified to drive on these streets, and it's total insanity out there. We'll just have to wait for Venkat to get back. Want me to order a pizza?" I waved the Pizza Corner menu, though by now I had it memorized. "We could try something different for a change. Something with vegetables?"

"Put some decent clothes on," Jay said, loosening his tie. "I'm going to change, and then we're getting out of this apartment. We're in India. Let's go eat some Indian food." He headed for the bathroom. A minute later, he let out a yelp.

"The toilet paper's all wet!"

"It's not my fault the toilet's in the shower," I yelled back, smirking. "How are we going to *get* to Indian food? I just said I wouldn't get in the car with you driving, remember?"

"Just like the Indians do. We'll take a rickshaw."

Just before I left, Kate and I were walking toward the subway at Seventy-Second and Broadway. Dripping wet from yoga, sipping spirulina smoothies, soaking up the late spring sunshine…and taking (though I didn't know it then) our charmed existences entirely for granted. We talked about India.

"Well, it's not like it could be any worse than *this*," Kate commented with disgust. Her slender arm, Hermes bracelets stacked three high, swept the air to indicate piled bags of garbage on the side of the street, the angry honks of passing taxis, the homeless guy in front of Gray's Papaya, wearing Lucky brand jeans and ashing his cigarette into a Starbucks cup. We climbed down the narrow stairs into the station, holding our breath against the subway smell of urine and popcorn and damp cardboard, shaking our heads, impressed with our own gracious tolerance for the dirty city we loved.

Had I really thought a comparison between India and the Upper West Side was within the realm of possibility? Wrinkled my nose at public transportation, thinking I'd seen and smelled the worst possible commute of the masses? Somewhere back in New York, a phantom version of me was still standing on that street corner, looking into a crystal ball, gazing at the *now* me, with one hand clapped over her mouth in horror and the other signaling gratefully for a taxi.

The *now* me was in a rickshaw, one hand clapped over my nose and the other clinging to Jay for dear life.

OK, I thought as Jay had led the way through Matwala Shayar's gates, the first time we'd ventured through them without the protection of several tons of steel and glass. *I can do this.* They were just like cabs, right? A mass of people clustered on what would have been the sidewalk if India had sidewalks. They all stared.

Madhapur Road was a major thruway. We stood at the edge of the road, waiting for a rickshaw to come our way. Were we supposed to hail one, like a taxi? Before I could assume my proper cab-fetching stance, one swerved across three lanes of traffic and screeched to a stop beside us, kicking up gravel and mud in its wake. There were three people already sitting on the bench in the back. The driver gestured to us. *Get in.*

On the side of the rickshaw, there was a red-painted sign: MAXIMUM PEOPLE'S FOUR WITH DRIVER. We would make six, with the driver, and that's if germaphobe Jay agreed to get into an auto with total strangers. Which he did not. We waved it on and waited for another.

Three more rickshaws pulled up. White people waiting for an auto was clearly unusual. A small crowd of bystanders gathered to watch the commotion. The drivers hopped out and began to argue, fighting over their right to take us. Negotiations began. One driver knew a few words of English. Jay waved the others away while I climbed into the back. A pair of fuzzy dice hung from the cracked rearview mirror.

The rickshaw swayed violently under my weight. Jay threw his hand out to steady it without missing a beat in his conversation. He wanted to make sure the driver knew how to get where we wanted to go, a restaurant called Ginger Court someone at work had recommended. The driver was concerned only with the fare. Useless, I sat in the back and kept quiet.

Finally they agreed on a price: seventy rupees. Jay joined me in the back on a rickety, pleather-covered wood plank. The driver floored it.

We were off.

The rickshaw maxed out at about thirty miles per hour, but with no doors or windows and only inches from the ground, that felt pretty fast. Two of the wheels creaked with each revolution; the third appeared to be on fire, casting a stream of black smoke in our wake. The rickshaw listed ominously to one side.

I clutched Jay, feigning affection. He didn't buy it.

"Maybe you should stay on your side. The weight is more evenly distributed that way."

I moved over. Sure enough, the auto shifted to the right and became perpendicular to the road. Jay smirked. I glowered. Fine. I'd be responsible for my own safety. Gulping back a sob, I gripped the bench with my thighs and began to pray. *Please, God, I promise I'll stop ordering pizza and learn to speak Hindi and have meaningful adventures every day if you'll just let us get there safely. Amen.* I wasn't sure if I even believed in God, but now seemed like a good time to start.

The driver was channeling Mario Andretti. He honked his duck-horn continually, a red rubber bulge mounted on the roof that reminded me of Bozo the Clown. He wove in and out of lanes, dodging potholes, cutting off two-wheelers, narrowly missing pedestrians every few yards.

We were SO going to die.

Jay was smiling. Infuriatingly, he was having fun. He was probably thinking it was like Disneyland, only without the crowds. We went over a huge speed bump at top velocity. The auto took flight. Jay's smile became a grin.

If we didn't die, I was going to kill him.

I hyperventilated as quietly as possible, not wanting Jay to realize how panicked I was. I resisted the urge to stop breathing altogether. From the back of an auto rickshaw, India smelled *horrible.* Urine, garbage, wet animals, sweaty humans, cooking spices, and exhaust from pipes that would never pass a U.S. emissions test. Plus the smell of burning rubber from the rear right wheel, which was still smoking.

Everywhere, men were peeing on the side of the road. A row of eight of them, like suspects in a lineup only facing the wrong way, aimed their streams at a wall painted with four-foot-high letters stating DO NOT PASS URINE HERE. Two dogs fornicated next to a traffic signal no one was paying any attention to. A cow bore down on us from the left lane. This one, I was pretty sure, really was a cow.

Was there no such thing as animal control? Was this because cows were holy? As uncomfortable as I'd been with the idea of Jay behind the wheel, I was beginning to regret letting him talk me into Mr. Toad's Wild Rickshaw Ride. The only way I liked cow was in the form of a nonfat latte with extra foam. Or on a bun with lettuce, tomato, and extra ketchup.

The cow was getting closer and closer. We were stopped in traffic. I could see flies buzzing around its ears.

Its tail flicked into the open side of our rickshaw. I saw horns.

Even distribution of weight be damned. I was about to be eaten by a cow. I dove onto Jay's side. The auto tipped dangerously to the right. The driver looked back and shouted something in Telugu, waving his arms. I ignored him.

Jay was still enjoying the ride.

Finally, the light changed. The cow decided to sit down for a while; our puttering little vehicle managed to outrun him. I said a quick prayer of thanks for not being eaten.

We pulled up to an intersection and the driver started speaking in rapid-fire Telugu, gesturing with his arms, neither of which were on the steering handlebars even though the rickshaw was still moving. Finally we got it—he wanted to know which way to turn.

We hadn't the faintest idea.

The driver got frustrated. The engine stalled.

Was there a string in the back somewhere, like on a lawnmower? I imagined being stuck in the sea of cars forever, stalled, too afraid to get out without a police escort or a waiting helicopter.

Some grunting noises, a revving sound, and the engine jerked to life. Jay and I were thrown forward as the driver vroomed up to meet another auto and ask for directions. After a brief conversation with the other driver (four hands gesturing wildly, not a single one on handlebars), our driver bobbled his head and took off, making a right turn from the left-hand lane and cutting off four lanes of traffic.

I couldn't take any more. I closed my eyes and prayed harder.

The auto slammed to a stop. I opened my eyes.

Jay dusted himself off and helped me onto the pavement in front of Ginger Court. He gave the driver one hundred rupees and told him to keep the change. The driver, dumbfounded, tried to thrust money back at us. The exchange went on for several awkward minute, neither party understanding the perplexing actions of the other. Finally we walked away, leaving him holding the money and shaking his head in confusion.

"See?" Jay said. "We made it. That wasn't so bad, was it?"

I felt like throwing up.

ꙮ

The inside of Ginger Court looked remarkably...unremarkable. Ordinary tables set with ordinary white table cloths, simple flower arrangements in green glass vases. I wasn't sure if this was comforting or disappointing. Lately I'd felt trapped between wanting things to feel exotic and wanting them to be just like home.

The maître d' beckoned us forward with a deep bow. "Welcome to Ginger Court, Sir and Ma'am. Would you like to be smoking or nonsmoking?"

We chose nonsmoking and were escorted to a cozy back table directly below the air conditioner. A purple electric bug zapper, the kind we'd had in the backyard when I was small, sat sentry in the corner, waiting to deliver mosquitoes to the next realm. Jay grabbed both of my hands and held them across the table, bumping the green vase with its single plastic lily. Water seeped onto the tablecloth. A waiter hurried over with a cloth, dabbing at the spill, apologizing like he'd knocked the flower over himself.

"Let's make this the first night of our adventure, OK, Wife?" Jay said, running his thumb along my wrist. "I know it's been a tough first week and we didn't exactly get started on the right foot. But now we're together, and we're out, so let's start all over." He lifted his water glass. "To India."

"To India," I echoed. "To holy cows and rickshaws with fuzzy dice. And to no more chicken fevers."

"No more chicken fevers."

"I think we should promise each other something," I said, spinning my water in the glass. I thought back to the night of his fever, how scared I'd been. How he'd needed me.

"What's that?"

"We both know it's going to get really hard sometimes, right? So I think we should make a deal that only one of us gets down at a time. That way it won't ever be too bad. The other one can stay positive. You know, balance each other out."

Jay smiled at me, lopsided, in a way that made my pulse race. I remembered why I'd followed him halfway around the world in the first place.

"Yeah, OK. I promise. It's a deal."

We shook on it across the table.

I was starving. In New York, there had been this great Indian restaurant, Sapphire, in Columbus Circle. On special occasions, we'd walk there and stuff ourselves full of *saag* and chicken *tikka masala*. But for some reason, none of those things were on the Ginger Court menu. Half the menu was for Chinese food, with dishes I'd never heard of, like "chili-fried American corn" and "veg Manchow soup." The other half was Indian, but there were no samosas, no deep-fried *pakoras*. The word "curry" was nowhere to be found.

The maître d' appeared again, this time with a tray of drinks… grass green, pineapple garnish, pink-and-purple paper umbrellas. The main ingredient was either Midori liqueur or dishwashing liquid. It was hard to be sure.

"Forgive me for intruding, but it is looking to me like you are celebrating, no?" he asked, presenting the tray with a flourish. "Please allow me to offering you specialty drinks on the house and inquiring what is the occasion?"

"It's our first night in India," Jay said. "Sort of."

"Ah, I see. How long will your visit be?"

"We aren't visiting; we moved. We'll be here for two years."

The maître d' looked delighted. "Well, then allow me to be making your acquaintance as your first official friend in India, Sir and Sir Ma'am. My name is Jena. It is my pleasure to be at your service. My wife and I, we are residing in Hyderabad seven years now. We have shifted from Chennai."

Seeing our menus still open on the table, Jena looked concerned. "Have you made your selections already? Or can I be of helping to determine your choices?"

Jay cleared his throat. "Uh, we were having a hard time finding some things on the menu. Do you have chicken curry? Or chicken *tikka masala*? Or samosas?"

Jena shook his head sadly. "Ah. Those are being delicacies from Northern India only. We at Ginger Court are specializing in Southern Indian cuisine, Sir," he said. "Hyderabadi food is being like no other food in all of India. Much flavor, much spice. May I be of suggesting a *murgh biryani*? Or some *palak paneer*?"

"What's '*murgh*'?" I asked.

"*Murgh* is as you are calling chicken," Jena said. "We are proudly serving non-veg delicacies here." He paused, looking at our confused faces, perhaps noticing our celebratory mood had faded. "I am having idea. What are your good names, Sir and Sir Ma'am?"

"Our good names?" Jay asked.

"Yes, yes, your good names. Like my good name is being Jena. Your good names, the names by which people call you?"

"I'm Jay. This is my wife, Jenny."

Jena nodded and bowed his head at each of us in turn, rubbing his hands together in excitement. "Jay and Jenny, Jenny is like my own good name, Jena. Is good fortune, Sir and Ma'am. As your first official friend in Hyderabad and maître d' at the finest cuisine restaurant in our city, I am making extra special arrangement with you. Allow me to be choosing your foods. Will you say yes?"

It didn't appear there was any other acceptable answer. Jena scurried back toward the kitchen. In moments, he was back with a fragrant bowl and two sets of forks and knives. "I am thinking you would prefer eating with utensils like our many Western patrons, no?" I looked around and noticed for the first time that everyone near us was eating with his or her hands.

Jena heaped a pile of corn kernels on each of our plates. "Is traditional American chili corn, Jay Sir and Jenny Ma'am! Specialty of Ginger Court House. Taste and find delicious, no?"

I took a bite. Deep-fried, spiced with chili flakes and dusted with a sweet, sticky sauce, the corn was one of the strangest things I'd ever tasted—but it was delicious. Jena watched my expression carefully. When he realized I liked it, his mouth broke into a big grin beneath his carefully groomed mustache.

"More delicacies to come," he crowed, dashing back toward the kitchen. "Next course being for authentic India!"

Jay and I looked at our green umbrella drinks, neither of us actually brave enough to taste the liquid. I took another bite of chili corn instead. It wasn't the chicken *tikka masala* I'd been expecting, but it was something. It was a start.

CHAPTER 5

Jena's benevolent, mustached face flickered before me like a mirage as I bent over the toilet bowl again, and again, and again. He'd looked so sweet. He'd treated us so kindly. The food had tasted so good. Nothing about Ginger Court's innocuous décor suggested it was secretly a breeding ground for gastrointestinal torture and doom. I curled into a ball on the shower floor, clinging to the toilet bowl for dear life. Was this why Indian toilets were installed in the middle of the shower? To make washing off easier when you were finished throwing up? I'd consumed half a bottle of sticky pink Pepto-Bismol (another gift from the ever-wise Alexis) and I still felt like death. This was food poisoning on a whole other level—the kind that made me think consuming *actual poison* was the only reasonable way out. When the waves of nausea finally subsided, I crawled back into bed, exhaustion forcing my eyes closed the instant my body collapsed against the unyielding wooden mattress.

"Are you alive under there?" Jay asked several hours later, his voice slicing through the electric hum of the air conditioner and my lovely dream about lattes in Central Park. He rubbed my back through the sheets. "I was getting worried about you. You sounded awful last night. I think this is what they meant when they warned us about 'Delhi Belly.'"

"I can't believe you're not sick," I moaned. "It isn't fair. We ate exactly the same things."

"My immune system is just better than yours," he said smugly. "I feel great. In fact, I'm hungry. Is there anything for breakfast?"

Sitting up in bed, I paused to assess my stomach's state of unrest. I felt mildly nauseated, but human. The worst appeared to be over. I stumbled to my feet, jostling a still-sleeping Tucker, and headed for the bathroom. I reached for the toilet paper, still barely awake, and shrieked in surprise. The roll was soaked through.

"JAY. Bring me new toilet paper. It's soaking wet AGAIN," I yelled. The door opened a crack and a new roll, the consistency of gift-bag tissue paper but blessedly dry, flew in.

"Oh good, you're out of bed. Any thoughts on breakfast?" Jay called back.

He appeared in the kitchen as I was putting the finishing touches on a peanut butter and jelly sandwich. His Armani suit looked strange against the backdrop of the idol-filled *puja* prayer room behind him.

"Again? We can't eat this forever, you know." He took the sandwich anyway, careful to keep the crumbs from falling on his jacket.

"We don't have any other food."

"Find some. You could at least toast the bread."

"There's no toaster."

"Find one of those too."

He left. I chugged the remaining Pepto-Bismol for my own breakfast and sat down on the elephant swing, Tucker on my lap, tracing the links of the swing's heavy chains with my fingertips. The metal felt cool even in the sweltering heat of the room. We swayed there idly, the tips of my toes making intricate paths through the grime on the marble floor.

Though I hated to admit it, Jay was right. The initial shock-and-awe phase couldn't last forever. We were going to be living here for two whole years. I didn't want to spend the entire time stumbling around with a *Made in America* bag over my head. We needed to settle in, to start making the expat life in India *our* life. And that meant buying groceries.

In Manhattan, groceries were a non-issue. We simply didn't need them. We ate our meals at work or in restaurants or had them delivered. Who needed a supermarket when there was a Thai place on the corner? Other people, non-New Yorkers, kept flour and sugar in ceramic canisters on their kitchen counters. We kept a stack of takeout menus in a special holder we'd gotten for our wedding.

Cooking wasn't a life skill; it was a hobby. Something to do on weekends, like visiting a museum or going for a walk along the river. We'd search for a recipe online, walk to Whole Foods, and buy exactly what we needed. Then we'd make an adventure out of making a meal. Weeks later, I'd throw away the leftover ingredients: moldy packages of tarragon, jars of tomato paste with one tablespoon missing.

I eyed the container of Skippy. It was almost empty. Ditto for the Costco-sized jar of strawberry Smucker's. Subu's weekly delivery of white bread and Amul brand (*Utterly, Butterly Delicious!*) imitation butter weren't much use by themselves. After the horrors of last night, I was ready to swear off Indian food altogether. But while avoiding Indian food might protect me from another round of "Delhi Belly," the way things were going, we might die of malnutrition instead.

I dialed Venkat's mobile. He answered, startled, like I'd woken him.

"Ten minutes, Madam. I be there ten minutes."

Venkat and I had an arrangement: if I needed him to drive me somewhere, I'd text him: *Come home*. Otherwise, I let him hang out at Jay's office building with the other drivers who didn't have accompanying spouses to ferry around. They whiled away the hours in BKC's cool underground parking garage, playing poker and smoking hand-rolled *beedi* cigarettes, escaping the heat of the day. It had to be more fun than being here, dozing behind the wheel of the Scorpio in the empty Matwala Shayar parking lot, waiting for me to muster the courage to actually leave the house.

The worst part of having a driver was the pressure to drive somewhere. I wasn't used to having someone—even someone as endearing as Venkat, with his hipster beanie and his ever-so-slight Reddy swagger—bear silent witness to my every move. Or lack of them.

"Where do I go for groceries, Venkat?" I asked, climbing across the backseat. Already, the air conditioning in the brand-new Scorpio wasn't working. I was beginning to think it was my fault, that my very presence in India was having some bizarre Mercury-retrograde effect on every appliance designed to lower the temperature. Venkat had been looking in the rearview mirror, adjusting his part. He stuffed the comb in his pocket, embarrassed, when he saw me approach. The smell of his Axe hair cream was overpowering in the hot car.

"Groceries, Madam?"

"Food? Supplies?"

"Ah. Some expat peoples be going Food World, Madam. But maybe for you, Q-Mart."

"Q-Mart?" I remembered Alexis mentioning an imported food store on the night of the aspirin run.

"Yes, Madam. Madhapur Road. Much American foods." The Scorpio's wheels spun as he swerved out of the Matwala Shayar lot, spraying the sleeping street dogs with mud.

"Venkat!"

"Madam?"

"The dogs!"

"Only dogs, Madam. No thinking. No mind."

"I mind."

"Sorry, Madam."

The ride, like every ride, felt endless. I looked out the window. Female construction workers in saris and those yellow plastic hard hats knelt along the side of the road, digging rocks from the earth with bare, blistered hands. I looked down at my own hands, cuticles ragged where I'd been gnawing them. Yesterday, I'd been complaining to Jay about how badly I needed a manicure.

The air was stifling. I stared at the back of Venkat's head and silently cursed him for his obsession with styling products. Outside the window, a herd of buffalo ambled along, oblivious to the chorus of honking horns that tried to scare them out of the way.

"Where are being buffalo U.S., Madam?" Venkat asked, observing my fascination.

"There aren't any."

"NO buffalo, Madam?!"

"Well, maybe there are some. In the zoo. Or maybe Montana. But they don't look like this. They're…fuzzy. And they don't walk in the road."

"But what about *city* buffalo, Madam?" Venkat asked. "Where living *city* buffalo?"

I told him our cities don't have buffalo. Venkat frowned pityingly, like he thought it was a shame.

We came to a stop at the Jubilee Hills check post, the only landmark in Hyderabad I'd learned to recognize. There was no actual post, which was perplexing. I cracked my window to get some air.

"NO, Madam!" Venkat shouted. At the same time, a set of brown fingers slithered into the car, pressing against the window glass, trying to gain more access. I leapt across the backseat to the other side.

"Please! Hungry! Rupees! Ma'am! Look at me!"

The Scorpio was crawling with ragged Indian boys. Screaming and laughing, they leapt onto the car, fearless, brazen with common purpose. They were everywhere—clinging to the sides, dangling from the roof, hammering the doors with practiced fists. A grinning boy, no more than five years old with stick-out ears and dressed in shredded jean cut-offs, pressed his naked belly against the window. He pointed back and forth between his mouth and his stomach, urging me, through the tinted glass, to help him. Venkat opened his door and leaned out, screaming at the urchins in Telugu. They laughed and ignored him.

The traffic light at the check post finally changed. Venkat slammed the accelerator to the floor. The begging children scattered, hitting the ground running, dodging effortlessly through a wall of cars as they headed for refuge on a grassy median to await the next red light.

My heart hammered in my throat as I turned to watch them through the back window. The oldest, no more than twelve, shirtless and swaggering, talked into a cell phone. The others squatted in a messy circle at his feet, counting rupees into a dented tin can.

"Venkat, if they're beggars, how come they have cell phones?"

"Cell phones, Madam?"

"That big one. He's using a cell phone. A mobile. How could he afford that?"

Venkat followed my gaze in the rearview. "Is not his. Is for his leader."

"His leader?"

"Leader is in charge. Gets childrens from streets and villages. All rupees go to him."

"Does he kidnap the kids? I mean, does he take them from their parents?"

Venkat shrugged and hunched over the wheel. "Sometimes taking. Sometimes childrens have no homes. Or the parents are leaving them on the road. Leader gives them food. Places for sleeping.

"No opening windows, Madam. Much danger. They are being teach to open doors for cars like these." He dragged the car to a stop in front of a rickety staircase. "Q-Mart, Madam. We are being here."

At the foot of the stairs was a toothless woman in a brown cotton sari worn to rags, chewing a mouthful of grass and selling bunches of daisies dyed neon pink and Windex blue. She waved a handful in my face as I stepped around her, smiling with polite refusal. She scowled at the rejection, spitting phlegm at my heels as I walked upward.

"Welcome to Q-Mart, Madam!" cried a man standing at the upstairs entrance. Three male cashiers, idling lazily on bar stools behind ancient cash registers, looked up with interest. "We are so happy to be having you! Is it your first time?" He wore a white button-down shirt and crisp Dockers khakis. His hand-lettered name badge read "Srikanth, MANAGER."

"It is," I said, looking past him at narrow aisles jam-packed with boxes. Dust was everywhere. Already, without knowing the lay of the Q-Mart land, I knew I was in the right place. There were things I recognized. American things. Shaving cream. Ritz crackers. Six packs of Diet Coke.

Srikanth handed me a pink plastic shopping basket with a broken handle. I headed straight for the Diet Coke. If coffee continued to elude me, the least I could do was stockpile a different form of caffeine.

After weeks of nothing but peanut butter and jelly and Pizza Corner, I rejoiced in the array of American products. Pancake syrup. Ramen noodles. Ragu spaghetti sauce, something I'd been way too

snobby to eat on American soil. *Too many chemicals and preservatives,*
I'd sniff when Jay eyed the displays at Food Emporium. Ragu had
always been his favorite, a fact I never let him live down. Here, it
practically had a halo around it. I did a little happy-dance shuffle in
my flip-flops and started in the toiletry aisle.

Next to me, a blond woman in clogs was sweeping an armful
of Breck shampoo into her basket. "They *never* have this stuff," she
whispered, looking over her shoulder like someone was going to
come and take it all away. I leaned toward her, hoping to start a
conversation, but behind us there were sounds of commotion and she
took off. Curious, I followed.

"I saw it first, man," whined a dreadlocked white guy wearing
army green *dhoti* pants, Birkenstocks, and a wifebeater. He was in his
early twenties, a backpacker maybe. He was wrestling with a middle-
aged man in a polo and plaid Bermuda shorts, who was waving a bag
of—wait, were those *Doritos?*—high in the air, the sweat of exertion
glistening on his bald skull.

"*Non!*" said Bermuda shorts, in French or maybe German, as he
fought off Birkenstocks to keep his hold on the bag of chips. The
blond woman from the toiletry aisle rolled up the sleeves of her tunic
and put her basket on the floor, ready to join the fray.

"But they're just chips," I said to no one in particular. The Dorito bag
split open. Powdery neon orange triangles poured to the floor. Someone
scooped them up and put them back in the bag. The fight continued.

Srikanth appeared behind me, observing the drama. He did nothing to intervene.

"Only one bag, Ma'am, and they are very rare," he said.
"Sometimes ten or more peoples are fighting." He shrugged, his
expression bemused.

I wandered further. Along the back wall were several freestanding freezers. Designed like top-loading washing machines, they were stuffed to the brim, cartons and containers spilling over their dented aluminum tops. Every few minutes, the electricity would cut out, silencing their electric whines.

The one closest to me had legs sticking out of it. Upside-down, jean-clad legs that churned in the air like they were riding an imaginary, upside-down unicycle.

"GOT it!" A hand appeared next to the legs, waving a package of sausage links. The package was crushed and dripped condensation. I wondered how many times it had thawed and been refrozen.

"I KNEW they'd be here." The owner of the legs executed a perfect flip out of the freezer and landed back on the dusty tile floor. He turned the sausages over and checked for an expiration date. "February. *Nice.*" Without a word to me, he dove headfirst into the next freezer.

It was June.

ه

"What did you buy?" Jay asked that night, listening to my retelling of the Dorito battle royale with disbelief.

"You wouldn't believe it: they had cream cheese! Philadelphia! I bought the last four packages. And I got Captain Crunch, and salsa, and more toilet paper. And the September issue of *Vogue*." I lifted item after item, proud of my purchases.

Jay's eyes remained glued to his BlackBerry, where he and his co-worker Diana were texting back and forth furiously. Region 10 was having yet another crisis he was determined to solve. "You bought *four* packages of cream cheese? Were there bagels?"

"No, there weren't *bagels*. Are you out of your mind? I was lucky to find cereal."

"Did you buy milk?"

"Um. No. It came in a cardboard box and it was just sitting there on the shelf, not refrigerated or anything. It kind of scared me."

"So we're having peanut butter and jelly for dinner."

I looked around. It was true. After all that time shopping and so many bags lugged up the elevator and into the flat, there didn't seem to be much actual *food*.

"How much did you spend?"

"I don't know. I just put it on the credit card. It couldn't have been much, it's INDIA. Everything is cheap here."

Jay grabbed the receipt, an old-school adding machine strip printed in faded purple ink.

"Tell me you did not spend 3500 rupees and we still have nothing to eat for dinner."

"Is 3500 rupees a lot?"

He threw the receipt back down on the kitchen counter without answering and left the room, yanking at his tie. I looked at the issue of *Vogue*, brushing aside a thick layer of dust to read the price tag. Rs 500. My math skills had always been pathetic. I counted on my fingers, did some division.

So that was like…twenty bucks. For a nine-month-old magazine. That I couldn't cook for dinner.

⟨◯⟩

For two weeks, Jay worked like crazy, clocking fourteen-hour days while he learned the ins and outs of his new role in Region 10. He came back to the flat looking overwhelmed and exhausted, his mind consumed with the details of the task before him.

"The boys have a day off tomorrow," Alexis said, stopping by to visit one afternoon after she and Younus had dropped Peter off at work. Because Peter was in the tax group, he, like the rest of the short-term expats, worked hours designed to maximize contact with the Western world. I envied the large portion of daylight hours they got to spend together, sightseeing or cooking together in their flat. Alexis always invited me to join them, but I mostly declined. I hated feeling like a third wheel. But an opportunity for all four of us to spend the day together in the middle of the week sounded heavenly.

"Really? That's awesome. Why?"

"It's a Hindu festival. The whole company is on holiday. Peter and I are going to watch the parades. They're supposed to be fun. Do you guys want to come?"

"Sounds like something we shouldn't miss."

"Ganesh Chaturthi, Madam! Much meaning," Venkat said when I asked him about it later. "Is being mine favorite. Ganesh is Elephant God. Much power. Much protection."

"How do you celebrate?" I asked, curious.

"First ten days praying, Madam. Then singing in streets, much flowers and colors and dancing," he said, waving his arms in the air to demonstrate.

"Venkat! Keep your hands on the wheel!"

"Sorry, Madam. After singing and dancing is idols swimming. Peoples making idols of Ganesh and we are putting flowers and coconuts. Then peoples are singing and dancing them to the water for putting in."

"The idols go in the water?"

"Ganesh swimming much holy, Madam."

Venkat's description turned out to be exactly right, but it still didn't prepare me for the spectacle we watched parading down Hyderabad's streets. Shirtless men spray-painted hot pink danced and pounded drums behind makeshift carts bearing hundreds of different artistic renderings of the Elephant God—all different sizes made from plaster and plastic, wood and clay. Fireworks showered down from the sky as each Ganesh, borne on its own pedestal, made its way to the Hussain Sagar River to be immersed in the muddy waters. Many of the idols shattered to pieces when they landed, coloring the water pink and purple and green where they fell.

"This is so awesome," Peter said, snapping pictures like crazy. "Why don't we have stuff like this in the U.S.?"

"Probably because this would qualify as a riot," Jay said, overwhelmed by the teeming crowds.

"What a waste of art," Alexis sighed, watching an elaborately painted Ganesh go by, five feet tall and teetering dangerously in the arms of several hot pink teenagers. "I can't believe all that beautiful detail goes into something they're just going to smash in the river."

"What I can't believe is that they have Indian women with buckets on their heads building four-story shopping malls by hand, but they managed to find a crane to get a fake elephant into the river," Peter said, pointing. Sure enough, an enormous yellow construction crane idled by the riverbank, dangling a Ganesh statue by one enormous ear over the churning brown water.

"I guess festivals take priority when it comes to heavy machinery," Alexis said, pushing her way to the edge of the crowd for a better view. I hung back, wanting to stay as inconspicuous as possible. People were already staring.

"Madam," Venkat whispered behind me. I jumped.

"Venkat, you scared me."

"Is heart attack?"

I grinned. "No, not quite that bad. Not this time."

"I giving you something. Is gift. Much secret, not for swimming. Just for keep." He pressed something into my palm.

It was a tiny Ganesh idol, carved with perfect detail. Below the elephant's crossed legs was a rat.

"Rat meaning is real, Madam. Only where is rat is real Ganesh. Others no good. Much bad fortune."

I caressed the tiny statue with my thumb. "Thank you, Venkat. I love it."

Venkat bowed his head, the tops of his ears blushing red. Then he slipped back into the crowd of dancers, smudges of hot pink visible on his jeans.

"Wow, did Venkat just give you a present?" Alexis asked, joining me again. The pounding drums surged in the background as the crane lifted the giant Ganesh even higher. "Ganesh is perfect for you. He's called the Lord of Beginnings and he's also the patron of writers and artists. My art teacher honors him at the beginning of every class."

"Wow. I had no idea," I said, tucking the gift in my pocket to keep it safe.

Behind us, the giant Ganesh dangled from the hook of the crane. A hush fell over the crowd as the driver extended the boom over the lake as far as it would go. Even the drums observed the briefest moment of silence before pounding to life again with renewed fervor. Whoops and yells rang out as the elephant swung dramatically back and forth, poised for descent. Everyone pushed together, jostling one another for a better view. The air was electric with anticipation.

Ganesh fell. The idol made an elegant arc despite his awkward heft, swan-diving down and disappearing beneath the surface for one breathless moment before breaking through again, face up and serene, his massive trunk broken but majestic just the same. The revelers cried out with joy and dove in after him, tossing flowers around him as he bobbed in the current. Petal-covered *aarti* lights, their ghee-soaked wicks reflecting hundreds of tiny flames across the river's surface, floated everywhere. Alone on the shore, we jumped up and down, cheering along with the crowd, our confusion trumped by the contagious elation of everyone around us.

CHAPTER 6

I'd expected to be good at this.

In New York, Jay and I would sit up in bed late at night and talk about our grand adventure: the places we'd visit, the people we'd meet. It all sounded so glamorous and foreign—the exotic animals, the smells and sounds, the ancient ruins, and the crowded bazaars. As soon as Jay uttered the word "expat," I was hooked on my new persona. I'd be like Katharine Hepburn in *The African Queen*, but without all the war stuff. And the swamps and parasites. Or like Audrey Hepburn in *Roman Holiday*, minus the princess part (unless being an American princess counted). What could be more exciting, more sophisticated than becoming a seasoned traveler, a citizen of the world?

Gazing out over the Hudson River, the New Jersey lights twinkling in the distance, I was sure I'd be the perfect expat housewife. I'd barter effortlessly in the open air markets. I'd learn local recipes and wow my new expat friends (because *of course* I'd have a whole bunch of glamorous expat friends) with my effortless transition into Indian culture.

But now, almost a month into our grand adventure, I still couldn't figure out the exchange rate and had swapped my visions of home-cooked *biryani* for a thirteen-dollar jar of Ragu. The Dorito scuffle in Q-Mart hardly counted as the sophisticated expat social scene I'd been dreaming of. I still hadn't found a decent cup of coffee. When we visited Alexis and Peter in their Delta block flat, they looked like they had it all together. Their living room was decorated with vases and carvings they'd picked up at local bazaars. Peter told stories like he'd been living here forever. Alexis even looked the part, wearing embroidered tunics and dashing off words of Telugu while she strained chick peas over the kitchen sink. Was I the only one getting it all wrong?

Still, it was early. We'd landed just a few weeks ago. Maybe getting into a groove in Hyderabad would take longer than I had anticipated. The journey was still new and our living situation was temporary— Venkat and I spent hours each day scouring the city for a house to rent. The all-night parties were wearing thin; I longed for some peace and quiet, a good night's sleep in my very own bed, and freedom from Subu's impromptu visits. Soon we'd have neighbors, maybe even some new friends. Wouldn't someone show up with a Bundt cake sooner or later?

"If you want to be meeting other expats, you should be heading for the Taj tomorrow," Subu told us one Saturday, watching us return from another fruitless house-hunting trip. "Everyone will be gathering there on Sunday morning. You'll like it—they are having live music and much Western foods."

"Should we try it?" I asked Jay, willing him to say yes. He continued to come home exhausted, a combination of the long hours and the difficulty of his new role. Heading out again was probably the last thing he wanted to do. Still, I was feeling desperate. I employed my biggest puppy dog eyes, already mentally planning my outfit.

"I'm fine going. Alexis and Peter usually go and say it's pretty good." I threw my arms around his neck. "Yes!"

Jay laughed and held up a hand in warning.

"But it's Venkat's day off, remember? If you still refuse to let me drive the car, then we need to take a rickshaw."

I closed my eyes for a moment. Brave another Mr. Toad's Wild Ride through the streets of Hyderabad or miss an opportunity to be social?

"OK. Let's do it."

؏

Sunday morning. Formerly a time we reserved for lazy walks in Central Park, Starbucks in hand, watching Tucker romp with the other dogs enjoying the pre-9:00 a.m., no-leash-required rule. Our old life had been so jam-packed with work and school and dinners and friends that we'd craved that one day of unstructured solitude. Now, I was thrilled to have somewhere to be.

Jay and I arrived at the Taj Krishna hotel a little past noon. Uniformed doormen, all in white with gold-braided turbans, bowed deeply and swung open the giant double doors with synchronized precision. The lobby was exactly what India looked like in the movies. Dark glossy wood carved into elephants and peacocks and lotus blossoms. Faded brocade upholstery on overstuffed furniture. Flaking gold leaf everywhere. There were giant palms in brass planters and crystal chandeliers. The air smelled like mildew and cherry pipe smoke.

I was red-eyed and achy from a fitful, sleepless night beneath the broken air conditioner. Still, with the promise of other expats and the possibility of making new friends, I'd dressed for the occasion—floral sundress from Rebecca Taylor, wedge espadrilles, giant Chanel sunglasses (the better to pretend I didn't see all the stares). But the minute we walked onto the large outdoor patio, my outfit felt all wrong.

The expats were arranged in factions. In the corner farthest from the pool, next to the elevated fish pond, were the families. Frazzled, laughing moms in khaki shorts and embroidered tunics, their hair tied back in sensible ponytails, tethered their toddlers with one hand and clutched glasses of iced tea in the other. Sunburned dads in golf shirts, mobile phones at the ready, ignored the kid-related chaos around them and swapped corporate stories from Amsterdam and Chicago and Sao Paulo.

Close to the bar, next to the smoking barbecue, were the post-grads in concert tees and battered jeans. Raucous and hungover, they were tax accountants from Philly and Portland and Detroit, living it up on their first international assignment. Because they worked U.S. hours, they didn't need to clock in until 2:00 p.m. India time. Which meant they partied every night, playing poker and blasting hip-hop until three or four in the morning, when they crashed in Kingfisher-soaked stupors on whichever couch happened to be nearest.

Jay recognized some of them, smiled and waved. I lifted my eyebrows in a gesture I hoped would be interpreted as friendly, but the truth was, I had a different crowd in mind. Jay and I had done our post-college partying post college. Now I was ready for something more sophisticated. But there were no other housewives here, no "accompanying spouses" who would show me where to shop for vegetables or keep me company on sightseeing trips and yoga retreats.

Next to the pool, lounging primly beneath the shade of striped umbrellas and coconut palms, were the expat elders. Closer to my parents' age than mine, these were the empty-nester expats, the high-level executives with their kids off to college, living out their dreams of exotic golden years under the Indian sun. Some of the women wore linen suits and wide-brimmed hats; others wore traditional Indian "dresses," ankle-length cotton tunics worn over matching tapered pants. I recognized the clog-wearing woman I'd seen in

Q-Mart, now sitting beside an elegant man with salt-and-pepper hair and navy pants embroidered with tiny whales.

I glanced down at my sundress, smoothed it further over my suddenly too-bare thighs. The dress had looked so perfect, so worldly and elegant, when I'd examined myself in the sliver of bathroom mirror before we left Matwala Shayar.

I could feel an entire room of expat eyes watching as we made our way across the patio. Unsettled, I stumbled a little and cursed the wedges I'd maneuvered so easily down New York City streets. I'd been struggling to endure these past few weeks of relentless Indian stares, so often being the only white person in a sea of brown faces. I hated feeling like a sideshow curiosity. But was that a chuckle I heard from one of the elders, compressed beneath a set of manicured fingertips, or was coffee withdrawal making me imagine things?

"Jenny! Jay! Over here," called Peter. "Congrats on making it to your first brunch in 'Bad." Hearing my name spoken out loud after so many "Sir Ma'ams" and "Madams" and "Mrs. Jay Sirs" felt strange. In my old life, I'd been greeted by name dozens of times a day—at the yoga studio, on campus, at the neighborhood bar for happy hour. I'd been a co-worker, a classmate, a friend. Here, I was no one. A parasitic extension of my husband, a hanger-on in the world of corporate transplants.

Alexis and Peter were at a table in the back, half-hidden by a carved marble pillar. With them were Diana and her husband Kyle, who'd been our frequent dinner companions in recent weeks. Jay and Diana worked the same long hours. When they finally left the office, they'd come collect Kyle and me. The four of us would pile into the back of the Scorpio and head out to Ginger Court or Little Italy, commiserating about expat struggles over bottles of Indian wine.

Diana, from the Los Angeles office, was one of the other two senior managers sent to Hyderabad along with Jay. The two of them were fast friends—both obsessed with work, addicted to their Blackberries, and possessing the same uncanny ability to appear cool and collected in the face of any crisis. Diana stuck out in Hyderabad even more than we did. Not only was she tall and thin and blond, but she'd bought herself a tangerine orange-colored Scorpio which, half the time, she insisted on driving by herself. Every surface in Diana's office was covered with Hindu idols and empty cans of Diet Coke.

Kyle, Diana's husband, worked in Hyderabad too, the general manager for the mobile division of an electronic media company. He spent half his time on conference calls with elite international corporate powerhouses, and the other half playing World of Warcraft beneath a giant pair of noise-cancelling headphones. Tall, Asian, and a surprisingly harmonious blend of gentle and sarcastic, Kyle made the long work-talk dinners bearable.

The waiter appeared with a towel folded over one arm like a perfect English butler. "Can I be getting Sir and Sir Ma'am something to drink?" he asked.

"Cappuccino," I said, begging him with my eyes not to tell me there was no such thing.

"Vodka," Jay said. I raised an eyebrow. "With tomato juice," he amended, shaking a napkin over his lap.

"Very good, Ma'am and Sir," said the waiter, bowing.

"Have you guys been here long?" Jay asked Peter, who was scanning through pictures on his digital camera. Alexis lifted her own Chanel sunglasses an inch to smile at me, her eyes red-rimmed. She looked as dejected as I felt. She stirred an iced tea listlessly with a teaspoon, fanning her other hand in front of her face to swat away flies that circled the table.

I'd been avoiding Alexis because her contentment seemed

oppressive. I hadn't wanted to hear about her art classes, or the orphans she volunteered with, or how she thought I needed a project to occupy my time. She meant well, but I preferred being left to wallow in my misery. Seeing her now, I felt terrible about my self-imposed seclusion. She'd been a good friend to me. It wasn't her fault India wasn't anything like I'd imagined.

"You've got to see these buffalo," Peter said, pushing the camera toward Jay. "They stopped traffic forever on Wednesday. I had to call in and explain why I was an hour late getting back from lunch."

Kyle was chowing down on a plate of something orange and spicy-looking. Diana picked at a pile of wilted lettuce and sipped a Bloody Mary, squinting at her BlackBerry from behind a pair of Ray-Ban aviators. Jay ordered a bowl of cereal with milk. I thought of the yellow cardboard carton of Nestlé Slim and wondered if the hotel had milk that came from a refrigerator. And if the kitchens were well secured. And what the punishment would be for stealing cow-related products if I were to get caught, say, *borrowing* some.

I scanned the menu, looking for something that sounded appealing. Spicy food had never been my thing. Anything stronger than 'mild' was a deal-breaker. Just looking at a bottle of Tabasco made me anxious. But in India, there seemed to be no such thing as 'mild' or 'bland.' Everything was five-alarm spicy, even stuff that wasn't supposed to be, like pizza and ketchup. Begging waiters to tell the kitchen "no spice" had absolutely no effect.

I wanted challah French toast from the Olympic Flame diner, or a spinach and feta omelet from Serafina. Even a fried egg and cheese sandwich from the guy with the cart at the corner of Sixty-Eighth and Broadway sounded like heaven.

Down at the bottom of the menu, tucked beneath a list of Indian pastries, was something called "Eggs Poached American with Style

Cream." Eggs sounded OK. I called the waiter over and asked what "style cream" was. He gestured with his hands as he explained that it was cold and white and served with a spoon. "Much good tasting, Madam. Shall I bring you a sample?"

"It's sour cream," said Kyle matter-of-factly, pouring himself another glass of orange juice from the pitcher on the table. "But they can't call it that here, because people will think it's actually sour. Like rancid. Gone bad. Ever seen a bag of Style Cream and Onion potato chips? They have them at Food World."

I closed my menu. "Poached eggs, please," I said as a blue Frisbee careened onto the table in front of me, knocking Kyle's orange juice into my lap. A red-haired toddler chased after it, weaving through my dripping legs and giggling. His apologetic mother brushed past, chasing after him as he headed for the pool.

"I'd never bring kids here," Jay remarked, handing me his napkin and taking a long sip of Bloody Mary. He winced and stirred it with a withered cucumber stick. "Too much to worry about. Jenny is enough of a liability."

"Very funny," I muttered, dabbing at my dress.

I couldn't imagine having children here with me. Being responsible for their nutrition, for their intake of clean water, for keeping them out of traffic and away from stray livestock that may or may not have rabies. Not to mention the mosquitoes. And the heat. And the cholera warnings. Still, I envied the young moms who were consumed with their offspring: teaching them phrases in Hindi, exclaiming over mango trees, letting them scrape curried lentils off plates with their fingers. Those women had purpose. They had routine. They had family.

"Your breakfast, Mrs. Sir," said the waiter, delivering two eggs swimming in a murky pool of white. A single slice of lime adorned the chipped ceramic plate. The eggs were shriveled like raisins, defeated-looking. I raised my fork and took a bite. Then I spit egg out all over the table.

"HEY!" Jay said, wiping egg bits off his shorts.

"*Vinegar*," I croaked, chugging down water. The "American style" eggs had been poached in vinegar. My appetite was ruined. My cappuccino had never arrived. Jay looked at me, sleep-deprived and caffeine-starved, my dress soaked and sticky.

"Waiter!" he called. "Get these eggs out of here. She'll have some cereal. And a Diet Coke."

On the way home, Jay was more silent than usual.

"What?" I asked.

"What?" he responded, watching a buffalo graze in the lane next to us.

"The eggs really were disgusting."

"I know, Jen."

"So why are you mad?"

"I'm not mad."

"You're silent. I can tell."

"I'm just…I want us to get settled in and be happy here. I'm not sure if your attitude is ever going to let that happen."

"What attitude? We just got here! I'm still adjusting! And you agree this isn't what we thought we signed up for, right?"

"All I'm asking you to do is try," he replied. He leaned back against the seat and tapped his fingers against the window, trying to get the buffalo to look at him. "Just try."

Settling in was not going according to plan. At least for me, it wasn't. Jay was making strides at work and forming friendships with some of his new colleagues. His fears about his leadership being rejected, about not being able to complete the task he'd been given, diminished with each passing week in his new role. He was even getting the hang of Indian expressions, tossing out gems like "Do the needful" in normal conversation.

But as his confidence grew, mine continued to waiver. My failures with the groceries, the cell phone-wielding beggars, those expat snickers I still wasn't sure if I'd imagined…they were all piled on top of each other in my mind, making it hard for me to focus on my next steps. Jay hadn't said anything about my bad attitude since that day in the car, but I still thought about his words, defending myself in my head against the accusation. *I'm lonely. Things are harder when you're the one at home all alone. Everything is so, so different.*

Everyone told me how foreign India would be; why didn't I listen to their warnings? The more time I spent analyzing my missteps, the worse my fears became. What if we never got used to it? What if it got worse instead of better? What if saying yes to the greatest adventure of our lives was really the worst mistake I'd ever made?

At work, Jay was focused and content, committed to the task at hand. With each passing week, he seemed more sure of himself. When I listened to his voice on the endless work calls he took from the apartment, he sounded confident and energetic. At home, though, my frustrations seemed to rub off on him. He was withdrawn and easily annoyed. There was an edge in his voice when he talked to me. If I weren't here, dragging him down, would he be happier? A good housewife was supposed to be supportive, and I wasn't even doing that. Jay was right. I needed to try harder.

In the meantime, the laundry situation was becoming increasingly troubling. More than a month had gone by; we'd been wearing the same clothing over and over again. The dirty clothes pile rivaled the size of the Statue of Liberty. A good housewife would do laundry every day, whistling merrily, making perfect corners with fitted sheets that smelled like Snuggle. Except we had no washing machine. We had no dryer. We didn't even have a bathtub. I'd uttered the words "fabric softener" to Srikanth in Q-Mart only to enter into a conversation so convoluted and confusing ("You are wanting your fabrics to be softened, Madam? First I will be needing to know what was done to make them hard?") I got a headache and gave up.

What we did have was a bucket and a filthy clothesline, covered with bird droppings and dead flies, out on the balcony.

One morning, Jay didn't bother to conceal his frustration as he pulled on yet another crumpled work shirt and tried to smooth the wrinkles out with the back of his hairbrush.

"I can't keep going to work like this. The partners are all in town. I have meetings." He dug in his cubby, searching unsuccessfully for a clean pair of socks. He sat down on the bed, narrowly missing my feet beneath the blanket, and pulled his shoes on without socks, grunting with exertion. Or merely for effect; I wasn't sure.

I was failing as a housewife already. It had only been six weeks.

I called Alexis.

"How do you do your laundry?" I asked. "Jay might divorce me if he has to go one more day without a clean pair of socks."

Alexis laughed. "I've been there. Dial Subu. Matwala Shayar has a laundry service; he'll come to your flat and pick it up."

"Do you think it's safe to use?"

"Is anything safe to use here? So far, we've been pretty lucky. You should give it a try."

It felt like a domestic cop-out to delegate the task. But it was looking like I was out of options, at least until we found a place of our own.

I had three more houses to visit this afternoon; maybe one of them would turn out to be perfect and I'd need to risk the Matwala Shayar laundry just this once. I called Subu and told him I needed to send out the wash. He arrived at our flat hours later with his assistant Ritu in tow. She was a sullen girl dressed in blue jeans and a bright orange *kurti*, a long-sleeved Indian tunic. It was an outfit that modern Indian teens wore to bridge the gap with the West and to annoy their parents. As a formerly rebellious adolescent, I appreciated the impulse.

Ritu took our laundry basket, dumped it on the floor, and examined the contents, holding up each piece for Subu's inspection. Subu nodded his head and took notes on a carbon-paper pad.

Things had different names here. As they went through our dirty clothes and itemized each piece, Subu recited the categories out loud. My tank tops were "slips." Jay's boxers were "short pants." His shorts were "medium pants." Anything longer than knee-length was "pants," including all of my skirts and dresses. At the last minute, I snatched back my underwear—my lovingly curated collection of Hanky Panky, Cosabella, and Victoria's Secret. Perhaps a test run was in order before anything delicate took the Indian laundry plunge.

Three days later, Subu let himself into the flat carrying a large bundle tied up in a sheet. Ritu followed closely at his heels. I'd been lying on the floor reading the September issue of *Vogue* for the ninth time. It was cooler on the floor. Tucker, who'd been curled underneath my knees, leapt to his feet and growled fiercely. Subu froze in the doorway. I hauled Tucker into the bedroom and locked him in. He whined and scratched in protest, his black nose poking through the crack beneath the door.

Subu, visibly relieved, unknotted the edges of his bundle with a flourish and separated the clothing into stacks.

"See, Madam? Laundry finished."

Now I had to go through it all and give him my approval. I had to do this or he would never go away. I tried to stare him down, telepathically willing him to leave, but he bobbled his head and shifted from foot to foot until I gave in and began to thumb through the piles.

Huh.

I didn't know Jay had a shirt that said "MUSHROOM NATION" on it. And what were all those V-neck undershirts? Jay hated V-necks. An Oklahoma University football jersey? And did those socks have… HOLES in them?

This was SO not our laundry.

Subu looked befuddled and consulted his list. Panic mounting, he dug through the stacks himself until he unearthed some things that did actually belong to us: Jay's gym shorts, my shirt with the Israeli paratrooper logo on it, a pair of boxers with devils all over them I'd bought Jay for our first Valentine's Day. A lacy demi-cup bra I'd overlooked, now grayish and misshapen. This was embarrassing.

After counting the total number of items in the pile, Subu determined that all of our laundry was accounted for. It was just that there was *extra* laundry that needed to be identified and returned to its rightful owner. So, beneath Subu and Ritu's fascinated stares, I began the unpleasant task of removing Joe Schmoe's holey socks, yellowed undershirts, and stained, pilly boxer briefs from our (vastly superior) pile of clothes.

Finally, Subu left. I freed Tucker. Now I could get down to real housewifely business: putting my husband's clothes away. Grocery failure? OK, possible. But the laundry thing seemed to be in the bag. Moving the pile from couch to bedroom, I heard an odd crinkling noise. I looked down to make sure I wasn't stepping on something.

I wasn't.

I took a few more steps. The crinkling continued.

There was NEWSPAPER. In our CLOTHES.

Inky, dirty pieces of newsprint were folded in between each and every piece of our clean laundry. Jay was going to freak. Newspapers were high on his most-toxic-germ list, along with doorknobs, car keys, and elevator buttons. I removed the newspaper and refolded the clothes. I hid the evidence in the kitchen trash.

Jay came home from work and asked if the laundry had come back. "Yes, honey," I said, all cheerful and housewifely. I showed him the clean clothes put away in his cubby.

He lifted up a sock.

"Um."

"Yes, dear?" I asked. Always the concerned, supportive spouse.

"Notice anything funny about this sock?" he asked. I took a closer look.

The sock was three feet long.

Literally.

Jay's feet were NOT three feet long.

It was very Rudyard Kipling. I tried to remember if the Limpopo River was in India or Africa, and what the chances were of Jay's socks having somehow fallen into it.

I called Subu.

"Subu, why are Jay's socks long?"

"Long, Madam?"

"Yes, Subu. Long. Taller. Stretched? Much longer than they were when we sent them to you."

There was a pause.

"Well, sometimes, Madam, the socks will be getting longer after ironing is finished."

"You're IRONING his socks? Thanks, but it's really OK. No ironing, please. Just wash."

"Sorry, Madam. Everything must be ironed. That is the way good laundry is being done in India, Madam."

Since I had no idea how to do "good laundry" in India or anywhere else, I was out of talking points. I hung up and shut the door to Jay's cubby before he noticed the newspaper smudges all over his white undershirts.

Jay took a shower and I put the rest of the clothes away. I slipped a tank top over my head and prepared to luxuriate in the cozy feeling of freshness.

But the shirt was stiff as a board and smelled horrible. Burnt. Smoky. Like…

Barbecue. My tank top smelled like barbecue. That smudgy, mesquite stench that clung to you after you spent hours flipping burgers over a charcoal grill.

Ugh. I ripped the shirt off and threw it back in the laundry basket. Maybe that one hadn't made it in the wash or something. I tried another.

Barbecue again.

Jay came out of the bathroom, dripping wet, his nose wrinkled in disgust.

"My towel smells like it's on fire," he said. "Can you get me a new one?"

Subu was now number-one on my speed-dial.

"Subu? There's something wrong with our laundry. It smells like barbecue."

"Barbecue, Madam? I am not sure of what is 'barbecue.'"

"Smoke? Coal? *Fire?*"

"Oh yes, Madam, *coal.* That would be from the ironing, Madam."

"Why would ironing make our clothes smell like coal?"

"Well, Madam, it is owing to the irons. They are being heated in pits of coal. That is how good laundry is being done in India, Madam." He muttered something under his breath. Probably Telugu for *you idiot.*

Jesus freaking Christ.

I'd failed at the groceries. Failed at the laundry. But there was

85

one last thing I could try, something that would ease the sting of my less-than-victorious attempts and make Jay forget all about peanut butter and jelly sandwiches and coal-pressed undershirts. I found one last clean pair of Hanky Pankys and slipped them on, tucking myself behind him and rubbing my hands along his shoulder blades. I kneaded my fingers into his skin, trying to release the stiff tension there. "Can't I make you forget about the laundry?"

Jay shrugged out of my embrace and grabbed his toothbrush.

"Forget it, Jen. I'm beat." He smiled his lopsided smile. It wasn't enough to take the sting away.

India. The birthplace of romance. Wasn't Tantra invented here? We were practically in the shadow of the Taj Mahal, the most stunning physical tribute to eternal love ever built. We were on an adventure. We were newlyweds. But already, we were fading from each other, trapped beneath our disappointments, paralyzed by the unspoken fear that we'd made a mistake we could never take back.

I tossed the underwear in a corner and changed into an old sorority T-shirt that came down to my knees. Trying to shrug off the sting of rejection, I closed my eyes and pictured the New York skyline the way it had looked from our bedroom window on the twenty-second floor. Twinkling lights and tall buildings, a whole world of possibility small enough to hold in the palm of my hand. I remembered the promise we'd made to each other, that one of us would always have to stay positive, and wondered whose turn it was now.

We got into bed, tucked beneath sheets that smelled like the backyard on the Fourth of July. Jay pulled his sleeping hat down over his nose. Just looking at the stupid thing made me even hotter.

"Fine for you," I grunted. "What am I supposed to do?"

"Find somewhere else to do the laundry," he said, turning away from me, already drifting off.

CHAPTER 7

With the exception of Alexis, Peter, Diana, and Kyle, we'd made little progress on the social front. Hyderabad was nothing like the elite jet-set scene I'd imagined it to be. The one Matwala Shayar party we'd gone to had been in a crowded living room full of twentysomething tax accountants, all male, playing beer pong and, as Alexis had warned me, consuming flaming shots of anise-flavored alcohol so potent it was illegal in the United States. Hip-hop blared too loudly on the stereo. Everyone wanted to get wasted. No one wanted to talk about ashrams or silent meditation retreats. No one had been to Dubai or taken a yacht around the coast of Bali. We stayed twenty minutes before ducking out, saying good-bye to no one, the pulsing bass following us back to our flat on a wafting plume of hash smoke.

One morning, someone from Team Assist slipped the Hyderabad Expatriate Society newsletter under our door, the March edition even though it was August. The newsletter was faded and ironic on purple mimeograph. It stated new expats needed to apply for membership at the HES weekly gathering, an "informal cocktail hour" at the Walden Club on Tuesday nights.

"I don't want you to get your hopes up, Jen," Jay said, watching me reapply lip gloss for the seventh time. "I don't think this is exactly what you had in mind. Peter said no one our age ever goes to these things. We're better off just hanging out with the tax guys."

"Let's give it a try, at least," I said, giving my makeup one last check in the mirror. "I love Alexis and Peter, but we need to broaden our horizons. They won't be here much longer. I don't want to end up with no one when they're gone."

Alexis and Peter's departure date was marked on the calendar in ominous red ink. I needed to find people who were here for the long haul, who could show us the true inner circle of expat society. For Peter and Alexis, three months in India wasn't much more than an extended vacation. But for me, this was life. For two whole years.

We arrived at the Walden Club almost an hour late. Traffic, combined with Venkat's poor understanding of my directions, made a timely entrance impossible. I wore my highest heels and a pashmina, which I hoped would protect my bare shoulders from hungry mosquitoes looking to feed. Jay wore jeans and flip-flops. He rolled his eyes when I suggested he might have gotten a little more dressed up.

"I'm not trying to impress anyone," he said, glancing at his watch, ready to leave before we'd even walked in the door.

A bow-tied attendant guided us up a narrow staircase to a rooftop deck strung with saggy, faltering Christmas lights. A dozen plastic folding chairs were arranged in a circle. Off to the side, there was a card table with a silver urn, a stack of miniature Styrofoam cups, and a crystal bowl filled with anise seeds. It looked like an AA meeting in a church basement. Except instead of coffee, stale doughnuts, and a microphone, there was a teapot, some Styrofoam cups, and a swarm of ravenous mosquitoes.

No one looked up as we entered. I saw the woman from brunch at the Taj, clogged feet crossed delicately at her tanned, thin ankles. She spoke in rapid, American-accented French to a woman in a *salwar* suit with a sleek black bob. The silver-haired man, her husband probably, smoked a pipe beside her. His pants were red now, with flamingos etched in Pepto pink.

"Um, hi. I'm Jenny, and this is my husband Jay? We called about joining?" I hated how uncertain and childlike my voice sounded. I'd always been on the inside, always at the center of things. I didn't know how to be the new girl.

"Yes, of course." The blond woman glanced at her watch, then rose from her chair, regal before a crowd of no one. She was old enough to be my mother. "My name is Carole. I'm the president. We're almost through here, but won't you join us for a few minutes?" Her smile started and ended with her thin, frosted lips, never reaching her eyes.

A painful half-hour passed—literally painful, because Jay kicked me in the back of the shin every few minutes to express his desire to escape the plastic-chaired circle of hell. Carole and her husband Robert asked us a few perfunctory questions before turning their attention back to the French couple they'd been chatting with.

Jay gave a final kick, and this time, I agreed. As we rose and said our thank-yous, Carole tapped my shoulder.

"If you're available for lunch tomorrow, I'd like to take you out and show you around," she said. "Shall we say Waterfront on Necklace Road, around one?" She handed me a smooth ivory card with her name followed by a long string of numbers. "My India mobile. Call me if your driver needs directions."

In the car, Jay snatched the card away from me.

"Well, that was a waste of time. You're not really going to go out with her, are you? She's like a hundred. And she's awful."

"She's the queen bee around here, Jay. If anyone knows how to get into the expat scene, it has to be her. So yes, I'm going. As long as it's not too long to leave Tucker alone."

When BKC first asked us to move to India, I'd had one steadfast condition: the dog went too. I made them put it in the contract, business class dog airfare and all. Tucker was my child; I wasn't going anywhere without him.

"But he'll get *eaten*," wailed my mother. And my cleaning lady. And the man behind the counter at the bodega on Seventy-Second street where I bought my coffee in the morning.

"I'm not going without him," I told them, rolling my eyes. "And they don't eat *dogs* in India."

By general standards, Tucker was…indulged. He slept in our bed every night, was never left alone for more than a few hours, ate only organic free-range dog food. Jay liked to comment that our future children were doomed if the way I treated the dog was any indication of how overindulged my kids would be. "They'll be spoiled rotten," he said. "We'll be shelling out thousands of dollars for therapy before they hit third grade." I wasn't amused. I wasn't trying to spoil him. I just treated him like…well, a child.

The absence of sidewalks and the deadly traffic along Madhapur Road meant that Tucker's daily walks were limited to aimless loops around the Matwala Shayar parking lot, often with a band of Indian children following in our wake. They giggled and whispered when they saw us coming, Tucker in his Red Sox leash and harness, me in my rubber Havaiana flip-flops. Sometimes they asked questions:

"Does he bite?" "What does he eat?" "Will he get any bigger?" But mostly the kids just stared, pointing and following us, until their parents called them inside again, or until Tucker couldn't stand it anymore and snarled in their direction, scattering them, shrieking, like a flock of pigeons.

Every Indian person who came into our apartment was terrified of him: the cleaning women; the tech support guy who endlessly, unsuccessfully tried to supply us with Internet; Subu and Ritu. Subu made me lock Tucker into the spare bedroom when anyone came into the apartment. Every time I left the flat, someone from Team Assist let themselves in to perform some task or another. Usually a task I hadn't requested in the first place.

In the United States, such a thing would be unthinkable, a total violation of privacy and tenancy laws. But in India, the parameters of privacy were blurry. Servants—drivers, housekeepers, security guards—were everywhere and knew everything. Our belongings were subject to scrutiny and scavenging: garbage cans, cabinets…the maids even cleaned my hairbrush daily, collecting the stray hairs to sell to wig-makers for an astounding price. My long brown hair was inexplicably falling out by the fistful, a fact I found disturbing. The Indian women who cleaned our flat, however, were thrilled.

At nine pounds, floppy-eared and brown-eyed, Tucker's unfailing ability to provoke fear and panic among Indians was perplexing to me. The street dogs that prowled the perimeter of Matwala Shayar in packs, mean and starving, pawing through garbage with emaciated limbs, seemed truly menacing. But those dogs were just part of the landscape, while Tucker stood out, a canine spectacle in furry white bas relief.

Subu regarded Tucker with a combination of horror and absolute fascination. One afternoon, he noticed me on the sofa brushing through Tucker's fur with a fine-toothed comb, detangling the tougher knots with my fingers, cooing to him soothingly when he started to get wriggly.

"That animal, it is being like your child," Subu said, part question, part statement. "You are treating it like Indian people are treating their childrens."

I laughed. It wasn't the first time I'd been accused of treating Tucker like a human. It was just that in Manhattan, home of doggie day cares and canine day spas and pet taxis, the behavior wasn't unusual. In India, simply owning a pet was uncommon. Loving one like a family member seemed to be downright unheard of.

Tucker had been a favorite recurring character on my New York blog, and now my blog readers were eager for stories of Tucker's Indian misadventures. I tried to oblige, using my Blackberry to post blogs written from his perspective and pictures of him in unusual places—lying on his camouflage-print dog bed surrounded by Hindu idols in the *puja* room; teetering on top of the elephant swing. At least Tucker was still appreciated back at home, no matter how misunderstood he was in 'Bad.

My biggest fear living at Matwala Shayar was that someone would let Tucker escape and he'd be lost forever. If he got as far as the street, he'd be toast. The wild dogs, the murderous traffic, the so-called canine-eating culture…it kept me up at night with terrible dreams. I'd wake up sweating, only to find Tucker curled safely between us, Nestléd in his blanket like a little white bird, fur sticking up everywhere.

With so much change, Tucker was my silent, furry rock. His company got me through the long, lonely hours while Jay was at work. Tending to his needs—his walks, his meals, combing his tangled fur—gave structure to days that were otherwise mindless and endless.

So much had been taken from me—my job, my friends, my love affair with Starbucks—but Tucker remained, loyal and comforting, a familiar face in a country full of strangers. But worrying about him was keeping me tied to Matwala Shayar. I'd promised Jay I'd try harder: be more adventurous, do some exploring, find some friends. But with Subu entering the apartment at will and the dangers that lurked beyond the door of Alpha 112, I was reluctant to leave Tucker alone for long.

Before I left for my lunch with Carole, I sequestered him in the spare bedroom with his bed, food and water, his blanket, and Bear. He whimpered at me through the closed door, sticking his black nose beneath the frame and the marble floor, sniffing wildly, furious with his captivity.

"Sorry, buddy, but I'm trying to keep you safe. And Mommy needs to make some new friends, OK? Maybe one of them will even have a dog for you to play with." Doubtful, but I had to try and make it sound like I was abandoning him for both our sakes.

❧

The restaurant was lovely. Waterfront sat directly on Lake Hussain Sagar, Hyderabad's manmade lake. We sat eating Thai food and sipping watery glasses of Sula chardonnay. Through floor-to-ceilings windows we had a perfect view of the eight-foot Buddha statue floating in the middle of the water. Hyderabad, for the most part, was a "dry" city, which made imported wine nearly impossible to come by. The Indian-made Sula, with its notes of dishwater and rubbing alcohol, was an acquired taste. Carole, icy beneath her Goa tan, was on her second glass, deep into a story about her chef's mulligatawny soup ("You can't find a decent one *anywhere* else south of Mumbai") when my mobile rang. Subu.

"Sorry," I murmured when Carole paused, eyeing my phone with disdain. "It's the apartment manager. I don't know why he'd be calling right now." I hit "end" and shoved it back in my bag.

Carole raised a well-groomed eyebrow. "Is that Yves Saint Laurent? The Muse?"

I smiled, pleased she'd noticed. "It is. It was a graduation gift. My pride and joy." I added a conspiratorial wink. Finally, someone who appreciated my taste in fashion.

"Hardly appropriate for your situation, though, is it? I prefer to use something a little more…functional, myself." She patted the black floral LeSportsac hanging from her chair. "Much less ostentatious. And it holds up well with all the dust, and the rain."

"Oh."

"Well, anyway. I suppose we should go into the things you need to know about living here. It would appear," she said with a pointed look at my ripped jeans and lace camisole, "you still have a great deal to learn about navigating the expatriate waters. After lunch, we should do a little shopping." She drummed her polished fingernails on the tablecloth, swishing her wineglass with her other hand, consulting some inner checklist on my expat shortcomings.

"I'd really love to know where I can get a good manicure," I said. I missed my weekly manicures almost as much as I missed Starbucks.

"Why, the Taj, of course. It's the only place to get a good *anything*, really, unless it's my Bookhur's mulligatawny. Which reminds me, do you have a cook? A housemaid? Because I'm happy to assist you if you're having trouble finding appropriate help. As president of TEA, I like to make sure everyone is well situated with reliable servants."

My phone rang again. Subu, a second time. This couldn't be good. I held up an un-manicured index finger and answered. Carole sighed heavily and tipped the remaining Sula down her throat.

"Ma'am! Ma'am! The dog is out," Subu shrieked.

Oh. My. God. My blood ran cold. I couldn't breathe. All I could picture was Tucker running away, scared, looking for me.

"GET HIM BACK, SUBU!" I screamed into the phone. Panicked, I hung up.

Fighting back sobs, I called Jay at work.

"I'm on my way."

I said a silent, fervent prayer. India wasn't making me any more sophisticated, but it sure was making me religious. *Please God, let Tucker be OK. Let him still be in the building and not out on the street. Please let Jay get there in time.* I pictured the starving, feral dogs. The ten people camped outside Matwala Shayar who seemed just as hungry. Suddenly, the idea of dogs getting eaten in India didn't seem so far-fetched after all.

I tossed a handful of sweaty rupees on the table in front of Carole. She stared at me, lipsticked mouth agape.

"I need to go. It's an emergency. My dog is in trouble."

"You have an emergency…with your dog?"

"Thank you so much, this was lovely, so sorry to leave this way!" I called over my shoulder as I raced out of the restaurant. I wasn't actually all that sorry. Venkat, idling in the Scorpio outside, saw me coming and revved the engine. He could tell by my face we needed to leave in a hurry.

"Matwala Shayar fast, please, Venkat. It's the dog. The dog is out. I need to get home." Venkat nodded and gunned the engine.

I called Jay again, my panic level escalating with each passing minute of uncertainty. "We need an interpreter, someone who can get the whole story out of Subu! Can you have Anish try?" Anish was Jay's most trusted colleague in Region 10. He'd been the de facto head of BKC's forensic practice while the team awaited Jay's arrival.

Now Anish was Jay's right-hand man. Without Anish to show him the ropes and pave the way, Jay's transition to the India office would have been almost impossible. Now, I was hoping Anish could save the day on the home front too.

Anish called back a few minutes later. Ah, the language barrier.

It seemed that by "the dog is out," Subu meant "at large in the apartment," rather than locked in the bedroom where I'd left him. When Subu and the cleaning woman came to the apartment, Tucker erupted into a frenzy of ferocious barking and they were too scared to open the door.

"He seems really frightened of the dog," Anish informed me.

"I know. I don't get it." I collapsed across the backseat, limp with gratitude.

Anish laughed. "Don't take it personally. He's a good dog. They just don't understand him."

I told Venkat he could slow down. The emergency was over.

When we finally made it home, Tucker was lounging serenely in his bed, which he'd pushed back into the living room where it belonged. He was curled around Bear and munching on a plastic bottle cap. He'd eaten all his dog food and finished his water and knocked both dishes over, his signal for wanting more.

His tail wagged with pride as I showered relieved, grateful kisses on his furry little face.

Good boy, Tucker.

They probably weren't going to eat you…but good job scaring them off. Just in case.

CHAPTER 8

Jay walked through the door one afternoon holding an enormous, filthy cardboard box with wires sticking out of the top. I should have known right then something was suspicious.

I was working at the computer. So far, instead of posting cool photographs and telling exotic travel stories on my blog, I'd been ranting about dirt, germs, and Subu—if I bothered to write at all. Creatively, I felt stuck. India was supposed to be making the writer in me come alive. Instead, I was forgetting why I'd ever thought I could be one in the first place.

"Oh good, you're writing," Jay said, letting the box slide to the floor with a loud crash.

"Just on the blog. Trying to get caught up while the wireless is working." I got up and kissed him, keeping one suspicious eye on the mystery box. I made a move toward it, but Jay put his hands on my shoulders and steered me back to the table.

"Go finish your post. I have a few things to do with Venkat anyway."

"What things? And what's in that box?"

"You'll see. We found an awesome way to blow off some steam. I'll be back in an hour or so for dinner. Alexis and Peter are coming too."

"Great. Q-Mart had tortilla chips, and I dug out this random block of cheddar from the bottom of one of the coolers. I'm making nachos. We still have that bottle of Old El Paso from last time."

"Peter said he was bringing some stuff over. He's going to grill on the balcony."

"Grill? Like, as in BBQ? I didn't know they had that here."

"He said he has a system. He uses Indian coal."

"Yikes."

"See you later, Wife," Jay called from the driveway. The Scorpio door slammed.

❧

Peter walked in with a Weber camping grill under one arm and a Costco-sized package of Hebrew National hot dogs under the other. "Dinner's here," he said with a grin.

Behind him, Alexis held a bag of something black and sooty and a loaf of white bread.

"We got the last bag of *kolya* they had," she said. "You would die if you saw this place. I think I have post-traumatic stress. It's next to a *halal* butcher and it was lamb slaughter day. Blood was literally gushing down the street. I couldn't even get out of the car. We made Younus get it."

"Kolya? What's that?"

"Indian charcoal. It's like little sticks of burned wood. You can't get the regular kind here."

"I didn't think you could get hot dogs, either," I said, drooling a little at the sight of the familiar red-and-yellow package.

"You can't," Peter said with pride. "Or salami or hamburgers or *carne asada.* That's why I became a meat smuggler. It's the only way to survive."

"A *meat smuggler?* Isn't that, like, illegal?"

Alexis rolled her eyes. "Don't get him started. He'll talk all night and we'll never eat. Do you have a blow-dryer?"

"This I need to see," Jay said.

Peter built a small pyramid of *kolya* on a piece of aluminum foil, then carried it to the stove and placed it carefully on a burner. I retreated to the living room. The Indian stove, with its external gas tank and manual starter, terrified me. After a few minutes, I braved a peek. Curls of smoke swirled up from the center of the pile.

"Get the blow-dryer!" Peter called to Alexis, rushing out to the balcony. He held the smoking foil between two pairs of tongs. Alexis produced an extension cord from her purse and handed him our new Q-mart blow-dryer. Peter squatted over the low camping grill. Ignoring a swarm of mosquitoes that circled hungrily, he aimed the hot stream of air directly onto the coal pile. The flames surged upward.

Alexis and I retreated to the kitchen.

"Does he do this a lot?"

"All the time. I try to cook Indian food when I can, but Peter can't live without his meat. Subu thinks we're totally insane. We had to ask him for a second freezer. And if he knew the extra freezer was stuffed full of cow, he'd probably freak out."

"Hot dogs smell good though," I said, sniffing the air.

"It's the little things that get you through in 'Bad," Alexis said sagely, cutting cucumbers for a salad.

⠒⠕

The boxes contained explosives. Commercial grade fireworks, to be specific, the size and scale of which you'd find at Disneyland or the Boston Pops Independence Day Spectacular, properly packaged and set off by a team of trained professionals. Not sticking out of cardboard boxes in a complex tangle of stripped wires and sketchy-looking fuses, about to be ignited in an empty Indian field by two clueless corporate guys wearing homemade earplugs.

Like I didn't have enough problems. Now Jay was going to blow himself to kingdom come with a Bic lighter and some sticks of dynamite, all in the name of "needing to blow off some steam." True, his work was stressful. He deserved a break. I'd been thinking of ways to surprise him—a massage, a weekend trip to Goa. Staying home while he ran around like a ten-year-old with flammable objects (or "inflammable," as they said in India) wasn't at all what I'd had I mind.

"You and Jenny don't have to come. In fact, it's probably safer if you don't. We'll go, get set up, and then…POW!" Peter and Jay slapped each other five. "Remember how sad we were when there was no celebration for the Fourth of July? This is totally going to make up for it. Just stand on the balcony and we'll send you a text when it's time to look west." Peter giggled and leaned back in his chair, tapping his fingers together like Mr. Burns on *The Simpsons*.

"I can't believe you guys are even considering doing something this dumb. Or this dangerous." Despite Alexis's cheerful front, there was tension in the air between her and Peter. I wondered if something was going on.

Tucker whined and scratched at the sides of the boxes, some doggie sixth sense telling him what was inside. He hated fireworks. Every year on the Fourth of July, I spent hours stroking his fur, trying to calm him down, while his small body shook with fear at the thunder-clap explosions that rang out long into the night.

"Must you do this to Tucker?" I asked. "And what about all the street dogs out there? And the PEOPLE. You don't know if there are people living in that field. There could be dozens of them, maybe hundreds. You're going to make them think the world is ending."

"If they're sleeping outside, they have worse problems than a couple of fireworks going off," Jay said. "Besides, the Indians are used to it. They use them for festivals and stuff, and there's one of those practically every other day. They'll probably be excited to have their own private show. It'll be an extra celebration, courtesy of their American neighbors."

"I really don't like this. It's just not safe. If we're going to continue to be stuck here, I want you all in one piece."

"Jay, I'll meet you outside," Peter said, heading for the door.

Jay pushed back from the table and started collecting dishes. He dumped them in the sink and put a pot on the stove to boil. The sink taps only ran cold water, which, even in conjunction with mountains of dishwashing soap, was not sufficient to kill food bacteria, according to my germaphobe husband. From the louder-than-necessary clank of silverware in the pot, I knew his mind was made up about the fireworks.

Alexis and I settled on the balcony with a bottle of Sula Madera and a box of Oreos I'd scored at Q-Mart for seven dollars. They weren't the same without a glass of milk.

"Is everything OK?" I asked, pouring more wine for both of us. I felt a pang of guilt for spending so much time sulking by myself instead of being a good friend. I wished her unfailing optimism about India didn't make me feel even worse about myself.

"Sure," she said in a way that suggested she was anything but. She swirled the wine in the bottom of her glass, watching the sediment rise in mini tornados. "How did you find the Madera? I thought there was a nationwide shortage."

"There is. I sent Venkat around to every hotel in Hyderabad to ask if they had any left and made him buy every bottle he could find."

"Wow. That's awesome. Did Venkat think you were insane?"

"Doesn't he always?"

Alexis laughed. "Yeah, Younus too. Nothing we do makes sense to them. It must be like watching aliens from another planet run around all day."

"Imagine what they go home and tell their families. Madam this, Sir that…we're like their very own soap opera."

"Younus saw us fighting today." Alexis fidgeted in her chair. "He looked totally freaked out, like he wasn't sure whose side he was supposed to be taking. Peter packed all my suitcases and put them in the hallway. He says he can't deal with me here anymore."

"I didn't know you were having problems."

"We don't like to talk about it. Well, Peter doesn't like me to talk about it. But it's going to be OK. It's just hard, you know? Being the 'accompanying spouse' is so not what it's cracked up to be. And I'm not even his wife." She toyed with a loose piece of rope sticking out from the edge of her chair.

"It doesn't get any easier when you are," I said. "Some days I think Jay might be sorry he married me." I'd never so much as thought those words before, let alone said them out loud, but as they hung in the air between us I realized how true they were, and how sad they made me feel. Part of me was relieved that Peter and Alexis's life in Hyderabad wasn't all joy and roses like I'd imagined. I didn't want them to be unhappy, but knowing I wasn't alone in my misery was comforting.

A mosquito buzzed near my wrist, sniffing out the best possible spot from which to suck my blood and infect me with something parasitic and incurable. I reached below my wicker chair and grabbed a blue plastic electric tennis racket. *Wham.*

"What is *that*?" Alexis asked. "Did you just kill a mosquito with that? Where did you get it?"

I handed her a yellow one. She smacked at a mosquito hovering near her left ankle and hit it on the first try. It sizzled wetly, like bacon on a griddle. "Wow. That's better than therapy. I already forgot what we were talking about."

"There's a bunch of peddler guys selling them at the Jubilee Hills check post. Jay is totally obsessed; he bought two for every room," I said, waving mine in the air. The size of a ping-pong paddle, the racket had an electric current that took down bugs like nobody's business with a satisfying *ZAP*. Before India, I'd never so much as stepped on a spider, preferring to scoop them up with Kleenex and set them free on the balcony. But in Hyderabad, bugs were more than just an inconvenience—they could literally kill you. In the battle for survival, I'd become an insect-murdering machine.

"Oh my GOD. Look!" Alexis scrambled on top of her chair, waving the racket in front of her with frantic horror. I looked. Scuttling near the half-empty bottle of Madera was a cockroach the size of a mouse. Or a mouse wearing a cockroach suit. It was hard to tell which. All I knew was that it was big, it was ugly, and it was headed straight for my flip-flops.

I swatted at the repulsive insect from above, the electricity from the racket sweeping through the air with a deadly crackle. The cock-roach looked bored. It changed course and headed for the Oreos.

"Not my Oreos! Those were expensive!" I bent over and swatted again, hitting it this time. The tennis racket zapped. The cockroach didn't even blink.

"Step on it!" Alexis shouted.

"I can't, I'll feel it squish. It'd be like killing a small animal, like a squirrel or something. I'd feel its bones."

"Cockroaches don't have bones. They have shells."

"You come down and crush it then."

Alexis shuddered. "No way."

I ran inside and grabbed a plastic takeout container from the kitchen counter. The cockroach, sensing danger, moved with alarming speed, taking cover under the patio table. I circled, trying to scare it out so I could pounce on it from behind.

Alexis reached down and grabbed the cookie box.

"Here, cockroach!" She tossed an Oreo toward the far wall.

The cockroach took the bait, scurrying toward its reward with repulsive verminlike wriggles. I threw the takeout container on top of it. It continued, undeterred, toward the cookie, hidden from view beneath the plastic like something straight out of a Hitchcock movie. Or a Looney Tunes cartoon. When it hit the balcony wall, it stopped, moving in angry circles inside the container, spinning it futilely against the concrete.

"That's so gross," Alexis said, coming down off her chair and eyeing the bucket. "We are so making the guys deal with that. Assuming they make it home. You know what I want?" She took a deep sip of wine, wincing at the taste. Fortified by the alcohol, she continued. "I want them to do it for a day. Just one day, where they sit here with the power off waiting for *us* to get home."

"Go to Q-mart. Argue with Venkat about the radio station. Or Subu about the laundry."

We laughed. I'd missed her.

"You want to go do something tomorrow? I need to get out of the house more. I'm turning into a hermit. Plus I promised Jay I would stop just sitting around."

"Have you been out to Golkonda? It's supposed to be cool, palaces and ruins and stuff. I can have Younus take us. He's been a bunch of times before. It's, like, a thousand steps to the top or something."

"That sounds awful. It's, like, a hundred degrees out," I said. But even as the words came out, I could feel my stomach bulging over the top of my jeans, the result of eating too many pizzas, too much time spent pouting on the sofa. "I guess I could use the exercise. Some real sightseeing would be nice too. Jay's been so busy we've barely done any."

Just then there was a deafening crash. Then another and another. The night sky, pale with smog, lit up red and purple and green. Alexis and I stepped to the edge of the balcony and leaned out as far as we could. Between flashes of color, we could see shadows darting across the field—small ones shaped like dogs and chicken, then larger ones, people, waving their arms over their head and pointing to the sky. I could hear laughter and shrieks, whoops of joy. The field was alive, all those shadows dancing together as the sparks streamed down toward the earth. Smoke curled in long fingers toward the sky.

My phone lit up with a text.

Did you see that, Wife? Crazy!!! Coming home now. Love you

Relief coursed through me. I let out a huge breath I hadn't realized I was holding. I stared at the keypad, trying to compose an appropriately sarcastic response that would both mask how scared I'd been and communicate how stupid I thought he was for going out there in the first place. But in my mind, I kept seeing those flashes of light, the shower of sparks falling from the sky. A celebration of nothing, and everything. Confirmation we were all still here.

I saw, I typed back. **It was beautiful**.

CHAPTER 9

I just don't get why everything has to be complicated," I said. "It's always no when it should be yes, or yes when it should be no. It's like they see my white face and decide to sell me the biggest line of bullshit they can come up with."

"We're always going to be outsiders. There's just no way around it." Alexis flipped through a dog-eared guidebook. "Can you believe this place used to be the diamond-mining capital of the world?"

"Really? I thought Golkonda was a fortress or something."

"It was both. According to this, the Hope Diamond was mined here."

"Isn't that the one that was cursed, the one that got Marie Antoinette beheaded or something?"

"That's the one."

"Figures."

We drove past a baobab tree, ancient and massive, protected from a crowd of Indian tourists by a tall metal fence.

"Elephant Tree, Ma'ams," Younus yelled over the techno music blasting from the speakers. "Much famous Hyderabad. Criminals hiding inside in olden times." With all those bulbous earlike branches, the tree did look sort of elephantlike.

Just beyond the tree was Golkonda fort itself. Majestic and broken, it towered over grassy green hills. The six-kilometer ride from the city had been the usual combination of empty fields and dry, dusty desert. But now there was an explosion of color. It was like we'd stumbled into Middle Earth. Any minute, I expected orcs and hobbits to scramble over the crumbling battlements.

Younus followed us out of the car.

"I told him he could come with us," Alexis said. "He's driven here dozens of times but never been inside."

"Come on, Younus," I called, beckoning for him to catch up and walk with us. But he shook his head, staying a few carefully measured paces behind.

At the entrance gates, a tour guide took our admission fees—the five rupee "Indian rate" for Younus, one hundred each for Alexis and me—and handed us a site map. "Don't forget to clap at the entrance to the main hall," she said, demonstrating. "It is the most wonderful feature of Golkonda. Your clap will be heard all the way at the pavilion summit. It is how the guards used to warn the Kakatiyas against invasions by the Mughals."

The grounds spread out before us. Hallways leading to ancient tombs, gates to gardens that were once magnificent, but now ruined with age and neglect. There was a ceremony taking place in a darkened anteroom; through the doorway, I glimpsed an arrangement of spices in brass bowls, dozens of flower petals in patterns on the floor, and a man leading a goat on a wooden rope toward a makeshift altar. I looked away fast. Something told me the goat wasn't just there as a guest.

"Where should we go first?" Alexis asked, looking at the map.

"Let's do the steps before it gets too hot. We can eat lunch up on the pavilion." I pointed to an entryway that led straight through the outer palace to the beginning of a winding path.

"Wait," Alexis said, grabbing my arm. "We forgot to clap."

On a silent count of three, we clapped. The sharp sound echoed louder off the clay walls, vibrations climbing higher and higher until they disappeared altogether, making their magical acoustic ascent to the summit. I wondered what it sounded like on the other end, if the clap was an exact replica or if it got altered in the translation. How could something as insignificant as a hand clap, so small, fleeting, and precise, exist in two places at once without losing its essence along the way?

With Younus following a few steps behind, we began to climb. The ruins spread out on either side of the uphill path. There were 382 steps to the top, haphazardly placed, winding up the side of a cliff strewn with boulders and debris. Daily scenes, like hieroglyphics, were scratched into the crumbling granite walls. There was a Hindu temple carved into the side of a giant boulder, with painted murals of a blue-skinned goddess with four arms and a fierce, red tongue adorning the sides.

"Ma'am! Ma'am! Please, will you photograph with us?"

A family of Indian tourists was clustered at the front of the temple, posing for pictures. The photographer, a man, gestured frantically for Alexis and me to join the group. I looked at Alexis. She shrugged. We stepped respectfully to the back. Alexis and I were around the same height, barely five foot five, but we were a full head taller than anyone else in the frame.

"*Neeli aankhen! Neeli aankhen!* Blue eyes, blue eyes!" a little girl cried. We were jostled and bumped to the front of the crowd as the family crowded around us, each of them wanting to be immortalized in their vacation album standing next to a blue-eyed white person.

"Blue eyes," I hissed to Alexis. "Do you think that's why they want us in the pictures?"

"Maybe," she whispered back through lips frozen in a camera smile. "Do you think they're almost done?"

Finally we pulled away, amid a chorus of elated thank-yous. We'd barely climbed another few steps before a second group pulled us off the path and requested pictures of their own. We looked to Younus for help, but he just laughed, sipping water from a paper cone while he waited.

Four rounds of photographs later, we made it to the next level, where a mosque topped with four minarets stood overlooking the vast green lawns below. I collapsed against the side of the cliff, hot and thirsty and out of breath. A giggle from behind made me turn around, alarmed. Alexis, snapping photos of the minarets against the cloudy sky, turned too.

A gaggle of preteen boys, lanky and barefoot, leaned backward over the metal railing, watching us and laughing. Younus glowered in their direction. Disappointed that my moment of rest was cut short, I heaved to my feet and started to climb again, slowly, hoping they'd get bored and move past us. But the boys hung back, mere steps behind me, so close their presence made the skin on my lower back prickle.

The gang followed us up the winding stairs, whisper-quiet in one moment, raucous with teenage hilarity in the next. Their relentless attention felt worse than the staring I'd begun to accept as a fact of Indian life. I didn't feel unsafe, exactly, especially with Alexis by my side and Younus trailing faithfully below. But the boys knew, as so many teenage boys do, which buttons to push to make me feel uncomfortable. A tense, threatening vibration between us stopped just short of danger.

We passed the minarets. The summit, and the looming pavilion above, was almost within reach. I wished I'd counted the steps as we climbed; I had the sudden, intense longing to know exactly which step I stood on, how many more lay between me and the place I was trying to go.

Alexis glared at our unwelcome entourage. "They're kind of ruining this for me. Do you want to turn back?"

I took one more glance toward the top and suddenly felt defeated. "Yeah. I do."

We took the downward stairs double-time. Younus, sensing our urgency, ran ahead, carving a path through the packs of Indian tourists who reached out and grabbed our arms, begging for pictures. The pack of boys was relentless, cackling at our heels. I'd come here to be a tourist, to marvel at ancient ruins and appreciate the culture of my adopted city. Instead, Alexis and I became the real tourist attraction, our otherness ten times more compelling than the crumbling fortress beneath our feet.

❧

"Ma'am, is something not to your liking?" asked Jena, wringing his hands. "Is your favorite dish, no? Can I be making you something other?"

I'd been pushing a pile of *aloo palak*, creamed spinach with potatoes, around my plate for the past half hour. Jay and Anish talked on, oblivious, about their latest work crisis. Next to me, Anish's wife Sunita smiled encouragingly. I knew how important it was to Jay that I make a good impression on his favorite colleague, but every time I opened my mouth to speak, I couldn't think of a single interesting thing to say.

"Jay tells me you went visiting at Golkonda today," Sunita said. She wore an exquisite turquoise *salwar* suit in thick raw silk. Tiny gold-edged mirrors adorned her bell-shaped sleeves, and a dozen fili-gree bangles dangled from her slender wrists. She scooped up a portion of rice with a piece of *tandoori roti*. "It's always been one of my favorite places in Hyderabad. Did you make your way to the summit?"

"No," I admitted. "We wanted to, but…something stopped us along the way." I explained about the boys, the tourists with their cameras, the stares.

"Hyderabad is a wonderful city," Sunita said, looking out over the balcony to the rush of traffic below. "There is culture here. Much strength. My family has lived here for centuries; we are proud of our history. But all this, it is moving very fast. We are not like the big cities, Delhi, Mumbai. It will take us some time to grow into the new Hyderabad. We were very accustomed to the old."

She looked at me with understanding. "My whole life I have been close to family. My children run in and out of my house, into their aunts' and cousins' houses, cared for by their grandparents the same as by their mum and dad. This is what home means to us. I imagine a life without family would be very lonely for you, when you and Jay are being so very far away."

"Yes," I said, playing with the tablecloth. I couldn't meet her eyes. "Jay says your children are lovely. Do you have pictures?"

Sunita reached into her bag and pulled out a folding cascade of snapshots. I examined each one with an enthusiasm I only half-felt. I envied her connectedness—to her husband, to her children, to her city. To Sunita, "home" was something identifiable and real. But my home wasn't anywhere. My life in New York, and the person I'd been there, felt a million miles away. We still hadn't found a home of our own in Hyderabad, and the Matwala Shayar flat felt more foreign every day. I didn't know where I belonged anymore. If anywhere would feel like "home" again.

MONSOON SEASON

CHAPTER 10

S *ightseeing. Indian food. Food poisoning.*
  Grocery shopping. Chai *stand. Food poisoning.*
Bookstore. Coffee Day. Food poisoning.
Walk the dog. Take a nap. Do the laundry. Food poisoning.
Repeat.
Repeat.
Repeat.

Somewhere between episodes of "Delhi belly," as my weak American stomach rejected everything from Indian *biryani* to Indian bananas, I realized that for all my fretting about the laundry and the groceries, I'd failed to address even half of the task at hand. I'd given up my job, put my writing career on hold, left behind everything to become the world's most perfect expat housewife…and then forgot all about the word "wife."

Secretly, I loved the idea of turning into '50s June Cleaver: cookies in the oven, lacy apron starched white, pink-lipsticked smile over perfectly even, TV-Land teeth. *Welcome home, dear. Here are your slippers. How was your day?* Wifely responsibilities didn't just include putting roasted chickens on the table and making sure everybody had clean socks. Women were supposed to nurture their families, be good listeners, right wrongs. But in the first year of my marriage, the same intimacy shorthand we'd employed when we were dating seemed to do the job just fine.

Even in New York, Jay worked all the time. I was a graduate student working a full-time job. In the odd hours we spent together, we tossed "sharing" and "listening" back and forth like hot potatoes, going through relationship motions as fast as possible on the way to something else: dinner reservations or a movie screening or the dog park. It was like those hospital dramas where the writers, who don't know any actual medical terminology, fill their scripts with "MEDICAL! MEDICAL!" in places where real doctors and nurses would yell things like "CODE BLUE!" or "Blood pressure one-ten over sixty!" or whatever. Later, real medical professionals would go through the scripts, making the scenarios feasible and inserting proper technical dialogue in all the right places. But Jay and I had no such professionals.

"Graduate Thesis! Graduate Thesis!" I'd say. To which Jay would nod sympathetically for a minute, eyes on his BlackBerry. And then he'd say: "Fraud Investigation! Fraud Investigation!" And I would cluck my tongue and smile, my yellow highlighter never missing a stroke across the pages of *Anna Karenina*.

Jay and I talked to each other. We supported each other. Even at our worst, we loved each other like crazy. But in seven years together, seven *so very busy* years where we were traveling and corporate-ladder-climbing and studying and working and partying, did we ever really *talk* to each other? Or were we just throwing out terms like wobbly Little League pitches, imprecise but cheered for anyway, a mutual unspoken agreement to swing regardless of what was actually coming over the plate?

Six years of dating before we tied the knot made us complacent. There had been an indefinable moment when I'd stopped listening, stopped taking in new information about the man I'd chosen to spend the rest of my life with. I had the basics down: *intelligent, funny, handsome, affectionate, driven. Flips pizza dough in the air with one hand. Wears long-sleeved shirts in 100 degree weather. Will make an incredible dad one day.* And then once all that settled into gray matter, as permanent as if it were carved in stone, somehow I stopped paying attention. I had only the most rudimentary grasp on concepts that, as his wife, I should have understood as effortlessly as the multiplication tables I'd memorized in third grade.

It was only after six weeks in the damp mustiness of the Matwala Shayar flat, countless hours of toilet bowl hugging and traffic, groceries and boredom, even more hours spent waiting for Jay to come home and tell me about his day, his job, his career—to give me the chance to prove how very June Cleaver I could be—that I realized we'd screwed up some key element of communication in a tragic, fundamental way. Because when he did come home and told me about his day and his job and his career…I hadn't the foggiest idea what he was talking about.

It didn't help that we were never alone.

Privacy just wasn't an operating concept in India—somebody was always around. Venkat, Subu with his key and his unannounced visits, Ritu with the laundry deliveries. The cleaning ladies with their stick brooms and their downcast eyes. And those were just the people who were around out of necessity and Indian custom. It's hard to properly dote on your husband when there are ten other people at the table, drinking Kingfisher and yelling over each other, waving pieces of *tandoori roti* in the air for emphasis.

"*Technology! Technology!*"

"Gigabyte! Gigabyte!"

I was perpetually in the background, Jay's plus-one. The person who *didn't* have any reason to be in India except that legally, I was supposed to do whatever he did and go wherever he went. But nowhere in my marriage vows had it said *I promise to follow you to a third-world country and smile politely while you drag me along to work dinners and ignore me until the car ride home.*

In New York, we'd rarely been alone either—there were too many friends to see, social gatherings to attend. Jay and I chatted in the backs of cabs on the way to other places, which gave us just enough alone time to hit the highlights (*"Writer's Workshop! Writer's Workshop!" "Forensics! Forensics!"*) before we morphed into our other, public selves, drifting away into separate conversations, coming back together for a quick kiss, a drink refill, a slight nod that meant *come on, babe, it's time to go home.*

However flawed, it was a system that worked. We were happy. We fought about normal stuff like credit cards bills and paint colors for the bathroom wall. On Sundays, we'd cook together in our tiny kitchen or curl up on the couch with a DVD and a batch of homemade pop-corn, making up for the rest of the *we're so busy,* disconnected week. Those small moments where the whole world was just about the two of us were enough to make everything else feel balanced.

Part of this housewife thing, I knew, was to be shiny and bubbly and supportive, a yin to his yang, an anchor of support in the rocky professional waters he was navigating. In New York, I took my cor-porate wife role seriously, trying for the perfect blend of charm and grace. When it came to steering conversations away from office talk, I always had something to bring to the table. I was a whole person, interesting and ambitious, enjoyable to be around.

In Hyderabad, I had no job, no academic career, no *New York*

Post to give me worldly knowledge or celebrity gossip. The *Times of India* was filled with Bollywood celebrity sightings and random acts of violence and horror: wife slayings, accidental drownings, cooking fire mishaps. My days consisted of Ragu-scavenging trips to Q-Mart, walks with Tucker, and naps on the living room sofa. Not exactly fascinating stories to tell over non-veg appetizers at Fusion 9.

Jay was flourishing. He grew more vibrant and Technicolor with each passing day. All those years of not paying attention to the nuances of his career left me wide open to be dazzled by him now: his tenacity, his innovations, his success in circumstances that would drive others straight down the path to failure. India, no matter what the sacrifices were, had been the right choice for him.

But if India was making him sharper and clearer, proving his rising stardom in his complicated, corporate world, it was making me fade. Spending entire days being stared at and misunderstood—ignorant of the language, ignorant of the culture—was making the old, charming me disappear. Frustration and bitterness hung over my head like thunderclouds, coloring my moods dark. Struggling to survive food poisoning and teaching Tucker not to attack Subu was not enough to keep me sane. I needed more.

"Maybe you should get a job," Kyle suggested over pizza at Little Italy. The novelty of Chef Boyardee-inspired cuisine had long since worn off, but we still somehow ended up there several nights a week.

"Doing what? And besides, I don't have a work visa."

"I could hire you. Do you know how to play video games?"

I brightened for a moment. "You mean, like Super Mario Brothers? Or Donkey Kong? I used to be awesome at Donkey Kong."

Kyle grimaced. "I meant something a little more…current."

"What about tutoring people in English?" Diana suggested, dipping a piece of garlic *roti* in a bowl of tomato sauce. Her blond hair, tied back in a messy bun, caused several people to stop by our table and stare.

"I'd need to speak Hindi for that. Or Telugu. I'm having enough communication problems on my own. I probably shouldn't be responsible for anyone else's."

Jay looked up from his BlackBerry. "Well, there's always waitressing," he said, nodding toward a man staggering under a platter of giant trays. "Maybe Little Italy is hiring."

"That's not funny," I said.

"Who said I was joking?"

Every couple of days, in that brief evening window when the electricity stayed on, I tried to write. For all the bragging I'd done about coming home from India with the world's greatest novel tucked under my arm, I'd never felt less like a writer in my life. My heart wasn't in it. I wanted to dash off exciting posts about third-world adventures, but when my fingertips touched the keyboard, still all that came out were my frustrations about Pizza Corner, anecdotes about Tucker, and my lingering fear of cows. The manuscript for the novel I'd been working on remained untouched.

It was the middle of July and unbearably hot. There were actual thunderclouds in the sky every day, but no storm ever came. Every day was the same: dull, smoggy. Life was an ever-brewing storm, never breaking, a permanent state of *just about to happen*. The heat was so thick it felt three-dimensional, like you could scoop it out of the air and mold it like clay. There was constant, invisible pressure in the air, contradicting movement, making normal things like walking and breathing and smiling feel like herculean tasks.

"Rain coming, Madam," Venkat said each morning, staring moodily through the Scorpio's dirty windshield. "Rain coming soon."

"How soon, Venkat? When are the rains coming?" I couldn't wait for the monsoons. They were late this year—according to the calendar in *Lonely Planet*, they should have started weeks ago. I'd always loved the rain. It made me feel peaceful, hopeful, like the world was being drenched with new possibilities. I loved the sound of raindrops against windows and splashing in puddles with my tall green Hunter rain boots (a major score on sale at Bloomingdales). Rainy days in New York were my favorites—cozy inside with books and soup and blankets, Tucker curled up in my lap.

The word "monsoon" made regular rain sound exotic and fun. *Monsoon Wedding* was one of my favorite movies. Secretly, I was hoping it would be like that: all romance and excitement and dancing on the sidewalks, with drops that shimmered down from the sky and made everything prettier. A change in season was just what Jay and I needed. A new outlook on life for me, something to drag me out of the slump I was in. And for Jay, something to distract him from the nonstop work and the office drama. A wet reminder that life was still spinning outside Region 10's walls. *Hey! This is India! Come outside and get wet!*

Venkat didn't seem so excited about the monsoon. As the days passed and the rains still lingered behind a curtain of ominous clouds, his mood grew darker. I tried to cheer him up.

"Look, Venkat. That guy is lighting his cooking fire with lighter fluid! No safety!"

He didn't even look up. I wasn't used to this kind of a role reversal. Usually I pouted in the back while he tried to lift my spirits with the most jaw-droppingly dangerous things he could find. He pointed out collapsing temples and hand-strung scaffolding and exposed power lines—whatever he thought might make me smile or gasp or recoil in horror. I didn't know what to do with this sullen, withdrawn Venkat.

"Is there something wrong, Venkat?" I asked one afternoon. We were on our way to Shilparamam, the local craft village. Sunita had recommended the artisan bungalows there when I'd mentioned wanting to do some souvenir shopping. I leaned forward into the front seat so I could read his expression beneath his pulled-down beanie. Wearing the hat was a bad sign too; Venkat's greatest pleasure in life was styling and restyling his glossy black hair. When the beanie came out, it either meant it was "cold" outside…or that something was weighing on his mind.

"No rain so long, meaning bad rains, Madam," he replied, dark eyebrows knit downward. He looked, in that moment, less like the rakish teenager he was and more like a middle-aged man, careworn. "I am fear for mine mother and sisters in mine village. Bad rains, no good fortune. No fruits. Animals dying, bringing fever to water. Much danger."

"You mean because the monsoons haven't started yet, they'll be worse?"

"Yes. More worse. Rains bad, bad for mine village. Bad Hyderabad." He scowled deeper, then brightened and patted the wheel of the Scorpio. "But you and Jay Sir lucky, buying much good car. Much safety in the rains."

Venkat's first vehicle had been a tractor on his village's farm. From there he'd graduated to driving the "biscuit truck," a delivery lorry for a local Indian company cookie manufacturer, which Venkat drove back and forth from Hyderabad to Bangalore twice a week. Finally, he'd logged enough driving hours to move to the city and become a "personal driver," the most prestigious and highly coveted transportation job of all. But Venkat was a farmer at heart. Someday, he'd go back to his village to raise livestock and tend fields, his memories of city life fading as the years went by.

We pulled up outside the towering, dusty clay walls of

Shilparamam. Two stone warriors on horseback, painted red and gold, stood two stories high in front of the elaborate entrance gates. Tucker was along for the ride. Since the craft village was outside, I figured no one would mind if he walked with me on his leash along the greens. I paid twenty-five rupees to the guard at the gate and kept Tucker hidden in my bag. Here, at least, there was no inflated foreigner admission fee.

Shilparamam was enormous, sixty-five acres that stretched across an otherwise empty expanse along Madhapur Road just outside of HITEC City. Craft artisans from all over India came to sell their creations to tourists and locals alike. At night, the whole place was lit up with red and green lights. Several nights a week there were live concerts. Hundreds of people would line up at the gates. Pushcart vendors hawked their wares long into the night—heart-shaped helium balloons, fresh young coconuts with painted wooden straws, steaming mounds of sweet-spicy *chaat,* and greasy yellow *pani puri* dough balls.

But during weekday daylight hours, Shilparamam was all but abandoned. Tucker and I went unnoticed as we walked around the greens. Everywhere square plots of sod were stacked two and three feet high, waiting to be turned into the green grass checkerboards that passed as lawns in Hyderabad. A grounds man in billowing red harem pants was trimming a patch of grass with a pair of huge brass scissors. Tucker sniffed at an empty fountain and lifted a leg. I glared at him. He put it down and trotted back to my side.

The craft huts themselves were tiny, with baked clay walls and thatched roofs. It was midday and hot. Many of the artisans had stretched out on woven rugs to take naps or sat cross-legged inside their huts, scooping up handfuls of rice and yellow lentil *dal* from steel lunch pails called *tiffins*. Trying to stay as inconspicuous as possible, I moved from stall to stall, admiring hand-carved Ganesh key chains and woven prayer blankets and papier-mâché bracelets. They'd make perfect souvenirs to send back to the life I'd left behind.

As the vendors finished their lunches and woke from their naps, they observed my progress with ravenous eyes, beckoning me with gestures and guttural, incomprehensible clicks of the tongue. I smiled and tried not to make eye contact, which I knew would open the door to a hard-sell that rivaled the ones from the faux-Louis Vuitton peddlers on Canal Street.

At a booth selling gorgeous dyed leather bags—hand-laced, weathered, and soft to the touch—I caved and looked the elated artisan straight in the eye.

"*Kitne*?" How much? One of my only Indian phrases so far, other than *dhanyavad* or *shukriya* for "thank-you" and *kuta* for "dog."

"Ah, lovely American lady, for you, two thousand rupees only. Made from the finest buffalo leather. So very soft for you to be touching, carrying needs for all essentials." The man—shirtless in a maroon *dhoti*, scarred arms stained with dye from fingertips to elbows—pulled the prettiest bag off the hut's display table and stroked it suggestively with his fingers. The bag was a golden saffron yellow, casting a bright, tempting glow in the afternoon's gloom.

"Too much," I murmured, moving ahead to a rack of leather slippers covered with gold embroidery.

"No, no too much. Is bargain, you will never be of finding such authentic fine item where you are from. You are from London, Australia, yes, Ma'am?" He sidled close, not quite touching me, but enough to force me to take a step back.

Tucker, back in my bag so as to attract less attention, popped his head up and growled, sensing someone invading our personal space. The leather man shouted and leapt back, horrified. Only a moment passed before he recovered, turning the shocking discovery of a small white dog in my purse into a sales pitch.

"Ah, I see you have the finest taste and need for the strongest materials," he said, holding out the yellow bag again. "Look where there is room for your animal, your mobile, your money and possessions, all strong and much secure where you are needing it to be."

"Five hundred."

"Five hundred and my family is starving, Madam. Five hundred and my hands are being stained and broken for nothing. To make my family suffer in this way is much cruelty."

His tone suggested this wasn't at all true, but I caved anyway. Jay would kill me if he knew this conversation was happening. He was a ruthless negotiator. I, on the other hand, was the world's biggest pushover.

"One thousand. Final offer." I reached into my bag and took two five-hundred rupee notes from my wallet. I needed to ditch the YSL anyway. I hated to admit Carole was right, but the purse was frivolous and impractical in Hyderabad, mocking me with my naïve fantasies every time I picked it up. The yellow bag might not be designer, but at least it was one-of-a-kind, handmade by a tradesman who would use my thousand rupees (*which was how much, again?*) to feed his family. I hoped.

The leather man snatched the bills from my fingers in a practiced, invisible movement. He hid the rupees in the folds of his dhoti and handed me the bag with an elaborate bow. I smiled and thanked him.

CRACK. There was a clap of thunder, so loud I could feel it vibrate down through the base of my spine. Tucker whimpered. Storms, like fireworks, terrified him. I looked around and saw mayhem. The vendors were throwing grass mats over their clay bungalows as fast as they could, dumping items into plastic trash bins, racing back and forth in total panic. I looked at the sky, trying to see what they saw, and then the clouds opened up and it was Armageddon.

Rain. Not droplets, not even sheets, but *oceans* of rain crashed down from the sky. Already water was pooling around my ankles, rust-colored, mosquitoes swarming in from nowhere to take part in the madness. I shielded Tucker with my body and ran as fast as I could toward the exit. In seconds I was drenched—rain sluicing off my body, jeans water-logged, T-shirt soaked and see-through. My flip-flops skidded in the mud as I hurtled through the iron gates and straight into the Scorpio's open back door, boosted in by an already-waiting Venkat. His wool beanie was soaked through, dripping into his eyes as he climbed into the driver's seat and turned on the engine. The monsoon's arrival seemed to have lifted his cloud of anxiety.

"Rain coming, Madam. No good rain coming," he said with a grin.

I rubbed at Tucker's fur with tissues. He was soaked through and shivering, half his normal size without his fluffy pile of white fur. His skin was freckled and pink. He looked miserable and confused, more drowned rat than purebred dog.

The streets were chaos. Not the usual, controlled, life-in-India chaos I was getting used to, but the sheer madness of panic and survival. The roads were already bottled up with cars, horns shrieking over the crash of water that continued to pour from the sky. The Scorpio glided along, steady and sure, over the muddied dirt roads. For once, I was grateful for the hulking, diesel-sucking Scorpio. The smaller cars, tiny Tatas and Marutis, were hydroplaning dangerously. Cars were stranded along the side of the road, some of them abandoned, others with worried faces inside, pressed up against the fogged glass windows, watching the rain. Most terrifying of all was watching the motorcycles—average number of passengers, four— tip frantically back and forth, riders clinging to each other, the drivers stoic and determined to keep themselves balanced on the undulating road.

Animals were everywhere. Chickens, dogs, the ever-present buffalo—it was like all of India's living things had come out to brave the monsoon together. There was nowhere for them to take shelter. For the first time, the story in the Bible about Noah and his ark didn't seem so far-fetched after all. A pair of soaking-wet goats circled an abandoned motorcycle, nuzzling against it like a long-lost mother. Venkat seemed to feel for the plight of the goats more than the people who were huddled together on the side of the road, cowering under newspapers and plastic bags, helpless and immobilized by the deluge.

"Goats sad," Venkat said. "Much wet. No good fortune being for goats."

"Do you have goats in your village?"

"Yes, many. Making cheese and milk. My village will keep them no wet," he said, shooting an accusatory scowl toward the absent, negligent goat owners responsible for the ones currently suffering beside the Scorpio. "No taking good care of goats, no good fortune for peoples." I tried to reconcile these two Venkats in my mind, the baggy-jeaned swaggering one who loved loud music and street *chaat* and hair gel, and the gentle, goat-protecting farmer he must have been before he left his village.

The Scorpio inched through the streets. The windshield wipers worked furiously. The rain had done nothing to abate the heat; steam rose up in columns from the street, shrouding everything in dense, soaked fog. Venkat hunched over the wheel, navigating the treacherous roads with confident determination. He saw me watching and read my mind.

"Mine driving good, Madam. Much safety."

The rain beat down against the floor-to-ceiling glass windows of

Jay's office building. The security guard, swaddled in a garbage bag, waved us through from the safety of his small booth without bothering to check Venkat's personal driver badge. We pulled down into the parking lot of C block. Jay was already waiting by the elevator.

"This is crazy," he said, climbing in beside me. "I was watching from the windows. There's, like, *roosters* floating downstream out there."

I curled against him, Tucker still shivering in the crook of my elbow.

"You're wet! And what on earth happened to the dog?"

"We got caught in the rain. I'm freezing. Make me warm."

Jay pulled his jacket off and wrapped it around me. I pressed closer to him.

"You don't have a dinner tonight?"

"Everyone left early because of the rain. It's a bad night to be on the roads. I thought we'd just grab Pizza Corner on the way home. Extra cheese American style, thin crust no veg," he teased, bobbling his head. He picked up his BlackBerry, started to scroll.

"Don't. Please. Just for the ride home. Just be with me."

To my surprise, he nodded and put the phone in his briefcase. The rains crashed down around us, beating furiously on the Scorpio's roof, sluicing across the windows and turning the world blurry and dark. The orange glow of headlights lit the path before us, only a few feet visible, blind faith and Venkat steering us forward. In that moment, there was only us, and the dog, and the rain. I wanted to stay there forever, wrapped in Jay's jacket, shivering in his arms, safe and close while the monsoon turned the world to chaos around us.

CHAPTER 11

July passed into August. It rained for weeks and weeks, just like the guidebooks promised. Rivers and oceans of rain, rain so infinite that you forgot any other state of being was possible. Every afternoon, just for a few minutes, the downpours would stop. A held breath like a baby's hiccup, an eerie pause where the sudden absence of sound was somehow louder than the roaring of the storm itself. The clouds would roll and shift and I would run outside to the parking lot to walk Tucker before the sky cracked open and it all started again. And then, there was no better excuse to hole up inside in my sweatpants with a stack of books and a cup of *chai*.

At first, the monsoons were as beautiful as I'd imagined. The skies filled with rainbows that peeked from behind power lines and half-demolished buildings, the dichotomy making the majestic arches all the more magical. In the mornings, children ran from their tent villages, racing into the fields holding lumps of soap made from sandalwood oil. Boys and girls chased each other across the muddied earth and lathered themselves with giant clouds of suds. The air was full of the soap's woodsy fragrance and the hypnotizing sound of their laughter. Naked and gleeful, spared from their usual tasks, the children played games in the rain, opening their mouths to taste the drops the way I'd tasted snowflakes on cold winter days.

But the monsoons were terrible too. The streets were thick with water, every surface covered with slow-moving rivers of feces, waste, and debris, knee-deep in places, toxic everywhere. In a city that had endured monsoon season for centuries, the total lack of drainage was mystifying. Despite the never-ending construction, there was no new infrastructure in place to prevent or restore the damage: fallen trees, ripped-out power lines, dead animals floating downstream. Posters that shouted *Beware Typhoid—Do Not Walk!* and *Caution: Danger of Cholera!* printed on official green-and-white City of Hyderabad paper in English, Hindi, and Telugu were plastered on every electrical pole. The poles themselves—fraying wire bundles shooting sparks toward the ground, the occasional stray cable flailing in the hurling winds— were hardly the place for the warnings.

Every day, somebody was electrocuted or run over or drowned. Venkat reported the monsoon casualties every morning with detached enthusiasm, like he was filling me in on the details of a particularly good football game he'd watched on television. When he wasn't giving us damage reports, Venkat was preoccupied and anxious. The roads that led to his tiny village eighty kilometers away had been impassable for weeks. There was no news of his family. Venkat lived with his sister and her husband in a different part of Hyderabad, sleeping on the floor of their tiny flat. We gave him Sundays off, an unheard-of luxury for drivers who were usually made to work twenty-four hours a day, seven days a week. Some Sundays he would stay in the city to see a movie or hang out with his friends. But mostly he hitched a ride on the back of someone's motorcycle and made the journey home, to bring money and supplies and be treated like a returning hero. Now the rains made those visits impossible.

"Are you homesick, Venkat?" I asked.

"No sick, Madam, much good health," Venkat said, offended.

"No, 'homesick'…are you missing your village, your home?"

"Oh, mine village." Venkat's eyes glazed over like they did when I stepped too far into the personal landscape of his mind. "I am happy working for you and Sir. I am liking Hyderabad. But mine village always missing, yes. Home is being nowhere else."

I knew the feeling.

He flicked on the music, another movie soundtrack. Venkat was obsessed with Bollywood. "What is your home like, Madam?"

It was the first time he'd asked. Knowing about the West was a badge of pride for Venkat; he didn't ask a lot of questions because he liked to impress us with knowledge he already had, mostly accumulated from movie posters and commercials for toothpaste—his sister had recently acquired a television. So I told him. About airplanes and subways and storm drains that took all the water away when it rained.

"Where is the water going, Madam?" Venkat asked, fascinated.

Good question. I made a mental note to google the answer later. We took infrastructure for granted in the West in a way I could no longer even wrap my head around. Skyscrapers and ambulances, sidewalks and electricity and 911. All there for us to use and ignore, never appreciating the planning, engineering, and funding that preceded their existence. Venkat was particularly interested in airplanes. He'd never even been on a train. The eighty kilometers of dirt road between his tiny village and the city of Hyderabad were the extent of his travels, though he'd clocked enough miles between the two to have gone anywhere: Delhi, Mumbai, Istanbul.

"How many kilometers before your home, Madam?"

"Eight thousand miles." 8,054 to be exact. Not that I was counting.

"In kilometers?"

I did the math on my phone. "Thirteen thousand."

"Too big number, Madam. Mine home could never be so far away."

We were on the way to yet another rental house. Our sea shipment had finally arrived at Hyderabad customs and we needed someplace to put all the stuff we'd sent…beds and appliances, sheets and towels, the rest of my wardrobe. I couldn't wait to be with my own belongings again. If I could only make India feel just a little bit like home, everything might turn out better.

So far, the houses we'd seen made Matwala Shayar, with its faulty elevators and all-night poker parties, look like luxury accommodations. One was in a development so mosquito-infested I refused to get out of the car without swaddling myself in mosquito net and spraying a layer of OFF! on top of that. Another had tiny, windowless rooms that looked more like jail cells than living spaces. Still another was so far out of town, Venkat had to stop and ask for directions twice. It was bad enough being stuck in the Indian city…being in the Indian suburbs would be flat-out torture.

Jasmine Heights was a gated community just five minutes from Matwala Shayar on the outskirts of Madhapur, next to the newly constructed Novotel hotel and Hyderabad Convention Center. Still months away from completion itself, the development consisted of three dozen houses on tree-lined streets, clustered around a half-built swimming pool, a tiny park, and a community building that would one day boast a gym and a rec room. Jasmine Heights had been developed with the wealthiest Indians in mind, the top 1 percent, and boasted the luxuries of elite living: twenty-four-hour security, servant's quarters, two-car driveways, and bright, spacious *puja* rooms. Which were all nice features, of course, but I was really looking for the holy grail of Indian residences: a washing machine.

Venkat pulled up to the security gate. Jasmine Heights was very much still a construction site; only four or five of the homes were complete. Evidence of building-in-progress was everywhere. There were metal-framed wooden wheelbarrows filled with bricks and bamboo poles piled six feet high, ready to be turned into makeshift scaffolding with bundles of heavy twine. There was a tent camp, bustling with activity, near the gate—women cooking, children hanging laundry on clotheslines or chasing chickens away from the blue tarp-covered shanties. The security guards, armed with two-foot-long wooden clubs, shooed people away as they began to swarm the Scorpio, curious and eager for a peek inside the black-tinted windows. A goat ran by. Venkat smiled.

Most Indian homes were comprised of all the things I hated in architecture—small rooms, narrow passageways, a total absence of windows and light. The darker the home, the cooler it would be in the blazing Indian heat—so windows were small and used sparingly. In houses like these, it was likely to be more than just the nuclear family: there were in-laws and cousins and servants all under one roof, so the more rooms, the better. And all those cubbies without a closet in sight? Indian clothes were made to be folded. Mine, however, were not. I closed my eyes as we crossed the threshold of Plot 39 and prayed for a full-length closet.

When I opened them, I knew we'd found our place. The two-thousand-square-foot first floor had a wide kitchen with plenty of wooden cabinets, plus a modern-looking gas range with a hood. There was an open living room and dining area, plus a bedroom with a bathroom—toilet AND shower, on opposite sides. The shower, made of clear plastic panels, had four actual walls. Everything was covered in several inches of construction dust. Beneath it was the glitter of black marble.

Upstairs, there were three more bedrooms on two floors, all with their own baths. The floors and staircases were the same glittery, smooth black marble. The second and third floors had wraparound balconies as wide as the bedrooms themselves. And best of all, at the top of the very last staircase was a freestanding, electric washing machine, still wrapped in manufacturer's plastic. I was home.

In front, there was a tiny, gated yard. We could plant a garden, with pomegranate trees. Tucker could run free. After months of being a housewife with no house of my own, I was finally about to become the mistress of my own domain.

We met Kyle and Diana at Fusion 9 for dinner to celebrate.

"What's going on out there?" Kyle asked, sliding into his seat with a bewildered look. "There are like a million people dancing and banging drums in the street. Traffic is even worse than usual." His shorts and T-shirt were wet with rain. I handed him a bottle of Kingfisher, which he accepted with a grin and an appreciative sigh.

"It's *Bonalu*," Diana informed him, signaling the waiter to ask for a glass of wine. "They're honoring the Goddess. It's a huge festival in Andhra Pradesh. People at work have been talking about it for weeks."

"Isn't every day a holiday in Andhra Pradesh?" Jay asked. "Every time I turn around, the guys at the office are asking for more time off. I keep telling them that's not the way we operate in the U.S."

"Ah, but you're not in the U.S. anymore, remember?" Kyle said. "In India, there are plenty of reasons to relax and take time off. It's one of my favorite things about this country. There's always something to celebrate."

"Our new house, for example," I said. "Maybe the Goddess had something to do with finding us Jasmine Heights Plot 39."

"If she did, you better start leaving her offerings in your *puja* room," Diana said wisely. "You don't want to mess with that kind of divine intervention."

"No way. Subu isn't around to tell me what to do anymore. That *puja* room is all for Tucker."

෴

Summer turned into fall. The rains continued. Negotiating the lease took several more weeks; the application process seemed like it would never end. We had to prove our residency in India, our income, our previous income, our previous addresses and landlords dating back ten years, which was more time than we'd actually been living on our own—ten years ago, I'd been a high school senior. We had to state our father's names and occupations, our religious preference, names and addresses of people who could provide character references in India. I sent in applications for a phone line, a bank account, a gas tank for the kitchen stove. I packed up the Matwala Shayar apartment and shopped for housewares at Shilparamam.

Finally, the paperwork was signed and we scheduled moving day. Venkat dropped me off at Plot 39 with the last of our Matwala Shayar belongings. Then he and Jay went to customs to claim our sea shipment. Anish went along to assist him; we'd been warned there might be delays. I sat in the empty house and watched Tucker sniff corners and skid across the empty marble floors. I waited.

Hours went by. I tried Jay's mobile, but he wasn't answering. I ordered Pizza Corner and waited two hours for the driver to figure out where the Jasmine Heights development was—the mere five-minute drive from Matwala Shayar may as well have been two cities away. The pizza came cold. I ate it straight from the box, offering some to the family who was living on our front porch: a husband and wife, plus another man—a brother? a nephew?—who was mentally disabled. They were migrant workers who had been living in the servant quarters in the back of the house, doing small jobs and keeping an eye on things during construction in exchange for a place to stay.

"Once you move in, you'll be needing to remove them," Anish had warned.

"Remove them how?" My first reaction was to want them gone immediately, but I'd gotten used to their presence. They'd been sleeping on the porch for days, waving at me cheerfully as I unpacked loads from the Scorpio. They were a motley crew for sure, but they made me feel less alone.

"It is no good for them to be here while you and Sir are residing," Anish said, his eyebrows knit together in warning. "You must be hiring them for work or sending them on their way. Letting them stay for free will only lead to sorrow."

"Sorrow for me? Or for them?" I asked.

Anish just laughed.

So far, the three porch people had been quite helpful, shooing away stray dogs, sweeping the porch and the main floor with their own brooms, opening the metal driveway gate for Venkat when they saw the Scorpio coming. I hadn't the foggiest idea how to make them leave, and besides, where would they go? All of their belongings were in our shed. The covered porch was the only refuge they had from the rains.

Restless, I called Jay again, then Venkat, then Anish. No one answered. I began scrolling through a mental film vault of worst-case scenarios—traffic accidents, buffalo attacks, a freak live wire crashing into the road. The rains slowed. Outside, it was foggy and humid.

It was almost dusk when the trucks pulled down our street. I heard the rumble of the Scorpio, then a metallic clank as Venkat opened the manual driveway gate. I raced outside. Three barefoot movers were already loading boxes, assembly-line style, onto the front porch.

"What happened? Where were you? I was really worried," I said accusingly. "That took all day! I thought you were taking off the day so we could unpack everything together."

"Sorry. My phone died. You have no idea what that was like," Jay said, rubbing his temples. "First there was this dog. It had been hit by a car, and it was in bad shape." He shuddered. "And these guys were just beating it with a stick, trying to make it die. It was the most horrible thing I've ever seen. So we chased them off and moved the dog out of the road. This other guy was there, an Indian guy, in a suit. He helped me. We called every number we could find for veterinarians, trying to make someone come and pick this thing up. It was just so helpless, you know?"

Behind us, the movers were carrying box after box up the slippery marble staircase. I raised my eyebrows at Jay, waiting for the end of the story.

"The dog? Was it OK?"

"I don't know. I had to leave it. It was awful. I would have taken him home, except…well, we wouldn't have been able to take care of its injuries, and with Tucker…" Jay put his head in his hands, cringing at the memory. "I gave these guys on the side of the road five hundred rupees and made them promise they'd wait until the people from animal rescue got there. I don't know if they did. He didn't have a whole lot of time left."

I slipped my arms around his waist. He buried his nose in my hair. We stood there for a minute, watching the movers carry our furniture through the front door. I'd grown so accustomed to Indian-made things that our New York belongings looked like mirages, as incongruous as a bubbling fountain in the desert in their new Far East surroundings.

"I'm sure they got to the dog in time." We both knew it was unlikely, but I couldn't think of anything else to say. "Did customs go OK?"

"God, it was a nightmare. They almost arrested me. For all that wine we packed. I guess Hyderabad is stricter about alcohol than almost anywhere else in India. Somehow they knew it was in there—they found the right crate and everything. I had to pay the guy in charge eight thousand rupees to let me go. Thank god Anish was there, or I might have ended up in prison or something." He produced a bottle of cabernet from behind his back and grinned. "Got to keep it all, though." He looked around the kitchen at the array of soggy, dented boxes. "What are the chances of finding a bottle opener anytime tonight?"

At 2:00 a.m., the movers finally left. They'd dumped the contents of each and every box unceremoniously on the floor, insisting through frantic arm gestures and rapid-fire Telugu translated by Venkat that the relocation company would punish them if they didn't take every inch of cardboard and every speck of packing material with them when they left. Jay gave them each a tip, several hundred rupees in cash, which seemed to surprise them. They bowed and nodded as they scuttled out of the house, collecting their rubber sandals from the front porch.

We sent Venkat home with the rest of the pizza and a cash bonus for the long day. Jay dug an opener from a pile on the kitchen counter. I poured wine into plastic cups with pictures of fruit on them, another Q-mart purchase. Orange slices for me, cherries for Jay. We sat down on our old blue couch, the one we bought for our first apartment in Boston. I chose my favorite spot, the short L part of the sectional, and draped the back of my knees over the arm like I'd done a million times before. Jay lay down the long way, so that our heads were touching, our feet pointing in opposite directions, in a position so familiar and so forgotten that it felt surreal. This still existed. We still existed.

"To our very own home."

"To the nicest house we'll probably ever live in," Jay replied.

I swatted at him. "Don't say that! I don't want the nicest house we ever live in to be in a foreign country."

"OK, to no more Subu. May he find new expats to torture."

"Amen."

"I can't wait to finally get a good night's sleep," Jay said drowsily, his arm up over his head, playing with the fraying strings on the torn knees of my jeans. "God, that wooden bed. Never again."

"No more loud parties. No more soaking wet toilet paper. The shower has actual walls, can you imagine? I might never get out of it."

"You'll get out. The water tank isn't that big. This place might be brand new, but it's not exactly *modern*. You know that, right?"

"It's perfect. Tomorrow I'm going to set everything up, buy some furniture. Make it ours. We need curtains, and a clothesline, and an oven, and…"

"Easy." Jay yawned and got up, pulling me up with him. "One thing at a time. Let's go to bed."

There was a knock on the door. Jay looked at me. I peered out the front window. The porch woman, standing there with a cup.

"She probably just wants water," I explained, opening the door and taking the cup. I filled it at the kitchen sink. We still couldn't drink the tap water ourselves, but for the migrant workers it was likely the cleanest water they'd seen in weeks.

"Wait," Jay said as I started to close the door behind her. "Give them these." He dug out a pile of old blankets and pillows from a pile on the floor and handed them to me. "It's got to be so uncomfortable on that porch."

The porch woman bobbled furiously in gratitude. She looked at Jay and me, sizing us up. Meeting my gaze, she pointed to him and then her heart.

"I know," I said, understanding. And I did know. Even if lately I'd been forgetting.

We started up the marble stairs. I beckoned to Tucker, waiting for him to follow. He whimpered and stayed on the couch.

"Tucker, come on," Jay said. "Bed time."

Tucker shivered and flattened his ears against his head.

"I think he's afraid to walk up the stairs," I said. "Maybe they're too slippery."

"Like this dog could get any *more* spoiled." Jay scooped him up with a sigh.

In the master bathroom, we took turns brushing our teeth with bottled water. "A four-thousand-square-foot mansion and we still can't get separate sinks," Jay grumbled.

"The shower has walls. Stop complaining."

"Well, what about this crack?" Jay said around a mouthful of toothpaste, pointing to a long, jagged break down the center of the bathroom mirror. It distorted our reflections into crumpled, clownlike masks. "It's a brand new house. How could the mirror already be broken?"

"They must have broken it while it was getting installed," I said, running my finger across the sharp edge. "I'll call the landlord and tell her."

Our bathroom towels were yellow and orange, a threadbare set I'd had since college. When I was packing up the New York apartment, I'd been just about to throw them away, but a wave of nostalgia made me reluctant to let them go and I'd tossed them in the sea shipment, a sentimental afterthought. I buried my nose in a hand towel. It smelled like us, like home.

CHAPTER 12

My first shower in our new bathroom was glorious. I unpacked my lemon and sage scented body wash, which I'd wrapped carefully in duct tape and tucked into a plastic bag so it wouldn't spill on the long ocean journey. The smell, after weeks of nothing but Indian sandalwood, was divine. The water was hot, with actual pressure, and the presence of shower walls meant the steam stayed wrapped around me, cloaking me in warmth.

I soaked. I lathered. I tried out my new Ayurvedic apple cleansing shampoo, which the woman in the beauty aisle at Q-mart swore would make my hair stop falling out. It was still coming out by the handful, making messy piles on my pillow, on the counters, in the drain. All the shedding was driving Jay crazy. "It's like living with a sheepdog," he complained, flicking a hair off his toothbrush. "Gross."

Packed with my toiletries had been an aerosol container of Skintimate. Shaving with actual shaving cream, instead of a rough pass with the razor and plain old water, was a luxury I'd rarely had time for in my jam-packed Manhattan days. But now, in India, there was finally time to take it slow, to enjoy the little things. I massaged a handful of Kerastase deep moisturizing mask into my hair. If the Ayurveda didn't work there, surely high-end salon conditioner would undo the damage. I foamed a handful of Skintimate onto my legs, lathering them from hip to toe while the conditioner soaked in.

The water shut off. I screamed.

Frantically, I pulled at both handles, twisting back and forth. One came off in my hand. Still no water. Not even a trickle. I grabbed the bathmat, the closest towel within reach, wrapped it around myself, and headed downstairs, yelling for Venkat at the top of my lungs.

Halfway down the staircase, leaving a slimy trail of baby powder-scented foam behind me, I slipped. The combination of marble and water was deadly. My feet flew out from under me and I skidded down the last few steps on my tailbone, clutching the bath mat around me and clenching my jaw with pain.

I collapsed in a soaking wet pile just as Venkat burst through the front door, a tall Indian man wearing a hard hat and carrying a clipboard close at his heels.

When he saw me, Venkat let out a little girl shriek and shielded his eyes. The man with him moved away from me like a VHS tape on rewind, stepping back into the shoes he'd left by the door, edging backward onto the porch with his head tipped down so only his mustache was showing.

"What happened to the WATER?" I asked, failing to keep the hysteria from my voice. "And who are you?"

"I am Raju," said the man from the safety of the porch. "I am building manager for Jasmine Heights, Ma'am. I am coming to introduce myself to being at your service."

Great. I'd swapped a Subu for a Raju. I said a silent prayer for better luck with this latest Indian version of Mr. Roper.

"I was in the shower and it just shut off," I said, rearranging the bath-mat and gingerly feeling my tailbone for signs of permanent damage.

"The water tank is empty, Madam. You will need to have it refilled," Raju said, removing his hard hat and taking a few steps forward but still averting his eyes from the dripping, barely decent spectacle I was making in the middle of the living room floor.

"There's no automatic refill?"

"No, Madam. You will need to have someone standing on the roof and watching the water level in the tank. When it is being low, then they can go and attach the pipes for refilling."

"But I can't go on the roof and stand around watching the water tank all day!"

Raju looked aghast. He fidgeted with his clipboard. "Of COURSE not, Madam. The lady of the house cannot go. You will be needing a servant for that." He cleared his throat. "I'm sorry for the intrusion into your household. There were just a few things I wanted to review about your living conditions here. Is there a better time for which I could come back?"

I gritted my teeth and smiled the most sincere smile I could muster. Our no-Subu celebration might have been the tiniest bit pre-mature. "It's nice to meet you, Raju. Let me go get cleaned up and I'll meet you back downstairs in a few minutes. Feel free to make yourself comfortable." I gestured to the couch.

Raju took a step forward, about to remove his shoes again. Tucker growled and bared his teeth.

"On second thought, Madam, I'll be waiting outside."

ॐ

The last thing I thought I'd ever do was hire servants. In New York, we'd had Julia, a twice-monthly cleaning lady who talked incessantly in a high-pitched voice and spared me scrubbing toilets and base-boards. Everything else, I'd managed myself. Servants, I thought, were a bourgeois concept for a prehistoric elite. I was a Democrat. I was from Manhattan. I was here for enlightenment, to frown on the caste system and help elevate India's emerging middle class. I was not here to hire a man to stand on my roof all day, staring at my water tank and roasting in the sun.

I finally understood what Carole, the expat queen, had meant when she offered her assistance finding me "adequate help." Raju seemed startled every time he rang the doorbell and I opened it myself. "Servants still no, Ma'am?" he asked. In Matwala Shayar, practically a boarding house for workaholic twentysomethings, everyone got by with just Subu and his small staff. But in our own household, we were expected to have servants. Lots of them.

A cook, a couple of housekeepers, a security guard, a landscaper, the guy to watch the water tank, plus Venkat...it was too much. I was far from a feminist, but I liked being self-sufficient. And I liked privacy. Even Venkat sometimes felt like a burden. Having someone lurking around, waiting for me to need something, was stifling. The thought of someone *actually in my house* all the time—hearing our conversations, touching our belongings, scrutinizing our behavior—made me positively itchy.

Jay came home early one night so we could go to Anish's house for dinner. It was our first invitation to an Indian home, and I was excited. Anish lived in Jubilee Hills. A security guard stood sentry out front, rising from his metal folding chair to look us up and down before waving us forward. The massive carved wood door opened, as if with invisible hands, before I could even knock.

"Welcome, welcome," Anish said, gesturing for us to follow him into a small sitting room to the right of the entrance. Framed pictures of him and Sunita, clad in traditional Indian wedding attire, hung above a black imitation leather couch. Across the hall, a *puja* room was set with altars and idols.

"Your furniture is lovely," I said. "Where did you buy it?"

"Thank you," Sunita said, appearing with a silver tray. Her dark blue *salwar kameez* shimmered in the light. "All of our items were custom made right here in Hyderabad by local artisans. *Chai?*"

"How is your new home?" Anish asked me, offering a sticky golden ball of *gulab jamun*. I declined. It was a delicacy, I knew, and turning down food was considered terribly rude in India, but the globby, honey-covered balls of dough were one of the things my weak American stomach had never learned to tolerate. I hoped they wouldn't be offended.

"We're just getting settled, but it's great. I love being in our own place after being trapped in Matwala Shayar for so long." I blew on my chai to stall from having to drink it, wondering for the ten thousandth time why Indian people couldn't just drink coffee. A female servant appeared, gesturing silently toward the dining room. Dinner was being served.

In the hallway, Anish's little girl played with a nanny, counting out the pieces of a giant jigsaw puzzle. She stared at us as we passed. I gave her a wink and a wave, pointing to the leftover *gulab jamun* in the sitting room. Her eyes widened below her thick brown bangs. She grinned back at me. She wore a Dora the Explorer T-shirt and jean shorts, a surprising jolt of Western culture in Anish's traditional Indian household.

We settled around a massive table, covered in black-and-white block print linens. My seat faced the kitchen, where two cooks were conferring over a pot on the stove. The back door was open, revealing a clothesline covered with freshly washed laundry. A woman, older than my grandmother, caught me looking and stared back, her mouth full of clothespins.

"Have you hired your servants yet?" Sunita asked, following my gaze. "We have some contacts if you are having difficulty."

"I was thinking of maybe not getting any," I admitted. "We have Venkat, and Jasmine Heights has security at the gate, plus they patrol the development on bicycles overnight. I don't really think we need more than that."

"But what about the cooking and the washing and the yard? Who will you be sending to pay the bills or wait in queue at the vegetable stand?" Anish asked, breaking off a piece of *roti* with his hands and dipping in into his *dal*. "Running an Indian household has many challenges."

"I thought I'd do it myself," I said, a blush spreading down toward my neck. "It's not like I don't have enough time on my hands."

Anish smiled at me indulgently. "That is simply not the way things are being done in Hyderabad. You should be enjoying this type of luxury while you can. Think of it like this: you will be supporting many families by employing your servants. It is the Indian way."

"But I'm not Indian."

"But when in India..." Anish winked. A servant materialized behind me and spooned more *dal* on my plate. "Don't worry. It is much like the food. You will grow accustomed to it eventually. You simply cannot do everything yourself." He offered me more *roti*. "And besides...why would you want to?"

I opened my mouth to respond, but Jay kicked my leg under the table. I gave him a furtive, meaningful glare. Then I smiled for the benefit of the rest of the table, stirring the food around on my plate, trying to make it look as though I'd eaten.

When I came downstairs early the next morning, the kitchen was flooded.

Everything had been normal when I'd turned in for the night. We'd come home, said hi to the porch people, turned out the lights, and gone to bed. There had been nothing unusual, nothing amiss.

There had most definitely NOT been a three-inch deep puddle of water all over the kitchen floor.

I went back upstairs. Jay and Tucker were still sleeping, sprawled out on top of the covers. Now that we were sleeping in our own bed with our own sheets, Jay's sleeping hat had been retired to the nightstand drawer. I sort of missed it.

"Hey. Wake up. The kitchen's flooded. There must be a leak or something."

Jay grunted and flipped over, away from me.

"Seriously. You need to get up. I need help. There's water everywhere."

"Call Subu," Jay answered, the words muffled by the pillow he'd shoved over his head.

"Subu's at Matwala Shayar! We don't have anything to do with Subu anymore, remember?!"

"Oh. Right. Well, call someone else. Household issues are your administrative responsibility. This is my morning to sleep in; my first meeting isn't till ten. Can you reset the air conditioner when you leave? The dog and I are hot."

I stomped back downstairs. Raju answered the phone on my fifth call. He promised to send a plumber right away. Which probably meant "sometime next week." I got out the bucket and a pile of rags and started to clean up the mess.

Jay came down as I was wiping up the last of the water.

"You missed a spot," he said, pointing to a corner.

I ignored him.

"Listen, I want you to be at dinner tonight. It's with a couple of the partners in from New York, plus Anish and some of the guys from the office. We're going to Little Italy, OK?"

"Sure."

"Try not to talk about how much you hate it here. I want to make sure these guys know I'm fully committed, OK?"

"You mean you want me to pretend we love it here so they won't know you're only here because you have to be."

"Well, if you want to be literal about it. Just keep the nasty comments about the food and the dirt and stuff to yourself."

"You're making it sound like I complain all the time."

"Well, don't you?"

Outside, Venkat honked. Jay grabbed his briefcase and held out his arm. I leaned in for a hug, but he pointed to the sink instead.

"Looks like your leak is starting again." Sure enough, a stream of water was creeping across the kitchen floor. "While Raju is here, have him check the freon in the air-conditioning units. I think something might be wrong with the lines."

"Sure! Just leave! Everything's under control here," I called after him, but my sarcasm was lost in the roar of the Scorpio's engine and the cloud of dust left in its wake. I stood there on the porch, still holding the bucket full of soaked rags. Across the street, a woman—the owner's wife? a housekeeper?—stared at me from the doorway. I waved. She disappeared back into the house.

Three hours later, Raju arrived with the plumber. I showed them the puddle of water on the kitchen floor. They conferred for a moment. I mopped up more water. The plumber sat down in front of the sink with a wrench in his hand, peering up into the pipes. He asked Raju something in Telugu.

"He wants to know if you are having a flashlight?" Raju asked.

I handed him the electric camping lantern we used to find the stairs at night when the power was off. He bobbled his head and thanked me.

Twenty minutes passed. Twenty-five. The plumber clanked and prodded beneath the sink. Finally he stood, wiping his hands on his pants, which were soaked from ankle to hip from sitting in the puddle of water. He handed me back the lantern and spoke to Raju in clipped sentences.

Raju translated.

"No leak, Madam."

"What do you mean?"

"He is saying there is no leak. All is fine."

"But that's crazy. Of course there's a leak. Would I have called you here if there wasn't? And look, he's all wet. From SITTING IN WATER. Do you think I poured water all over the floor myself?"

Raju looked confused. "No, Madam, I am not sure why you would be doing something like that."

"Of course not! Why would I! Which is why there's a LEAK in my sink!"

The plumber shook his head, emphatic. "No. No leak."

Raju looked at me with his hands in the air, like *See? I told you.*

"Are you seriously leaving here without fixing the sink?"

"Be of having a wonderful day, Madam," said Raju, one foot already out the door.

INDIAN HOUSEWIFE AND MISTRESS OF MY OWN DOMAIN, WEEK 2

Number of appliances sacrificed to 220-volt electricity? Six, and counting. So far we'd bid farewell to the dust buster, the blender, the toaster oven, an electric toothbrush, and the hair trimmer we'd bought for

Tucker. There were no dog groomers in Hyderabad and he was starting to look like a tiny, overgrown sheepdog. Jay had insisted on cutting his fur as soon as I unearthed the clippers from a pile in the bedroom. The hair trimmer died midswipe down Tucker's furry back—no sparks, no smoke. Tucker looked ridiculous with a reverse Mohawk, but, thank god, he'd escaped the incident unharmed. My beloved Mr. Coffee, on the other hand, died an especially violent death. With no coffee grounds to speak of, I'd decided to plug it in and fill it with espresso from Coffee Day. It had glugged twice, choked, and exploded in fiery plumes that left smoke stains on the kitchen ceiling.

Venkat and I made three separate trips to the electrical shack, an open garage on Madhapur Road that was filled floor to ceiling with wires, plugs, and shiny metal coils. The proprietor swore up and down (in Telugu, via Venkat) that his converters would make my 120-volt American appliances work seamlessly with the raw, uncut 220-volt electricity streaming through our Indian outlets. With each new appliance death, I cursed him and his family to a lifetime of burnt toast and dust-covered floors.

I missed my dad. He was a genius with anything mechanical, using complex procedures to mend things with an arsenal of supplies like duct tape and wire cutters and Krazy glue. He'd have been able to fix it so the upstairs toilet would actually flush, or so I could use my electric frying pan without shorting out every circuit in the house. But he and his toolbox were ten thousand miles away, and I was stuck here with my broken Mr. Coffee and a trash can full of charred plastic.

Even Indian-made appliances turned out to be useless. There was a reason Indian housekeepers stuck to buckets of water, cloth rags, and stick brooms. Every day, at exactly 9:05 a.m. when Jay pulled out of the driveway, the electricity in the development shut off. Except for a few brief surges in the afternoon, when every light and fan went berserk with sudden, Frankenstein-esque life, the power remained off until 9 p.m., which was right about when Venkat pulled the Scorpio back into the driveway. Just in time for Jay to deny such an inconvenient, maddening phenomenon could possibly be happening.

"It does *not* go off *every single morning*," Jay said with a sigh. "You're exaggerating because you hate it here."

"I'm being serious!" I said, outraged. "Ask Raju if you don't believe me." Hating it here was one thing. Exaggerating to the point of flat-out lies was quite another. The accusation stung.

My non-electrical attempts at cleaning our all-marble mansion weren't going well, either. The floors were brand new, but inexplicably streaked with angry swipes of white and gray that no amount of scrubbing could erase. The construction dirt that blew in through the open doors and windows clung to every surface, leaving a brown, sticky film. Nothing was shiny. What was the point of having an all-marble house if it was as dull and matte as 1970s linoleum? The broken mirror in the upstairs bathroom remained broken.

"Try using Dawn," my mother suggested on our weekly call. "It really cuts through the grease."

"Mom, are you kidding? They don't have Dawn here. Our kitchen sink doesn't even have hot water. I'm lucky they sell dishwashing liquid at all."

"Maybe baking soda? Do they have that?" she asked.

I sighed tragically. "I doubt it."

My attempts to take out the garbage, hang up a clothesline, and water the lawn were as comical as they were pathetic.

"Servants would be fixing," Raju observed as he watched my efforts from the driveway.

I grunted from beneath an armful of soaking wet towels and ignored him.

"It's pretty filthy in here," Jay said, taking his shoes off at the door but leaving his socks on so his feet wouldn't touch the floor. I'd adopted the Indian custom of shoe removal prior to entering a home, but in our case it didn't seem to be helping with the dirt. Not that I appreciated Jay pointing this out.

"It's not my fault. It's the marble. It just won't get clean. There must have been a problem at the factory or something. It's defective."

"The factory? You mean the *quarry*?"

"Whatever."

"Did the phone get installed? The cell service here is awful. I really need to start making my calls from a landline."

"Our application got rejected again."

Jay gave me an exasperated snarl and stomped upstairs. Like it was my fault Hyderabad had more red tape than Capitol Hill when it came to utilities.

The water, tank refill issues aside, was controlled through the Jasmine Heights development itself. Which meant we had it, no questions asked. The electricity too was controlled through the community. A bill was slipped underneath the front door every two weeks. I sent Venkat to the electrical office with a handful of rupees to pay in cash. But the telephone line and the gas tank for the kitchen stove were totally different stories.

The fancy stove with the gleaming stainless steel hood I'd so admired on our first visit to Plot 39 was deceptively modern. There was no gas line to the house. In order to turn the stove on, it needed to be connected to a propane tank with an orange rubber hose. A hose that looked about as substantial as a drinking straw, one that might snap at any moment, filling the house with toxic gas, which, with an open cooking flame, would be enough to blow us and the house into a million little pieces. This particularly neurotic scenario of mine was on hold, however, because the city refused to give us a gas tank.

"They're all out," Jay had said, coming home empty-handed for the third day in a row. "I guess there are only a certain number of tanks, and someone has to turn one in before we can get ours. There's a wait list."

"That's ridiculous," I said. "How can there only be a certain number of *tanks*? Can't they just make more? And anyway, the neighbors got theirs yesterday and the people up the street got theirs the day before that. There can't possibly be a tank shortage." Our neighbors, and the people up the street, had also gotten phone lines installed. They were Indian. We were not. I was beginning to suspect this wasn't a coincidence.

"You want Ginger Court? Venkat's in the car waiting. Let's go meet Alexis and Peter."

Jena was thrilled to see us. He brought out a plate of chili-fried American corn without being asked. Peter and Alexis rushed in a few minutes later.

"Younus and Venkat are hanging out in the Scorpio, blasting music," Peter said, hugging us both hello. "Should we send them down some dinner?"

"Younus only eats veg," Alexis reminded him. "Jena, can we send some *chana masala* to the boys downstairs?" Jena bobbled his head and disappeared.

"What's happening in Bel Air?" Peter asked, slapping Jay on the back. "Now that you've moved on up, we never see you guys anymore."

"I hate to admit it, but I'm missing Matwala Shayar a little," I admitted. "The backup generator. The wireless. I'm even a little lonesome for Subu."

"Come over tomorrow and visit," Alexis said. "He'll barge in on us unannounced two or three times and you'll be cured."

Jay and Peter caught up on BKC gossip while Alexis listened to my housekeeping woes. "Sounds like you might be better off just finding someone to help," she said. "No one is going to think any less of you for it."

"It's not that. I just...I don't know who I am anymore. If I'm not being a housewife, there isn't a whole lot I'm supposed to be doing."

Alexis laughed. "I'm sure you'll figure something out." She launched into a description of her latest painting class, the traditional Indian still life she was working on of a gourd and a painted bowl. Even in India, she still identified as an artist. Alexis spent her days in museums, studying artwork and artifacts. She wore *kurti* tunics and taught drawing to Indian school children in the afternoons. She and Peter seemed to be back on solid ground, comfortable and happy together. I envied Alexis the unfailing sense of self that followed her around the world, as comforting and ubiquitous as a shadow.

In New York, I had belonged. I defined myself by where I worked, what I wore, the words I wrote. I knew exactly who I was—a writer, a yogini, an Upper West Side newlywed. The world made sense. Lights turned on and off when I expected them to; people smiled at me instead of stared; eating food made me feel full, not violently ill. My fierce independence was rewarded, not mocked. I was just Jenny—not Madam or Sir Ma'am or Mrs. Jay Sir. But in India, I was no one. Infamous and invisible at the exact same time. With no familiar world to tether myself to, I felt like a torn balloon in the sky, spiraling toward the earth in a free fall, desperate for a gust of wind that would lift me up again.

CHAPTER 13

By October, the rains had stopped. But despite the impending arrival of Hyderabad's "winter," it was hot.

So hot I could feel the sidewalk burning beneath my Havaiana flip-flops, so hot I couldn't shower until long after the sun went down because the water that came from the tank on the roof had literally boiled in the relentless sun. At Ginger Court, Jena tried to tempt us with "hot weather specialties" like mint soup and *anari raita*, but I just picked listlessly at the plates. Even the air seemed like it was on fire. The Indian city had an ever-present scorched smell that seared the inside of my nostrils with every breath.

"You sleep too much," Jay declared one morning, whipping the sweat-soaked sheet off my body. "Get out there and do something." I stayed still, curled into the fetal position, willing him to go to his air-conditioned, electrically sound office and leave me to my misery. He didn't budge.

"I mean it, Jen. This isn't good for anyone."

You mean it's not good for YOU, I thought to myself, but I got it.

I was slipping deeper into a semi-conscious state, hiding in bed and melting into a pool of nothingness while the Indian world marched on around me. It was too hot to shop, too hot to read, too hot to venture out into the crowded city streets for sightseeing. Venkat tried to amuse me by reciting the daily temperature and proclaiming the weather "Much worse hot climate ever, Madam" but his numbers were in Celsius and my brain was too scorched to do the math required to convert them to Fahrenheit.

One day, trying to manipulate our air conditioner to crank out more than a whisper of tepid air, I turned the dial all the way. There was a loud blast. Panicked, I jumped back. White smoke poured from the metal unit, filling the living room. I grabbed Tucker and ran outside, barefoot and screaming, begging for help.

No one came. Venkat was hanging out at the office. Raju was nowhere to be found. A handful of workers in the empty house next door looked up, snickered, and resumed their tedious brickwork under the pounding sun. A neighbor peered out from an upstairs window and then disappeared. Smoke continued to pour from the front door. I dialed frantically on my phone—Venkat, Alexis, Jay, anyone who would come rescue me—but I couldn't get a signal and eventually I gave up, sinking to the sidewalk with my head in my hands, Tucker trembling beside me. If the house went up in flames, maybe I'd get to go home.

ॐ

"What did you do all day?"

Jay asked this question, with no trace of irony, every night when he walked in the door. At first I thought he was being sarcastic. So I got creative, exaggerating the *nothing much* I'd actually done into epic tales of struggle and valor on foreign soil. *Just as I was crossing the street, the buffalo bared its teeth and started to charge!* Then I got defensive, indignantly standing up for my work-permit-less right to do nothing at all. *So what if I stayed in bed all day? It's not like I had anything better to do.*

I filled my days with *nothing much.* I shopped for souvenirs, met Alexis for lunch at Little Italy, went to Q-Mart or the vegetable stand. I stopped by the men-only *chai* stand on the side of the road, braving the stares of semi-hostile confusion to grab two shot-glass-sized Styrofoam cups of hot, sweet black tea for Venkat and me to drink in the car. It was a phantom nod to my afternoon Starbucks breaks, back in the old days when I'd had days I'd actually needed to take a break from. The *chai,* unlike the rest of India, was growing on me.

The brilliance of New York was the seamless blend of public and private, together and alone. Everybody was really, really busy—which meant no one had time to worry about what anyone else was doing. Everybody was different, which meant no one was. For a New Yorker, staring at someone—even if they were walking down Fifth Avenue wearing a chicken costume singing "Desperado" at the top of their lungs—was a dead giveaway you weren't actually from New York. Same as being nice to taxi drivers or pronouncing "Houston" like the city in Texas. You could ride the subway with a thousand other people, crammed into a space too small for secrets, and feel absolutely anonymous, blissfully alone. You could be as quiet or as loud as you liked, engage in the world or detach completely, and New York would go on in a liquid stream around you, supporting your decision with the endless buoyant swell of an ocean.

India was the opposite. There was no privacy, no delineation between the masses. Rich, poor, old, young—everyone was thrown together in forced intimacy. The tent camps directly outside the gated housing developments, the street urchins crawling over imported

C-class Mercedes sedans, pounding on the windows for spare change. There was no such thing as personal space, because there *was* no space. Everything was shared.

Our Indian neighbors never came to say hello, but I could see them watching us through the windows at night, staring into our lit-up living room like Jay and I were characters on a screen. Whispers traveled through the tent camps like feathers in the air. It felt like we were trapped under a microscope. I felt judged and ridiculed for being the exact stereotypical American princess I'd sworn I'd never be. I craved just one subway ride where I could slip back inside the security blanket of cultural anonymity. I wanted to disappear.

Tucker and I started most of our days in Jubilee Hills's KBR park, walking the long circular hiking trail, ignoring the occasional shout from the groundskeepers who didn't appreciate his presence. (I'd checked the official rules; nowhere, in English or Hindi, did it say *no dogs allowed*.) We were often alone in the early morning hours; only serious joggers were out braving the morning heat. The outer trail was a six-kilometer loop built around four hundred acres of conservation land that boasted six hundred species of trees, flowers, and plants, and 140 species of animal life. So far, we'd only seen peacocks and the occasional stray dog, panting and lethargic in the sun.

"Tigers, Madam," said Venkat solemnly when he dropped us off at the entrance gate in Jubilee Hills. "Much tigers inside KBR park. Much danger."

"I don't think so, Venkat," I said, strapping Tucker into his harness. "Do you want to come for a walk with us?" I always felt guilty when he was stuck behind the wheel of the Scorpio in a parking lot, roasting in the blazing sun, waiting for me to finish something or other so he could turn the engine back on and crank the AC.

"No, thank you, Madam. I am staying here." He climbed in the front seat and reclined it all the way, pulling a comb from his pocket. When he thought I'd walked away, he propped a wallet-sized photograph on the dashboard. The picture showed a girl in braids wearing a turquoise sari. I wondered who she was.

Diana, a fitness freak, ran KBR's full six-kilometer trail almost every weekend. Kyle, who was opposed to exercise of any kind, thought she was insane. Tucker and I hadn't made the full loop yet; we usually picked a point thirty minutes in to stop and rest before we turned around and retraced our steps. I kept an eye out for tigers, just in case. My favorite stretch was a straight uphill climb that ended at a lookout point, stone benches arranged beneath a banyan tree that overlooked the entire city. Even from here, the skyline was sepia: heat and dust, smoke from cooking fires and funeral pyres and garbage piles burning in the tent cities.

But it was quiet beneath the banyan tree, like someone had pressed a button to mute the car horns and the pounding construction. I stretched out in the rare luxury of shade. Tucker and I shared sips of water from a bottle of Himalaya. I liked this feeling, of being small way up above something huge. It was the same feeling I'd had when I sat on our tiny New York balcony on the twenty-second floor, looking out over the city lights to the Hudson River. Taking in the enormity of the world and feeling cozy in the tiny space I'd carved out within it. Up here, I could look at Hyderabad with that same kind of wonder, enjoying the vastness without feeling swallowed up.

I took my new journal from my pocket, hand-tooled in orange leather. It was a recent purchase from my bag-selling friend at Shilparamam; I'd been hoping it would bring me some Indian inspiration. I tried to capture my feelings on the journal's pulpy white pages. But the words didn't come. This brief space of silence wasn't enough to quiet the noise in my mind.

A family clambered up the hill, their laughter and shouts filling the air. A boy and a girl raced ahead of their parents to reach the summit. When they saw me, they stopped dead, brown eyes saucerwide. Their mother came up behind them, wrapping them into the saffron skirts of her sari. They all stared.

I tried a friendly wave, but their expressions were impenetrable. The sanctity of my moment under the banyan tree was ruined. Disgusted, I scooped Tucker up and started back down the hill, stomping my feet harder than necessary. Little clouds of dirt swirled around my ankles.

In New York, when life got stressful, I'd spent many a dejected hour soothing my sorrows at Barneys or Bloomingdale's, filling the hollow places in my heart with luxurious *things*. My credit card bills suffered (*cheaper than therapy*, I'd tell Jay defensively, shoving shopping bags into each other so it would look like there were fewer, or smuggling them into the house hidden under the dry cleaning), but my spirits never failed to lift once I became the proud owner of a new bag or a necklace or a bottle of imported perfume. Even a lip gloss at Duane Reade would do the trick. Maybe an Indian shopping trip would help me get out of my funk. A little dose of fashion would go a long way toward making me feel like the self I was losing. I'd get my retail therapy fix and maybe, with a new wardrobe, I'd fit in a little better too.

"Venkat, I want to go shopping."

"Q-Mart, Madam?"

"No. Clothing. Take me somewhere to get Indian clothing."

"Indian dress? You, Madam?" He looked doubtful.

"Somewhere nice, OK? Somewhere the other housewives would go."

"But…"

"Just drive, Venkat."

Snapping at Venkat always made me feel guilty, though I did it more and more these days. Really, Venkat was one of the only bright spots in my days. He was smarter than his position; kinder and more sensitive than his tough swagger let on. And while his English wasn't good enough to tell me, and his private nature prevented him from trying, I knew his dreams were different too. I wondered who he would have been if he'd been born on my side of the world, instead of in a village that raised goats and sent teenagers away to earn money for their families by chauffeuring rich Indians and expats like us.

In my upper-middle-class neighborhood, born to second-generation American parents, I was raised on the American dream, believing that anyone could rise above their circumstances if they worked hard and dreamed big enough. But that concept didn't apply in India. Someday, Venkat—with his fourth-grade village education and his limitless potential—would leave his personal driver days behind and go back to his goats. And he would be happy. But he'd never be everything I knew he could be. I wasn't sure which was the bigger tragedy: his acceptance of his linear fate or my inability to reconcile it.

We pulled up outside a white-washed concrete building, three stories high. Mirrored chandeliers like disco balls hung in the windows. Mannequins in head-to-toe sequins sparkled in the revolving light. A parking lot attendant rushed to open my door, speaking to Venkat in rapid Telugu.

"I am waiting for you here," Venkat said.

"I won't be long. Keep the air conditioner on for Tucker, please."

Inside there were rows and rows of fabric, sparkly and embroidered, sewn with tiny mirrors and jewels. My style had always been basic, classy, with a little bit of urban boho mixed in. I loved street jewelry with T-shirts, little black dresses and strappy gold sandals, jeans and chunky sweaters and boots. I liked dark, rich colors like navy and charcoal. India's riot of bright colors and shiny embellishments were the exact opposite of my New York uniform.

A trio of saleswomen appeared, their elaborate *salwar kameez* ensembles—calf-length tunics over matching pencil-legged pants—making them look as though they were gliding instead of walking.

"Can we help you, Madam?" They spoke in unison.

I ran my hand over my yoga pants, self-conscious. I probably should have gone home to shower and change first.

"I'm looking for Indian clothes. Maybe some long skirts or those…" I gestured to their *salwar* suits. Really, they looked like costumes to me, something that should be worn onstage for an International Day pageant, not as day wear. "Do you have something in black?"

One of the women clicked her tongue. They exchanged a meaningful glance.

"Black is an inauspicious color in India, Madam. You won't be finding many clothings available in that color here." She looked me up and down, estimating my measurements with a practiced eye. "We can allow you some options to try. But in truth, Madam, you are too large for Indian fashions. We are suggesting you might have better circumstances finding your clothings custom-made."

I was a size six. Too big to be a celebrity, but perfectly acceptable in normal life in a healthy, yoga-toned, mid-range BMI kind of way. Despite struggling with the same ten pounds my whole life, I'd never, ever been described as "large" before. It felt terrible. Face flushed and heart racing, I accepted a small pile of clothing and ducked behind the dressing room curtain, grateful for the privacy. The first thing I pulled on, a fuchsia *ghagra* skirt that reached the floor in accordion pleats, was atrocious. The fabric strained over my hips and thighs and bunched at my ankles, clinging in exactly the wrong spots. It was marked XL, but the elastic waistband was stretched to capacity over my stomach. I couldn't breathe.

Three more outfits, three more misses. I'd always been comfortable identifying as "curvy," but now my chest and hips seemed grotesque, fun-house-mirror distorted beneath the fluorescent lights. Worse, I looked like a parody of myself—a child playing dress-up on Halloween. I tossed the rest of the clothes into a clumsy pile and fled the dressing room, my expression of defeat as transparent as the smug looks of *I told you so* on the triumvirate of saleswomen waiting for me outside.

"Perhaps some jewelries, Madam?" they called after me. "Or a handbag?" I stopped at a display of bangles just before the exit. They were turquoise and orange and yellow, studded with tiny gems. I picked one up and tried it on. I couldn't get it past my thumb.

৶৩

There was a cow sleeping in the road. Horns painted pink, orange marigold garlands strung across its emaciated body. We were three cars behind the cow, listening to the angry cacophony of horns from in back of us that protested the delay. Impervious to the anger of hundreds of commuters, the cow dozed on, a peaceful expression on its bovine face. I was jealous. I also felt like screaming. Why was this allowed to happen? How, in a country that had existed for centuries, were farm animals still allowed to call all the shots?

Venkat put the car in park and reclined his seat, stretching his legs. He combed his hair in the rearview mirror. From his pocket, he took the photograph of the girl, taking a quick peek before stashing it away again.

"Who is she?" I asked, officially too curious not to pry.

Venkat looked embarrassed. I could see the tips of his ears turn red all the way from the backseat, reminding me just how much of a bashful teenager he still was behind his swaggering, village-boy-turned-city-man bravado.

"She is Swapna, Madam. Mine cousin. From my village." He paused, deciding how much to tell me. "She has thirteen years. When she has fifteen, I am marrying her. For two years I am waiting."

"Can I see the picture?"

Swapna was lovely, serious and small, with high cheekbones and skin the color of caramel. As if he could read my mind, Venkat pointed to the picture. "Much white, mine Swapna. Mine childrens will be Reddy and much white, both."

On television, there were commercials for whitening creams and powders, elixirs you could drink that promised to "pale your complexion." The ads showed men slumped over desks, being ignored and insulted at work, and then, post-whitening cream, winning the promotion and the cutest girl in the office in one fell swoop. Women stood on the sidelines, glum, watching wedding after wedding, and then, voila! A magic complexion powder would lead to a red sari, hennaed hands, and a groom on a white elephant. It made sense that Venkat was so proud of his betrothed's good complexion. My white skin was making me miserable in India, but for everyone else, it was the holy grail.

The cow stirred and stretched.

"Cow nap over," Venkat announced. "We going."

At the next intersection, we pulled up beside a tent city. In the early evening glow, it was alive with activity—men returning from a day's labor at the construction site, women stirring fragrant lentils and thick rice over cooking fires. There were community clotheslines strung between the rows of blue tarp–covered huts. Children were everywhere, hanging laundry, chasing each other in gleeful games of tag, lying on their stomachs alongside the roads, waving at the cars as they passed.

The Scorpio inched forward and now my window was directly outside one of the tents closest to the road. I stared inside, transfixed, my face pressed up against the glass. The entire space was half the size of my tiny New York kitchen. A man lay curled on a blanket in the corner, sleeping. A child, no more than five, sat cross-legged, rinsing rice over a pot. His sister drew lines in the dirt with a stick while their mother scrubbed at a length of fabric submerged in a tin bucket full of soapy water. In the corner, there was one cooking pot. Three more blankets were neatly rolled and stacked. Four pairs of plastic sandals waited just outside the entrance. There were four plates, four cups for water, and a worn wooden spoon. One worn sari and a pair of brown *dhoti* pants swayed on a clothesline. The boy spilled a few grains of rice on the ground and looked up at his mother, anxious. She smiled at him and rumpled his tangled black hair.

It was beautiful. So beautiful and immediate and real it made my stomach hurt. I was staring at some of the most visceral examples of poverty in India—a tent camp full of transients, a family of four living underneath a plastic tarp and working like slaves for less than a living wage—and instead of feeling pity or confusion or rage, I felt envy.

Everything was so clear. Their places in the world, their lives laid out before them like so many stepping stones on a predestined path. They had exactly what they needed to survive. There was no room for indecision or clutter or waste. There was no narcissistic hand-wringing of *what should I do, what should I be?* There was just food, shelter, family, survival. A pair of shoes was a blessing. A day's wage was a prayer answered. They had themselves, and each other, and a place to sleep under the wide open sky. Trapped behind the tinted glass, homesick and lonely, I watched that family and longed for what they had.

Was this what karma really meant? To travel halfway around the world only to find out I was nothing, and no one, in the face of people who knew real struggle and real sorrow and real joy? My whole life folded out in front of me, as silly and insubstantial as a game of Candyland. Sugary sweet, all lip gloss and handbags and self-important dreams, with obstacles as imaginary as the Lollipop Woods and Gum Drop Mountain. In the face of the tent city's true reality, my whole existence felt meaningless.

CHAPTER 14

"You're going to crash and burn here, ya know," observed the man behind me, snickering.

I was in line at Coffee Day. Being homesick and miserable was one thing; being homesick and miserable without Starbucks was quite another. Tetley English Breakfast and roadside *chai* just weren't cutting it. Desperate, I'd decided to brave the Indian espresso experience yet again. Rashmi, once again, was having trouble understanding my order.

"Latte, please. With *nonfat* milk. Fat-free? Skim?" Another snicker from behind me. I turned and looked at him, unused to being addressed directly without a "Madam" or a "Ma'am" and a head bobble attached. "What do you mean?"

The man was tall, six feet at least, wearing battered green cargo shorts, untied hiking boots, and a black, logoless baseball cap. Good-looking in a rugged, unshowered kind of way. His accent was thick and hard to place—English? Scottish? Australian? I'd had a friend from London once who did a Munch-face of horror every time I confused her accent with someone's from, say, New Zealand. Apparently there was a world of difference between them. To me, they all sounded the same.

"Your American accent is terrible. No one is going to be able to understand a word you're saying," he continued, resting his elbows on the counter and grinning up at me. He was cute. When was the last time Jay had grinned at me like that? Last year? Ever? The guy's accent was cute too, but as crippling to my ear as mine was to his. I could barely understand a word he was saying. For a moment, I waffled: enjoy the unaccustomed male attention or get offended at the unsolicited criticism? I chose option #2.

"I'm doing fine so far, thank you very much."

"I'm surprised they could even make you that drink you just asked for. LAAHTAY. Don't you find yourself getting a lot of things you didn't ask for around here?" He had the smug look of a backpacker, someone who rolled through town for a few hours and declared himself a local expert.

"It's not my fault they can't understand me. It's not like I'm speaking Chinese or something."

"I think what you have here is a failure to communicate, no?"

OK, fine. He had a point. No amount of pantomime seemed to get my point across to the drivers, vendors, and rickshaw operators I attempted to converse with. Even with subtitles, the Hindi programs on television were mostly incomprehensible. In a country whose national language was English, even my native tongue wasn't getting me very far. I grimaced.

"Do you live in Hyderabad?" I asked.

"Nah, just ambling through. I'm headed down to Goa tomorrow. Melbourne is home."

Exactly. No one who wasn't forced to *live* in Hyderabad—pay the electric bill, obtain a gas tank, fight the traffic, get stared at all day long—was entitled to make fun of my poor communication skills or my "terrible" American accent.

"Yeah, well. There's not a whole lot I can do about my accent. I'm stuck with it. Just like I'm stuck here."

The Aussie straightened, hoisting his backpack up higher on his shoulder. "There are worse places to be stuck."

"Somehow I doubt that. Have you tried the *biryani*? It almost killed me."

"Having some troubles fitting in, then?" Rashmi reached around me to hand him a cup. I could have sworn she batted her eyelashes. Maybe the key to expat success had less to do with accents and more to do with being a cute male.

"What makes you say that?"

"Have you looked in a mirror lately? No offense, but for a pretty girl, it looks like you might have seen better days."

I moved a self-conscious hand to my hair, which was thrown together in a messy bun on top of my head. It was still falling out in handfuls; no amount of lathering with the Ayurveda shampoo could make it look anything but lank and greasy. The water tank issues had made showering less of a luxury and more of a twice-a-week necessity. I couldn't remember the last time I'd worn lip gloss. Or mascara. Or perfume.

Rashmi held my latte in her hand, too busy watching our conversation to hand it over. I cleared my throat, raising my eyebrows in her direction.

"Excuse me, Sir and Ma'am, but if you are wanting my opinion, I am finding it much difficult to understand either of you, especially when you are speaking so quickly." She handed over the drink. "Has Ma'am considered Hindi lessons? You should be contacting Simrahn.

She is quite good at instruction." Rashmi pointed to the bulletin board just inside the door. "Her card is there."

"Can I join you?" asked the Aussie, following me out. He pointed to a table on the outdoor patio next to a pack of teens in stone-wash denim blowing grape-flavored hookah smoke toward the sky. "It's been a while since I've seen a friendly face."

I wasn't sure what he found friendly about mine, considering he'd just told me I looked like shit, except not in so many words and with an Australian accent. I sat anyway. I had nothing but time to kill. I glanced out the window, wondering if Venkat could see me, what he would think if he did. I wasn't doing anything wrong, but my pulse raced the way it used to when I was a teenager, right before I crawled out my bedroom window two hours past curfew. I wanted so badly to have a real conversation with someone. Someone who told me I was pretty. Someone who might still think I was witty or interesting. Or sane.

"What brought you to Hyderabad?" he asked, dumping pellets of saccharin into a cup of Americano as thick as tar. His face and hands had the same weathered texture, like he'd spent hours working in the sun. Even tanned, he and I were the only white faces in the cafe.

"My husband's job."

"He works a lot?"

"All the time."

"So you hang out in coffeehouses scaring people with your accent and complaining about the local cuisine?"

"Something like that. You?"

The Aussie laughed. "I'm on sabbatical, researching clean water efforts in Southeast Asia. India is nothing but inspiration, no? All this struggling humanity." He waved his arm to include the whole cafe.

"This isn't exactly a good sampling of the population. Everyone in here can afford a 250 rupee coffee drink. And flavored smoking tobacco. And blue jeans."

"You know what I mean, aye? Anyway, I'm not meant to stay long in Hyderabad. I'm stopping through on my way to Goa for a bit of a holiday." He sipped his coffee. The waxed paper cup was already disintegrating, crumpling into itself like a melting snowman. "Just fueling up before I go out into the field again. Taking down some notes." He held up a leather notebook similar to mine, but worn with use. It was literally bursting with pages and pages of scribbled pencil. I thought of my own empty notebook, the emotions and ideas that had once come so easily, but now vanished into the smoky Indian air long before I could turn them into words.

"I'm a writer too. Or used to be. I haven't felt so inspired lately." I ripped the empty saccharin packet to shreds with my ragged fingernails.

"She might be right, you know." The Aussie gestured over his shoulder with one thumb, where Rashmi still stood, watching our discussion with interest. I wished she'd paid such close attention when she'd been making my latte; espresso grounds floated on top of the foam like tiny insects.

"About what?"

"Learning the language. Sometimes the words only come when you teach yourself new ways to think about them. Plus, everything is easier if you find some common ground." He reached over to the bulletin board and plucked a slip of paper from the bottom. "Here, take this with you. Doubt she'll be able to fix that accent, but you might learn how to order a cup of coffee you'll actually drink." He pointed to my untouched latte. "Drink up; it'll make you feel better." He winked and stood up, crumpling what was left of his cup and tossing it toward the garbage can without looking. It went in.

"See you around then, beautiful."

"Yeah, sure." I blushed under his gaze. "Thanks."

Jay never told me I was beautiful. I'd been wounded by the absent compliment more than once, frustrated that he seemed indifferent to my appearance no matter how much effort I put in. *Don't you think I'm pretty?* I'd ask. *Of course I do. I married you, didn't I?* he'd answer, as though that were good enough.

I wanted him to think I was beautiful, or at least tell me so, even when I wasn't. Because I wasn't, always, but I longed for him to see me that way. My desire for his acceptance and approval hadn't disappeared the day he put a ring on my finger. Sometimes I'd stand in front of the mirror, staring at myself, trying to see what he saw, wondering what flaw rendered me so ordinary to the person who was supposed to love me most.

But mostly, I let it go. There were other people who filled that void. Whose compliments lifted me up and made me whole. My parents, my girlfriends, my co-workers and classmates. Years before the cultural phenomenon of the Facebook "like," we traded support like currency, banking a *gorgeous* here and a *brilliant* there, knowing that when we needed it, a whole slew of love-isms would come back to us in spades. Like standing on a giant pyramid, Jay and I balanced at the top, holding hands but facing away from each other, while everyone we knew stood below, shoulder to shoulder, forming the platform on which we stood, whispering the words that filled in all the empty places.

In Hyderabad there was no pyramid, no supporting cast of loved ones to keep us afloat in a sea of uncertainty. All those people were thousands of miles away. My face in the broken mirror was less recognizable than ever. Jay seemed to see me less and less every day. I wanted *him* to think I was beautiful, not a random Australian backpacker with a cute smile. I hated that Jay made me feel so insecure. I didn't want to be some simpering hothouse flower, needing constant attention in order to bloom. But I needed him to remind me where I came from and who I used to be. In the absence of everything familiar, I was losing myself.

India made me feel like I was falling down an endless shaft, untethered and uncertain, a thousand eyes watching but not a single hand reaching out to break my fall. Deep down, I knew if I never stopped falling, by the time I reached the bottom it would be too dark and too deep to ever climb back up again.

⁂

Jay and I drove home from dinner in silence, locked in trains of thought that traveled in two different directions. It reminded me of that old math problem: *If Train A was traveling east at a speed of forty-five miles per hour, and Train B was traveling west at a speed of sixty miles per hour, how long would it take for them to pass each other?* He was east, rooted here in this foreign world, filling his days with purpose and intention that moved ever forward, never looking back at the life we left behind. And I was west, yearning for a home I could no longer define, wishing I could run back to where I came from and stop trying to fit into a life I'd never asked for. We were supposed to be taking this journey together. I watched his profile, shadowy in the darkened car, and wondered if he'd ever turn my way again.

The sun had set hours ago, but the air still broiled with violent heat. We turned onto Izzat Nagar road, where dozens of people were sleeping on the concrete median. On nights like this, when it was too hot to sleep in the tents, the men from the camps would pile next to each other in a long line of slumber, blankets over their heads to shield them from the noise and the headlights of oncoming traffic.

Venkat took the corner fast, as usual, in a rush to get home now that his long day's work was done. Suddenly he whipped the steering wheel hard to the left, avoiding something bulky that blocked the road. I flew into Jay's lap, banging my head against the window. We never bothered wearing seat belts in the Scorpio; there were so many other hazards on the road that staying strapped into the car seemed like the least of our worries.

"Venkat, what was that?" Jay asked, annoyed. "A cow or something?"

"Guy. Dead," Venkat answered, steadying the car and accelerating like nothing out of the ordinary had happened.

"Dead? Like, a person?" I asked, craning around to look behind us.

"Yes. Guy dead. Man. Killed. No living," Venkat said. His tone was the same one he used to tell me the climate would be hot today or that we needed to stop for petrol.

"Venkat, Jesus! Turn around! We can't just drive by!" Jay leaned forward into the front of the car, shaking Venkat's shoulder. Venkat shrugged him off.

"No, Sir. No turning around."

"What? Why? How do you know he's dead? What if he's still alive and just hurt? We can call the ambulance. What's the number for 911?" I grabbed my mobile, realizing I had no idea who or where to call for an emergency.

"Dead, Ma'am. Police coming later, four, five hours. No now. Now nothing."

"Turn *around*, Venkat," Jay said angrily.

Venkat hunched down, chastened but clearly opposed to the demand. He made an awkward U-turn, oblivious to oncoming traffic. A flurry of infuriated horns sounded in protest. Venkat pulled back out onto the main road, then made the same right turn back onto Izzat Nagar. This time, there was no need for a violent swerve. He knew exactly what he was trying to avoid.

Sure enough, it was a body, lifeless and splayed awkwardly on the pavement, still wrapped in a purple blanket that revealed only thin, scarred ankles and filthy bare feet. There was no indication of what happened or who was responsible for leaving him there, denied even the dignity of being rolled away from the onslaught of cars and livestock that still threatened to trample him. His spot along the crowded wall was empty. On either side, his companions slept on, either unaware or unconcerned that while they lay dreaming, one of their own met his demise on the unforgiving road.

Venkat stalled the car across from the body, still sulking behind the wheel.

"Venkat, I want to call the police. Is there a number?"

"No number. No calling. They coming, later."

We stayed there, staring at the body in the road. Jay tried a bunch of different numbers but nothing went through. Finally, he called Anish and explained the situation. I couldn't make out what Anish was saying, but Jay's responses were mostly grunted affirmations, accompanied by a couple of shrugs and a furrowed brow that told me he wasn't satisfied with whatever Anish was telling him.

At the sound of Anish's voice through the phone, Venkat looked even more alarmed. Anish and his Brahmin family were powerful in Hyderabad, members of the highest caste. He commanded more respect from Venkat than Jay and I put together. It was Anish who had negotiated Venkat's salary and given him basic instructions for his position. It might have been me who handed Venkat an envelope of rupees at the end of each week, but as far as Venkat was concerned, Anish held all the power.

Jay hung up and slipped his BlackBerry back in his pocket. "Anish says he'll make some calls to the people he knows on the police force, but he doesn't think they're likely to do anything about it. And he says we need to get out of here because they won't like it if we start poking around asking questions."

"So we're just going to leave him here? Who won't like it, his friends on the wall? They're not doing anything; it's like they don't even care or something. This would never happen at home. Death *means* something there. How can they just leave him like this? He had a name, a family."

My voice broke, cracking beneath a landslide of emotion I barely understood. I felt useless and angry, so utterly foreign. It was like there was a missing piece to a puzzle that was forever buried beyond my reach. Everything I'd ever understood about the sanctity of life and death was suddenly blurry and out of focus. Did life mean more here, as I'd imagined when I envied the tent people their focused, contented lives? Or did it mean less because death was everywhere, imminent and unbiased, choosing as casually as a blackjack dealer with a deck of cards?

We were so out of our league, so poorly equipped to navigate an emotional and moral landscape that let us think we were superior for reasons that meant nothing at all. We had industry and innovation, airplanes and skyscrapers and supermarkets, but at the end of the day, at the end of a life, the only difference between the West and the East is that we would never stop spinning with the centrifugal force of our own self-importance. Here, there was life—celebration and love, joy and fear and sorrow—and there was death. It was only our perception that made the moment it all ended any different from the moment before it or the one that followed.

We pulled away and we left him there, lifeless in his purple blanket. I turned around and watched the body get smaller and smaller as we drove back past the tent camp to our gated development, our marble mansion, our protected lives that were equally as pointless as the one we'd just left behind. Jay put his arm around me. I hadn't realized I was shivering.

"You're letting this mean more than it should," Jay said, watching me as I lay in bed, eyes wide open, unable to sleep. "This happens all the time, every day. Maybe he was old or sick. Maybe he rolled off the wall on purpose. You just don't know. Things are different here. Life doesn't mean the same thing."

But that couldn't be true. Somewhere in all this poverty and filth, beneath the confusion and the chaos and the stares, there was truth like nothing I'd ever known. It glimmered on the edges of my consciousness, demanding my attention but refusing to show me a way inside. I was losing myself, watching my marriage crumble, forgetting what it ever felt like to be home. And the only moment that held any meaning, that let me glimpse the answers I was desperate to find, was seeing a dead guy in the road and driving away without doing anything at all.

CHAPTER 15

L adies and gentlemen, this concludes our Air India nonstop flight to
Singapore International Airport. Please remain in your seats with
seat belts fixed until the captain has signaled. Thank you for choosing
Air India. We hope your journey with us was pleasant. *Namaste*."

So far, our flight had been light years away from "pleasant." The
cramped, narrow cabin was full of coughing adults and wailing children. There were bugs. Germs. Sticky leftover food from previous
flights clung to the seats and left a sour stench in the recirculated air.
Periodically, flight attendants came down the aisle spraying clouds
of noxious fumes out of rusted metal canisters, killing mosquitoes.
And perhaps us too, had we been foolish enough to inhale during
the flight.

The loudspeaker clicked off. There was an instant flurry of activity: seat belts unbuckling, overhead compartments being opened,
suitcases being heaved into the aisles. I was in the middle seat. Jay
was in the aisle. The woman next to me, wrapped in a beige sari
with a stripe of crimson powder painted along the center part in

her dark long hair, had been slumped against the window, snoring loudly, for most of the flight, one arm flung across my right thigh. But suddenly she sprang into action, gesturing impatiently for me to get out of her way.

"Excuse me, please," she said haughtily, clearly inconvenienced by the fact that I was still sitting with my seat belt securely fastened. Because the fasten seat belt sign was still turned on. Because the plane was *still moving*.

I smiled and pointed up at the little lit-up picture of a buckle above us. "I think we're supposed to stay in our seats," I said. Around us, it was chaos. People were jostling each other out of the way for a better position in a line that had formed in the aisle. The flight attendants looked unperturbed. The woman looked like she was going to hit me.

"Please move aside and let me pass," she said, raising her voice. I looked at Jay. He shrugged and moved like he was going to unbuckle himself and let her by.

"Don't you *dare*," I hissed under my breath. This was a matter of principle. I turned to our aisle-mate. "Sorry. We need to wait until they turn the sign off."

My fake-friendly smile did nothing to placate her. She grunted and tapped her fingernails loudly on the back of the seat in front of her, standing so close that the bottom hem of her sari draped across my lap. She shoved a worn plaid suitcase into my shin, trying to physically bludgeon me out of her path to freedom.

The scene on the plane was exactly why I was categorically unfit for life in India. I was a born rule-follower, a lover of structure and boundaries. I colored inside the lines. My free-spirited mother's staunch refusal to ever park her minivan within the confines of one parking space caused me much teenaged angst. Jay affectionately dubbed me "hall monitor" from our very first date, when I refused to choose our own table at the restaurant because we were standing in front of a gold-framed placard that clearly stated "Please Wait to Be Seated."

India had no rules. Or, if there were any, everyone gave themselves carte blanche to blatantly disregard them whenever they felt like it. At a traffic signal—of which Hyderabad had precious few—a red light only meant "stop" if the drivers nearby felt inclined to obey. We passed alongside the DO NOT PASS URINE HERE wall every day; I'd yet to count less than five men relieving themselves there, using the giant painted letters as targets for their streams. If New York had been organized, purposeful chaos, then India was just chaos—loud, frenetic, unrepentant.

And then there was me. An ill-placed comma in a book I was reading plagued me for days. I glared at people who tried to sneak more than ten items through the express checkout lane at the grocery store. The clothes in my closet all hung facing left. Was it surprising, really, that I—a rule-following hall monitor practically since birth, who still kept my sixty-four-box of Crayolas organized by color, who had never jay-walked or double-parked or cheated at Scrabble in my entire life—was ill-suited to a world where rules simply didn't apply? Perhaps not.

This last-minute weekend in Singapore was a work trip for Jay. I was tagging along for a mini-vacation. It was the first time we'd left Hyderabad since the day we arrived six months ago. I was mildly concerned about the canings-for-chewing-gum rumors about Singaporean culture, but everything else about it sounded heavenly. Crosswalks and sidewalks and French restaurants with white tablecloths. I wanted to drown myself in *filet mignon* and *sauvignon blanc*. I wanted to crank the air conditioning high and sit around in a thick fluffy bathrobe, sipping cappuccino on the thirty-second floor of a fancy hotel with skyline views. I wanted to ride in a real taxi cab, with four wheels and actual doors, and stop at every traffic light. Just breathing non-Indian air sounded too good to be true.

We'd begged Venkat to stay in the house with Tucker, to which he agreed, reluctantly, only after I promised to listen to his pitch on why we should buy him a Yamaha motorcycle as soon as we returned. He wanted that motorcycle desperately. I hated to resort to bribery, but it was the only way I could leave the city and not spend the entire time worrying about my dog. I trusted Venkat. He and Tucker might not be the best of friends, but at least Tucker would be safe.

Outside, the humid air smelled amazing, like frangipani or maybe tuberose. The outside of the airport was even cleaner than the inside. There were no rickshaws, no smoking piles of garbage, no cows or buffalo wandering the roads. There were only palm trees, smooth white pavement, and expensive imported cars.

We grabbed our luggage and got into a cab. Just as the doors closed behind us, a tropical downpour burst over the city. I watched the city flash by as the rain spattered across the windshield and drummed against the roof, making me feel safe and cozy inside. It was light, easy rain—a far cry from the violent onslaught of the South Indian monsoons.

"There is much beauty here," said the cab driver. Jay and I nodded in agreement, transfixed by the scene outside our windows. "No trash. No filth. We are proud of our city."

Civic pride, I thought with a flash of bitter spite. Could we figure out a way to import that concept back to India, where, out on the street, you had to duck to avoid being hit with garbage people tossed out their car windows?

Singapore was the anti-India. Everything was washed and freshly painted and neatly landscaped. There was a Starbucks on every corner. There were taxi stands and skyscrapers and the fastest, sleekest subway system I'd ever seen. And there was shopping—real, true designer shopping. My heart leapt with joy every time we passed yet another familiar and beloved name on a shiny, glass-paneled storefront: Chanel, Prada, Louis Vuitton.

Best of all, it was *orderly*. People were standing in lines, waiting at crosswalks, putting on seat belts. Even the rushes of people walking on the sidewalks moved with a kind of synchronized rhythm. Nothing seemed accidental. Everything had purpose. The little hall monitor inside me turned cartwheel after cartwheel in my head, beside herself with joy.

Our hotel room was a fully automated modern masterpiece, all white carpets and glistening chrome. The curtains opened and closed with the push of a button. The shower had a huge rainforest spout. There were fluffy white towels and fluffy white bathrobes and fluffy white terry-cloth slippers laid out next to the bed. There were chocolates on our pillows and fresh oranges in a bowl on the table by the door. I hung my dresses in the full-length closet and stood back for a moment, admiring them. *This* was the way things were supposed to be.

Jay only had a few hours to spare before his meetings. After a lunch of sushi (*sushi!*), fresh-cut fruit, and handmade spring rolls hot from the fryer, we headed to the beach. A lifetime of living near oceans made living in landlocked Hyderabad feel claustrophobic. I ached for the hypnotic rhythm of the waves, to crush sand between my toes and let the ocean breezes soothe my troubled mind.

With limited time and so many beaches to choose from on the tiny island, we decided to visit Sentosa Island. Mainly because Jay was dying to travel by "cable car," a method of transportation we'd previously only seen before at Disneyland. The tiny, brightly painted gondolas hung precariously over the city, creaking in the wind along a cable track in the sky. We paid for our tickets and stood in line, Jay gazing eagerly out over the horizon, me sipping the best vanilla latte I'd ever tasted. My entire body twitched with the unaccustomed influx of caffeine.

I stumbled a little climbing into our red gondola car. To match the blue silk sundress I was beyond thrilled to be wearing, I'd chosen a pair of high-heeled strappy sandals.

"You couldn't have just worn flip-flops?" Jay asked, grabbing my arm to steady me.

"And miss out on the chance to look cute for a change? No way."

Like the cable car—and really, much of Singapore itself—Sentosa Beach had a curiously fictional feel to it, complete with rope bridges and torches right out of Tarzan's Tree House. There was a grass hut bar playing Jimmy Buffett songs, and a weathered wooden dock that extended into the water. Cheerful rowboats were tethered on either side, bobbing in the gentle surf. Jay and I slipped off our shoes at the edge of the sand and walked toward the lapping waves.

Our relationship was so unpredictable these days, an ever-shifting cloud like the pattern of an erratic hurricane. His moods changed and my moods changed, and our ability to weather each other's storms dwindled with each passing day. Once again, I thought back to the promise we'd made each other that very first week, that only one of us could be down at one time. Now we were just spinning our unhappiness in opposite directions, blaming each other for miseries neither of us could control.

We took a long walk around the island. My shoes became unbearable and I slipped them off, looping the straps over my wrist and walking barefoot on the immaculate sidewalks. Jay whistled while we ambled along, heading into the sun, taking our time. I'd always loved it when he whistled. It was a rare, childlike impulse he only gave in to when we were alone.

Back at the hotel, though, Jay's distracted frown returned. He went to the business center to make some calls. I changed clothes and hurried out of the room. If *Lonely Planet* was correct, Singapore truly was heaven on earth. Because there was a Bikram yoga studio. *In the hotel.* As I raced through the hotel to make the next class, I could swear I heard harps playing and angels singing. Beach, coffee, yoga. A trifecta of the things I loved most in the world.

Despite my former devotion to yoga, I still hadn't made it to a single class in Hyderabad. I'd craved Bikram every single day since we moved. I went from practicing yoga five days a week with religious determination…to absolutely nothing. The other day, I'd bent down to put on Tucker's leash, and for one terrible, paralyzing moment, I thought I couldn't reach my toes.

Contrary to its illustrious title, Bikram's Yoga College of India was not actually located in India. And it wasn't just Hyderabad; there wasn't a single Bikram studio in the entire country. Bikram had founded his yoga school's world headquarters in Los Angeles. If I wanted to rediscover my yogini roots, I'd need to find another lineage to follow. It had been the very top of my India bucket list: *study yoga with ancient masters*. But like so many items on that list, written in New York a million lifetimes ago, that dream had fallen to the wayside in the face of my new reality.

The studio was the nicest Bikram space I'd ever seen. Quiet and serene, the woodwork was lush polished mahogany. The whole space smelled like tropical flowers. Gentle chimes played in the background. In class, I let the familiar dialogue wash over me. Even Bikram's grammatical errors and linguistic impossibilities were music to my ears. My spine groaned in thanks as I worked deep into muscles I'd been sorely neglecting. The heat melted my limbs into blissful puddles of acquiescence. Even with sweat streaming down my body, my lungs gasping for air, I felt healed. Transcended. *This is my religion*, I thought during final *savasana*, deeply relaxed for the first time in months. *This is home.*

"We need to move," I told Jay at dinner. We were at Les Amis, a French restaurant on a quiet back street in the Orchard shopping district. Our darkened corner table was lit with a single tapered candle in a pewter holder, the perfect setting for an intimate night. I slathered cold, salted butter on a fresh baguette and moaned with ecstasy under my breath.

"What do you mean? We're not even halfway through yet. We can't go back to New York now, Jen. You know that."

"No, not to New York. Here! To Singapore! Wouldn't it be perfect?" Singapore was the answer to all of our problems. We'd still be expats, only the kind of expats I'd imagined all along—chic and cosmopolitan, with designer clothes and vacations in Bali and plenty of coffee. My writer's block would disappear. Instead of sitting around the house, rotting away in my own misery, I'd finally be happy again. I could be the wife Jay wanted me to be, the one he deserved. Jay could do his outsourcing thing here, and I'd spend my days writing like crazy, doing Bikram yoga, and eating dumplings at Din Tae Fung. What could be better?

"God, it's good to have an actual wine list. What do you feel like drinking?" Jay asked, sliding his hand onto my thigh under the table. His hands were strong, with smooth tanned skin and calluses I loved to rub my fingertips over. I'd fallen in love with his hands long before I'd made up my mind about the rest of him.

"Don't you think it's a great idea?" I persisted, taking his hand and rubbing my thumb across his knuckles. There was tenderness in his touch. I wanted to grab on to it and hold tight before he slipped away from me again.

"It doesn't work like that," Jay began, just as the waiter arrived to recite the daily specials. Jay ordered wine and changed the subject. The moment was lost.

When we got back to Hyderabad, everything was the same, except worse now that I had Singapore to compare it to. The unpaved roads felt aggressively bumpier. The airport, lacking air conditioning and carpet and a Coffee Bean, smelled mustier than ever. Even the mosquitoes buzzed louder and closer, welcoming me home with their subtle, ever-present threat of baseball-sized flesh wounds and malaria. The magical bubble of Singapore had popped, leaving all that was left covered in an oily film of disappointment. Vacation was over. Real life was here to stay.

"Why don't you do something fun tomorrow?" Jay suggested as I trudged upstairs, holding a traumatized-looking Tucker in one arm and my overnight bag in the other. The thought of unpacking my dresses, shoving them to the back of their cramped cubby to collect another six months' worth of dust, was unbearable.

"Fun?" I said, not bothering to turn around. "Yoga is fun. Going to the beach is fun. Eating out in fancy restaurants is fun. We left all that behind in Singapore, remember?"

"I'm sure if you think hard enough, you'll figure something out," Jay answered, duplicating my cold sarcasm with pitch-perfect tone.

CHAPTER 16

Jay's hours continued to get longer as he tackled Region 10's ever-growing challenges. I was proud of him for taking on such a huge task and making it work, against the odds, with no beaten path to follow. *You're doing great*, I wanted to say. I should have said it often and loud and with feeling, so he'd hear me and know how much I supported him, believed in what he was doing. But every time I opened my mouth to say the words, my misery took over and different words came out instead.

The power was off all day again.

You're working too much. I'm lonely.

I hate it here.

I want to go home.

I called my parents every couple of days, hating how pathetic I sounded but unable to stop myself from rattling off an ever-growing list of complaints.

"Hang in there. It will get better," my dad said, eternally optimistic. It was one of the things I loved most about him—and clearly something I'd failed to inherit from his DNA.

"We're coming to a visit in a few months. That should give you something to look forward to," my mother reminded me. They continued to believe I'd somehow triumph, that I'd make the best of my journey no matter how often and how loudly I complained. I felt like I was letting both of them down. They'd raised me to be a fighter, but all I could think about was crawling into a corner and giving up for good.

The walls closed in around me a little more every day. The house was a marble cage I was trapped inside, so many doors and windows but no way to escape. Some nights, when Jay stayed out late, finishing work at the office or grabbing beers with the team, I sat alone in the dark on the cool marble floor and waited. There was a tennis ball in his nightstand drawer, left over from the days when we used to play together, and I threw it in listless arcs against the bedroom wall, letting it bounce and echo in the darkness again and again and again.

Everyone but me was consumed with work. Diana spent even more time at the office than Jay did, leaving only to shower and sleep before she returned again, drinking lukewarm Indian Diet Coke by the case. Kyle had gone to China on a business trip, leaving me behind as the only non-BKC employee in our eclectic circle.

Peter's rotation in Hyderabad was over. We'd had one last celebratory dinner at Ginger Court, with Jena scurrying around preparing "bon voyage" drinks and fussing over every detail of their final Indian meal. We'd driven him and Alexis to the airport, helped them load their bags onto the conveyor belt, and exchanged one last round of hugs and handshakes and see-you-soons, even though we wouldn't. Then Alexis and Peter had walked away through the crowds, ready to return to their lives in Philadelphia, leaving me more friendless and alone than I'd ever felt in my life.

Electricity on. Wireless working. Such a moment was so rare and so sacred that, at first, I spun in helpless circles, trying to decide what to do first. I wiped a layer of orange dust off my laptop and fired it up, elated to find the Internet operating without a hitch. I opened browser windows and closed them, lifted the VOIP phone off the receiver and listened to the glorious sound of a dial tone. I reunited with the Internet like a long-lost lover, gorging myself on digital media. I scoured online newspapers and gossip magazines, shopped for clothes I couldn't wear on websites that wouldn't ship to India. I caught up on my favorite blogs and even wrote a new post of my own, uploading pictures from the Singapore trip and indulging in a whiny rant about how much better things were there. Then I opened up Google and typed in "Hyderabad hair salon."

The Singapore trip, brief as it was, had inspired me to start taking better care of myself. Just one yoga class had me sleeping better, moving more freely in my own skin. Staring at my haggard reflection in the broken mirror day after day made me slip deeper into the endless circle of my unhappiness. I looked the way I felt. I felt the way I looked. But in Singapore, I'd felt pretty. And it wasn't just the wine or the clothes or the makeup I'd finally mustered the energy to apply. It was my emotional landscape, radiating outward. Jay had looked at me differently in Singapore. Less like a liability, an endless source of complaints and tears he needed to endure. More like someone he wanted to be around. I wanted him to look at me that way again. Because most days, he didn't look at me at all.

One afternoon, reading *Gone with the Wind* and twirling a strand of hair around my index finger, I noticed something terrible: split ends.

When I'd told Nikki, my NYC stylist, that I was moving to India, she'd looked completely aghast.

"What about your *hair*?" she cried.

"What do you mean?" I asked, confused.

Forget malaria, cholera, monsoons…according to Nikki, India was going to be more hazardous to my hair than any other part of me. I left the salon with a list of strict instructions: no washing with tap water (contaminated), no drying with a blow dryer (high-voltage electricity), no sun (would wreck highlights), and no swimming (hyper-chlorinated water). And under no circumstances was I to *cut* or *color* my hair any farther east than York Avenue. If only she'd known how very true all of her dire predictions would become.

The split ends were the least of it. My hair was dry, brittle, and continued to suicide-leap off my head in tangled clumps. My gold highlights were slowly creeping toward my ears, but I knew better than to mess with those. I saw a blond woman at the Taj hotel salon once, blissfully unaware, sitting beneath a purple heat lamp while two dozen foils baked her hair a minty shade of green. The terrible roots would have to stay.

After some rigorous Google searching, I booked an appointment at Manea, the new L'Oreal salon on Banjara Road. Diana had already been and swore it was great. Her blond locks had been as carefully cultivated in LA as mine were in New York. Surely she wouldn't steer me wrong with something so important. Just to be on the safe side, I booked the appointment on a Tuesday. Tuesday was an inauspicious hair-cutting day in India. Very bad luck.

When we arrived at the salon, even Venkat—hardly one to stand on form—seemed reluctant to let me out of the car once he figured out what I was up to. But I figured the Tuesday thing guaranteed me the whole place to myself, so there wouldn't be any extra people staring. Besides, where I came from, there was no such thing as an unlucky day to cut your hair.

After a blissful Indian head massage and a hydrating scalp treatment, I settled into a revolving salon chair. This was turning out to be quite relaxing. Everyone in the salon was easygoing and professional, treating me like a valued client, not some white-skinned freak from another planet. The head massage had left me sleepy and agreeable, like I'd just finished a delicious meal. I stretched, catlike, in my chair. I could get used to this.

"Will you be wanting a whole new style, Madam?" asked Akbar, my L'Oreal International Certified Stylist, as he twisted his fingers through my hair, pulling it this way and that as he examined each strand.

"No, thanks. I just need a trim."

Akbar frowned at me in the mirror.

"The style you have is quite unflattering, Madam. I need to be recommending something more suiting."

"No, really. Thanks, though. I like it the way it is. Just a tiny trim, please."

Akbar nodded, scissors in hand. He lifted my long brown hair up high above my head. With a single flash of silver, he made his first cut.

Half my hair hit the floor.

I lost it.

Oblivious, Akbar snipped again, and again.

"It is proper Indian hair, Madam. Very becoming, highly in fashion," a distraught Akbar cried, wringing his hands at my distress when the haircut was finally finished. My reaction clearly astounded him. Between fits of hysteria, I felt guilty for causing so much drama.

"It's fine. Really. It's not your fault," I squeaked between gasps, tossing a handful of rupees on the counter and fleeing down the stairs so he wouldn't witness another single second of my sorrow. I'd just paid triple for a haircut I hated beyond words. I couldn't shake the feeling that it was somehow my fault, that my misery had culminated in an epic disaster of hair karma.

When I got to the car, I was crying so hard that Venkat thought I was ill.

"Hospital, Madam?" he asked. I stared at my reflection in the tinted glass until a fresh wave of sobs forced me to turn away. I looked terrible. Beyond terrible.

India had taken the last of me, stripped the final vestiges of the girl I'd been when I left New York. I wasn't a writer or a jet-setter or even a halfway decent Indian housewife. The transformation was complete. My image in the broken mirror was who I'd become.

"It's not so bad," Kyle said at dinner that night, forcing me to take the scarf off my head so he could examine the damage. He'd just flown in from Shanghai, jet-lagged and full of stories of why everything there was better than here. "I think it makes you look like Grace Kelly." I just scowled, fighting back tears. I'd written a tearful, self-pitying blog post describing the hair salon drama, but instead of making me feel better, like writing used to do, I felt worse than ever. I looked at Jay, hoping he'd tell me I looked beautiful anyway or, at the very least, acknowledge my distress. But Jay, absorbed in a conference call with New York, said nothing at all.

We were eating at Laguna, the top-floor restaurant in a newly opened, three-story shopping complex in Jubilee Hills. The menu featured veg and non-veg "Mediterranean delicacies," which mostly included flatbread pizza and a variety of deep-fried appetizers. Still, the change of scenery was nice. I missed Jena's comforting, hovering presence, but I was as sick to death of Indian food as I was of India itself.

The best part about Laguna was watching people fall into the moats. Narrow, concrete trenches snaked across the restaurant's floor.

Each trench was filled with a foot of dingy water, perhaps lending to the Asian minimalist aesthetic the management seemed to be aiming for. The moats wound through the restaurant in lazy patterns, dividing sections and cutting between tables. Laguna, like all the hip new eateries in Hyderabad, was so dimly lit it was almost pitch black. So it wasn't surprising that every third person being led to their table by a hostess in a chic black pantsuit walked right into a moat, soaking themselves to the knees.

Diana, early as usual, had been the one to warn us about the watery death traps. She'd sent the rest of us anxious SMS messages: **Look down when you're walking to the table. Very dark and water pits everywhere.**

"Someone could break an ankle or something," she worried aloud when we arrived, taking small anxious sips of her Diet Coke. Around her neck was an intricate gemstone necklace, rubies glinting in the dim light. Diana dealt with stress by shopping too. Her jewelry collection grew every time BKC gave her another impossible deadline. By the time our two-year assignments were up, she was going to need her own vault. "I can't believe they aren't warning people. This is a lawsuit waiting to happen."

I sipped my Sula chardonnay and watched people fall into the moat. It was a mean-spirited, *schadenfreudic* way to be entertained. But each unsuspecting splash and its accompanying outraged cry put a small, dark smile on my face.

Kyle, equally amused, caught my eye and smiled. Jay and Diana launched into yet another discussion of Region 10 drama. They gestured wildly and talked over each other, rehashing the events of yet another disaster Kyle and I knew nothing about. Kyle sent me a text under the table.

Do you think they'll ever stop?

No, I typed back. **Save me.**

Just keep drinking. At least we're somewhere that provides entertainment.

As I read the message, there was another giant splash, followed by a torrent of furious Hindi swears. Kyle and I laughed. He reached over and tapped my wineglass with his bottle of Kingfisher.

"Ah, 'Bad," he said, chasing a curried jalapeno popper with another swig of beer. "Just think of the stories we'll tell if we ever get out of here. I really do think you look like Grace Kelly, by the way."

I smiled wearily and looked away.

ॶ

"Ma'am. Please. Ma'am. Please. Please. Ma'am."

The old woman—clutching a tree branch, wrapped in rags—pulled on my sleeve, chanting for attention. She pointed to her toothless mouth and then her stomach, wringing ravaged fingers. "Ma'am. Please."

It was impossible to help all of them—I'd learned that the hard way. Beggars swarmed the car at stoplights and clawed at my clothes outside shops and restaurants. They camped outside our development at night. The sacks of coins I took with me into the city were never enough. For the polio-ravaged children. For the burned women, victims of "cooking accidents" after their lack of a dowry rendered them useless and unwanted. For the injured, limbless men too broken to get work. No matter how badly I wanted to, I couldn't help them all.

The bazaar was crowded. I scanned the streets, waiting for Venkat and the Scorpio to appear. The woman drew closer. I stepped away, trying politely to avoid the old woman's desperation.

"I'm sorry."

She moved closer still, blocking my view. I recoiled instinctively, wanting her out of my personal space. Wanting to disappear rather than face her naked, wretched need.

The action made her angry. She lashed out with an elbow, spilling my bag of groceries to the ground. As I knelt to pick them up, a single rupee coin rolled from my pocket and came to rest between us. She grinned, pounced—and then there were others.

Two other women, a man, several children, all drawn in by the glint of precious metal in the dirt. They circled around me, pulling at my clothes, backing me toward the street on my knees. Traffic whizzed past, so close I could feel rushes of air at my neck, and I scrambled to my feet, trying to run before I was fully standing, trying to shout for help above the clamor of the beggars' voices. "PLEASE MA'AM. PLEASE MA'AM."

And then there was an arm lifting me away from them, pulling me out of the heat and dust, into the cool, black fortress of the Scorpio. Venkat. He'd even saved the groceries. We didn't speak on the way home. The air was thick with silence as I tried to slow my racing heart, to forget the sound of the old woman's cackle as she pounded the ground with her stick to rally the crowd.

It was hours before Jay came home. When he did, I was huddled in the dark, shivering, hugging my knees to my chest. Glaring at him with accusing eyes. His fault, all of this. The heat and the beggars and the loneliness that crushed me from morning until night. I didn't belong here. I never would.

"Where WERE you?" I shouted. Anger radiated from my skin

like the hum of an electric fence. Venkat, replacing the keys to the Scorpio on the hall table, turned in shock.

"*Working*, that's where," Jay sneered back. "Something you have the luxury not to have to do." Venkat slunk out the door, giving me one last shrug of pity as he closed the latch behind him.

From someplace outside myself, I could hear Jay's voice shouting, the venom in my own voice as I shoved my pain into a ball and hurled it at him, desperate to be rid of it, desperate for any shred of relief from the misery that threatened to bury me alive. But underneath the shouts, something else, a taunting, painful memory, whispered at the edges of my consciousness.

I promise to love you always and follow you everywhere, to the ends of the earth and back again. I promise to respect you and cherish you and grow with you for the rest of our lives.

The wedding vows echoed in my mind on cruel, mocking repeat. When I'd spoken them that day, not even two years ago, I'd meant them with every cell in my body, intending to believe them and live them every day of my life. Now they felt like nothing more than an iron chain, binding me to a life I wanted desperately to escape.

CHAPTER 17

The days crept on. I locked myself in the bedroom with Tucker, eating Lays "Style Cream and Onion" potato chips by the bag and sleeping so much that my whole body hurt from being horizontal for so long. If I managed to leave the house at all, to Q-Mart or the Taj for a manicure, I'd snarl at anyone who so much as glanced in my direction.

Raju was terrified of me. Every time he came to the door, he put his hands out in front of himself, a defensive posture in case I hit him or something. (I hadn't, of course. Not yet.) Sometimes, after communicating particularly bad news ("electrician not coming today, Madam" or "leak not fixing today, Madam" or "gas main exploding broken, Madam"), he would become so distraught about my fits of fury that he would sneak off and call Jay at the office.

"Madam upset, sir. Madam upset."

I'd had enough. I was sick of spicy food and broken English and people staring at me all the time. I was sick of being trapped all day with dozens of strangers tramping through the house, leaving behind muddy footprints and puddles of water, fixing nothing at all. I missed my parents. I missed my friends. I missed my life. Finally, Jay couldn't take it anymore.

"You're going home," he said, watching me sob as I sprayed Raid onto thousands of ants swarming the kitchen cabinets.

"I'm not leaving you here."

"Yes, you are. You're going home. You can't stay here anymore. I'm booking your flight."

"I'll be fine," I sniffled, swatting convulsively at the imaginary ants I felt crawling up my arms.

"You're not fine. Look at yourself."

I didn't need to look to know what he saw. I thought of all those photo albums of our past years together: engagement, honeymoon, going away party. I was smiling, glowing, *happy*…and it showed in every picture. That kind of happiness has its own way of projecting beauty through the camera lens, its own language for capturing joy. Now, even without a photograph, I knew that depression had blighted my face, settled into my features. The girl in the broken mirror, as broken on the inside as she was in her reflection.

I didn't want to give up. I didn't want to lose. I'd wanted to return to my family triumphant. I'd wanted to be a whole different person, with hundreds of fascinating stories to tell and a new worldly attitude, enlightened and wise. Most of all, I wanted to stick it out for Jay's sake, supporting him while he did something big and important. But in so many ways, I'd already given up. I'd already lost. One night, Jay came home with a paper ticket in his hand and he forced mine. In that moment, we both acknowledged the truth. That my misery threatened to destroy both of us if I didn't leave India for a while.

Maybe forever.

~◯

"Why don't you just pack everything?" Jay asked, watching me cram a few last items into my carry-on. "We both know you're not coming back."

There was no accusation in his words, no intended barb. For once, we weren't using sarcasm as a weapon. It was just the resigned statement of a fact I wasn't willing to admit. Not yet.

On the way to the airport, we were quiet. We weren't fighting, at least not out loud. Our regrets hung like cobwebs in the stale air between us. Venkat hummed to break the tension until Jay barked at him to stop.

"What do you want from America, Venkat?" I said, trying to soothe his injured feelings. "Chocolate? Hair gel? Car wax?" Venkat's face lit up, but Jay interrupted before he could make a single request.

"Forget about it, Venkat. She's not coming back."

"Not coming back, Madam?" Venkat looked over his shoulder and eyed my one suitcase, Tucker shivering in his pet carrier. "Madam is coming back, yes?"

I couldn't answer.

Jay waited in the security line with me, stoic and silent. The guards let him come far enough to help me put my bags on the conveyor belt for security, then gestured for him to step aside. He hugged me once, hard. My throat closed on itself and I clung to him, wanting him to say something that would make all of this OK. He stared over my shoulder into the distance and stayed silent.

Half of me wanted to grab my luggage off the belt and run back to the car and drive back to Jasmine Heights, where I was supposed to belong. To climb into bed with my husband and let the flight take off without me, listening to the roar of the jet engine fly over our heads from the safety of Jay's arms. How could I just run away and leave him here? I'd promised him so much more than this.

But the other half of me saw the lights on the runway and thought *freedom*. Just a couple of hours and I'd be in the air, putting miles and miles between me and a country that was swallowing me whole. There would be sidewalks and electricity, family and friends to hug me and make me feel loved. I could walk out on the street and no one would stare. I could eat cheeseburgers and sushi and go to Starbucks five times a day. I could smile again, laugh again. *Breathe* again.

I didn't want all that to feel more important than my marriage. Had I really become so shallow and foolish that a cup of coffee was more compelling than my husband's arms? I looked up into Jay's familiar brown eyes, eyes that used to fill me with absolute wonder that someone like him could love someone like me. I wanted proof that he still loved me, that he wanted me to stay. If only there was tenderness behind his stoic gaze. But when he met my eyes, the only emotion I saw was a cold detachment. In his mind, he'd already said good-bye.

Panic made my pulse race and my breath short. The airport was spinning fast around me—lights too bright and sounds too loud, people turning in circles everywhere.

"Are you OK?" Jay asked, grabbing my arm to steady me. "What's wrong?"

"I don't want to leave you," I whispered. I couldn't look at him. His emotions were shut down, locked up tight, while mine were overflowing, spilling everywhere, irrational and beyond my control. It was like being trapped on an ancient playground teeter-totter, one of us flying into space while the other came crashing down.

"Please come with me. Come home. I don't want to be there without you."

"This is home, Jen," Jay said, more gentle than he'd been in weeks. "I know it's not the home you wanted. But this is where I need to be right now."

"I want to stay with you. I can make it, I'll try harder. I promise." I couldn't keep the tears back. Jay hated when I cried. I could feel him recoiling, incapable of facing the torrent of emotion.

"I'm not mad about it. We're doing what's best. Just not together. Not for right now." Jay hugged me again, harder still, and handed me a folder with my travel papers. "Everything is in here. Text me when you board so I know you're all right. It's going to be OK," he said, reaching up with one finger to wipe at a tear caught in my eyelashes. "I promise it's going to be OK."

Then he turned around and walked back to the Scorpio. He didn't look back. Venkat held the door open for him; Jay climbed into the backseat and closed the door. Venkat honked the horn to clear a path. The engine roared and they were gone.

Twenty-four hours later, I landed in Boston at noon on a perfect fall afternoon. In the cab on the way to my parents' house, I looked around and felt like I'd stumbled onto a strange planet I'd only visited in my dreams. It had been six months since I'd been on American soil. Everything was the same, but I was seeing it all with completely different eyes.

It was so clean. So quiet. No incessant honking horns, no mountains of garbage in the road, no men urinating in crowded streets. No one was staring at me. Everyone somehow looked familiar. Confused, I tried to figure out how I knew them all, where I'd seen them before, when I realized they were all strangers. They were just strangers that looked like me.

I sneezed. The cab driver blessed me. No one other than Jay had said "Bless you" in six months. And half the time, he forgot too. After so much time spent trying to understand and blend in to another culture, I felt dizzyingly relieved to experience the simplest of traditions in mine. I wanted to throw my arms around the driver in gratitude.

"Can we make a stop?" I asked instead.

"Sure thing." I waited for him to call me Ma'am. He didn't. I explained what I wanted; he shrugged and nodded. He pulled off the Pike at the next exit and made a few turns, navigating the familiar roads of the neighborhood I grew up in. And then there it was.

The green and white awning that embodied the American dream. The place I'd been pining for since the day we left New York.

Starbucks.

I shivered with joy as I ordered a grande house blend with skim milk and two Sweet'N Lows. Not a gritty, four-ounce latte made with black tar and buffalo milk. Not the medicinal-tasting, sugar-free saccharin tablets that floated on top of the cup. Just coffee. Exactly the way I liked it. Thirty seconds later, I held a cup in my hand that wasn't melting or falling apart at the seams, with a lid that actually fit on the top.

"Have a great day," the barista said. She smiled at me like handing me that cup of coffee was totally ordinary, not a miraculous epilogue to months of lonely, isolated, coffee-deprived suffering.

"You too."

And I walked out into the sunshine cradling my coffee like a cup full of gold between my palms. People were all around me, in their cars, waiting in the crosswalk for the light to change. I'd seen these things a million times before…and now, truly, I was seeing them for the very first time.

God bless America. I was finally home.

CHAPTER 18

My first week home was a blur of jet lag and skinny lattes and long hours on the phone with family and friends. The simplest things had turned into miracles: driving a car, paying a parking meter, hot water coming out of the kitchen sink. I spent hours at my parents' giant kitchen table, staring out the window at the river in their backyard. Like I'd just gotten off of a ship after months at sea, I was trying to feel the ground beneath my feet again.

In India, having nothing to do was nothing but a punishment. Back in my childhood hometown, it felt more like a luxury vacation. I walked Tucker through crisp fall leaves and learned to bake pumpkin muffins from scratch. I went to yoga class every day and out for drinks every night. The *everything-is-brand-new* feeling didn't fade; instead, it intensified as I gorged myself on all things American: sushi and cheeseburgers, Top 40 radio, bad reality TV. I lived inside a mini-tornado of gratitude, spinning through my once-familiar world with new wonder, new perspective, new thanks.

Everyone was captivated by my stories of life in the third world.

Holding court at the dinner table, I spun the tales exactly as I'd experienced them, playing up the high points, reminding my fascinated audience that everything they were hearing was as true as it was outrageous. Suddenly Venkat and Jena and Raju weren't just faces that filled the otherwise empty landscape of my everyday life. They were characters in my very own reality show, comic foils for my wacky, misguided expat adventures. The more stories I told, the more I heard unfamiliar emotions creep into my narrative voice: Amusement. Pride. And even…joy?

No, that couldn't be. I was telling stories about cockroaches the size of rodents and rodents the size of chickens. Of repairmen who said "No leak, Ma'am" and death-defying rickshaw rides and homeless Indian children dancing in the rain. My hair looked like death, Tucker was traumatized, and I'd had food poisoning approximately forty-seven times. But there were other stories too: of Jena and his green umbrella drinks; of Venkat and his sweet village romance with Swapna; of Shilparamam and illegal fireworks and the banyan tree in KBR park.

Joy had been missing from my life for so very long. Every moment had been filled with disappointment and misery and failure. I was too busy hating India to love it, too busy loathing myself to remember the person I'd set out to be. So where was this benevolent storyteller pulling her material from? Was it all glorified fiction to make myself look better in the eyes of the people I'd come home to? Or could there really be joy beneath the sorrow, laughter under my tears? In my own words, India didn't sound so bad.

It didn't sound so bad at all.

As the days went on, I started feeling restless. I was still grateful for every moment of American life, for electricity and supermarkets and well-spoken English. But as much as I loved my parents' quiet, idyllic house on a Charles River peninsula, it wasn't home. My keychain still held the thick brass key to apartment 22M in our Columbus Circle rental building, but that wasn't home either. Not anymore. I was unbound and drifting; headed, aimless, for nowhere in particular.

For my whole adult life, I'd been putting one foot in front of the other on the path that lay before me. Sometimes that path was complicated or broken or led me the wrong way. But karma always felt like it was there in front of me, giving intention and meaning to my movements. Never before had I felt so completely removed from my own life. The road I was supposed to take had all but disappeared. Without it, I was lost.

⟲

Jay flew in for Thanksgiving on a Tuesday. We'd spoken only a handful of times. He sounded the same. There wasn't much to say. The only difference now was that the distance between us was literal too. Thousands and thousands of miles between where we wanted to be and where we'd ended up. I missed him. I was afraid to ask if he missed me too.

I waited at the airport terminal for him to go through customs with a fresh Bruegger's bagel in my hand: sesame, scooped out, with light cream cheese. He might have mixed feelings about seeing me again, but I figured there was no way the bagel would fail to make him smile. Tucker waited on his leash beside me. He seemed as eager as I was to be a family again.

Finally, Jay came around the corner, dark circles under his eyes and a face full of stubble, his passport in one hand and his sleeping hat in the other. The sight of that red fleece hat made me feel like crying. We'd drifted so far apart, but he was still him. As conflicted and as lost as I felt, I was still me. And as long as there was that, there was still hope. Or so I wanted to believe.

Jay was quiet on the car ride home. He gazed out the window, not really seeing, like he was thinking about something a million miles away. I kept quiet too, waiting for him to say something. I asked a few polite questions about his trip, about Venkat and what was happening at the office. He answered them perfunctorily, eyes fixed out the window at the passing highway. The bagel sat untouched in his lap.

Later, after he'd showered and napped, I suggested we take a walk along the river. We bundled up in parkas and hats, protecting ourselves from the late fall chill. Jay, who'd gotten off the plane wearing shorts and flip-flops, was shivering even through his coat. He stuck his gloved hand in one of my pockets for warmth. Tucker romped through the leaves ahead of us, batting them up in the air with his paws and chasing joyfully after them, kicking up swirls of red and orange in his wake. The setting sun glinted gold off the river. I blew out long streams of breath that hung in the air.

"I can't take this cold," Jay said, cupping his nose with his palms. "It's freezing here."

"It's always been this cold in the winter," I said, tossing a rock into the half-frozen water. It skidded on the ice, startling a flock of sleeping geese. Their honks filled the silent sky as they scattered. "You're just not used to it anymore."

"I'd rather live in India and be warm than deal with winters like this anymore."

"I'd rather live anywhere than India," I retorted. "I'd live in an igloo on the South Pole."

"There probably wouldn't be Internet there either," Jay said, pulling his hand back and tucking it into his own pocket. Just like that, the moment was broken. We walked back to my parents' house in silence. When they asked us how the walk was, we smiled big and avoided each other's eyes.

The week passed quickly. During the day, we saw friends and visited family. At night, we crawled into bed on opposite sides, backs to each other. Tucker lay between us like furry Switzerland, trying to bridge an impossible gap. In the middle of the night, I'd wake up to the sound of Jay's breathing and stare at him, huddled under the sheets away from me. It was like I'd never seen him before. Nothing about him was familiar—not the way he smelled or the sweep of hair that curled beneath his sleeping hat, now worn for warmth instead of protection from germs. That hair, the darkest possible brown before we left New York, was streaked with shocking gray. Somewhere along my path of misery and self-pity, Jay had become a stranger. I curled into myself, fighting back the crushing wave of fear that nothing might ever feel right again.

I want to get out of here, I whispered to myself. *I want to go home.* But home was nowhere.

❧

The car's headlights cut through the fog in front of us in a swath of dusty yellow. We were driving home from dinner with friends, an evening that started out promising but ended up stiff and awkward as the tension between us grew too large for our companions to ignore. I'd had two glasses of wine, maybe more…enough to make every sound louder, every worry more pressing. I slumped against the window with my forehead against the cold glass, disoriented by riding in the front seat and on the right-hand side. I wondered if everything would always feel backward now, no matter where I was or which way it was supposed to be.

"I think we should get divorced," Jay said. His hands on the steering wheel were loose and calm. His tone was normal, like he'd asked me to switch the radio station or to grab him some change for the tollbooth.

"What are you talking about?"

"You aren't happy. We aren't happy. You hate India, and I'm going back in three days. Maybe we need to go our separate ways. Start over again."

A numbing cold spread through me. I stared at him. He didn't turn his head.

"I don't understand what you're saying. We just got married. You're being insane."

Silence.

"So we're unhappy. Life hasn't been easy. We live in a third-world country, for god's sake. It's not like these are normal circumstances."

"It's not the end of the world. People get divorced all the time. It's better than being miserable together."

"So now our whole marriage is ruined? India sucks and *this* is the best you could come up with? DIVORCE? What about 'move home and save our marriage'?"

He shrugged and kept his eyes on the road.

His lack of emotion hurled mine into overdrive. "So that's *it*? There's nothing between 'We're having a rough time' and 'It's OVER'?" I spat, halfway between disbelief and hysteria.

"I want you to be happy, Jen. I don't make you happy anymore."

"You make me happy. It's India that's making me miserable."

"That's not totally true. You know that." Dispassionate fingertips tapped on the gearshift between us. I dug my nails into the flesh of my palms, trying to make the pain prove this moment couldn't possibly be real.

"You can't mean this. Do you have any idea what you're saying? Look at me!"

He looked at me. His dark eyes, almost invisible in the dim dashboard lights, locked with mine for a split second. Just long enough for me to glimpse what lay behind his chilling, robotic words: sorrow, bitterness, regret. But what shocked me most of all were the cold threads of fear I saw there, breaking through the familiar placid mask he'd been wearing since the day I met him. My husband, the man who'd spent seven years being strong enough for both of us without so much as a flicker of doubt, who was fearless and powerful and more impossibly self-assured than anyone I'd met in my entire life, was afraid.

The blood in my veins ran colder still. I could feel my heart breaking with the crystalline catastrophe of shattering glass. I crawled across the seat until I was half on his lap, my head on his shoulder. I reached for his hand and held it between both of mine, so tight I could feel his fingers tremble and resist for a moment, then fall still between my palms.

"*No*," I whispered into the gray hairs at his temples, brushing my lips against them. Claiming them as mine.

و◯

Thanksgiving morning dawned cold and bright. Ignoring the lump in my throat that formed whenever I thought about India or my marriage or the future, I grabbed Jay and pulled him out of bed, eager to get started on a day full of sacred traditions. Thanksgiving was my favorite holiday. If I'd learned nothing else in my ill-fated time in the third world, it was that there was a whole lot more to be thankful for than I'd ever bothered to think about before.

"Get up. We have to go to Starbucks."

"What?" Jay looked at me through narrowed eyes, then grabbed a pillow and pulled it over his head. "I'm sleeping. It's early. Go away."

"We need to leave now or I won't have time to get back and start the pies."

"Pies?"

"Apple. Plus I'm doing the mashed potatoes and baking bread. But not if we don't get out the door in the next five minutes. I can't bake without coffee."

"I'm only doing this for pie," Jay grumbled on his way to the bathroom.

I handed him his toothbrush, fully loaded with Crest. "That's OK," I said. "I love you too."

All day, while I drank coffee and ate pumpkin muffins and peeled apples with short, inexpert strokes, I watched Jay when he wasn't looking. I watched the way he wrestled with the dog and helped my dad bring in firewood, watched while he poured oil into the turkey fryer with studied concentration and childlike glee. His features, warm in the glow of the fire, were familiar again, like I'd been gazing at him through a dirty window that was suddenly scrubbed clean. When my favorite Macy's parade float, the Sesame Street one, rolled into view on TV, Jay grabbed my arm and led me away from the dough I was kneading. On the mantel above the screen, our wedding portrait was framed in brushed silver. In the photograph, we smiled and squinted and held each other in the brilliant Nantucket sun. I wanted to crawl inside the frame and live there again, safe in the promise of our dreams coming true.

"You don't like the Macy's Thanksgiving Day parade," I said, wiping flour on the legs of my jeans.

"No, but you do."

I wanted this. I wanted him. I wanted Starbucks on Thanksgiving morning and apple pies and a bunch of kids with his dark brown hair and almond-shaped eyes chasing after him on a lawn covered with fallen leaves. If India was the bridge I needed to cross to get there, to get back to him, then I needed to figure out a way to cross it—without falling or failing or running away.

"I left you something on the bed," Jay said into my hair, his bare arms around me tight. He was shivering; he'd left his winter coat in the front seat of the car, not wanting to carry such a useless item all the way back to Hyderabad. His flight to Frankfurt took off in less than two hours. In twenty-four, he'd be in the car on the way back to Jasmine Heights with Venkat whistling behind the wheel. He'd unlock the door to the dark, empty house and crawl into bed without me.

"What is it?"

"Just wait till you get back. Call me when you get there. I'll still be waiting to board."

"No hints?"

"No hints."

I drove home. It felt strange to be behind the wheel after so many months of being a constant passenger. The setting sun blazed fiery pink as I headed west, toward my parents' house, farther from Jay and the life I might have left behind for good.

"Did Jay get off OK?" my dad asked when I let myself in the back door. He was standing in the door of the freezer, eating a carefully dissected half of a miniature Reese's peanut butter cup.

"Is there another one of those?"

He flipped the other half toward me. We sat down at the kitchen table and licked at our respective chocolate pieces in silence.

My dad cleared his throat.

"Remember when I dropped you off at college sophomore year? When you cried and told me there was no way you could do it, to turn around and take you back?"

My eyes burned at the memory. I'd hated school then, had almost failed out after my freshman year. I'd wanted nothing more in that moment than to dive back onto the bench seat of the rickety U-Haul we'd driven for 450 miles, to pack everything up and drive straight back home.

"You told me I could do it."

"And what else?"

"I don't remember." I got up and grabbed another peanut butter cup from the freezer. I tossed one at him. He caught it without looking and unwrapped it, slicing it down the center with practiced surgical precision.

"I think it was 'batten down the hatches.'"

"Fair winds and following seas. Yeah, you're right. Put up the spinnaker. Keep a straight course."

"Pull up the anchor and try not to sink." My dad smiled, pleased with the opportunity to speak sailor.

"Wear foul weather gear."

"I didn't say *that*."

"No, but if you're talking about India, you might as well say it now. I've got one more monsoon season to get through if I'm going back."

"You're going back," my dad said firmly, sweeping chocolate crumbs off the table with a triumphant flick of his wrist.

"How do you know?"

"Because I'm your father. I know everything."

❧

In the middle of the guest-room bed, which Jay had attempted to make in an adorable, inept way, was a plane ticket in a navy-blue-and-gold Lufthansa envelope. He'd refused to book me a return ticket when I'd left Hyderabad, maybe because he'd been plotting our divorce all along. But here it was, sitting up proud on top of my empty suitcase. Scrawled on the envelope, in black permanent marker, was a note.

I LOVE YOU, WIFE. PACK WHAT YOU NEED AND COME HOME.

MANGO SEASON

CHAPTER 19

"Hurry, Venkat! We need to get home fast."

"What's the rush?" Jay asked, pulling me closer to him in the backseat. "I still can't believe you're really back."

"Me either," I admitted, curling into the warmth of his sweatshirt. It was a few days past Christmas; the temperature in Hyderabad was the lowest I'd ever known. Which meant that at three o'clock in the morning, wearing a sweatshirt without melting into a sweaty puddle was actually possible. Five o'clock shadow aside, Jay looked like a little kid in the oversized blue zip-up, young and vulnerable, hood pulled up and sleeves rolled down over his knuckles. I liked him like this, a throwback to the cocky college kid he'd been when we started dating. His corporate self, all Armani and dry cleaner creases and Jean Paul Gaultier cologne, was nowhere near as endearing.

My emotions were all over the place: exhaustion from the trip, relief at being back with Jay where I belonged, fear and anxiety about what lay ahead. But mostly I felt grateful. I'd spent months feeling ashamed of myself in almost every way, but now I had a reason to stand up straighter and feel proud. Packing my suitcases and getting back on the plane had taken almost everything I had—but I'd done it. I was here. Here, with one more shot to do this journey right.

At the Jubilee Hills check post, a cow leaned into the window, pressing its damp nose against the glass. I wondered, since cows were holy and the stars invisible because of the smog, if it would be OK to wish on cattle instead. I closed my eyes and wished. When I opened them, Jay was staring at me like I was crazy.

"What are you doing?"

"Wishing on a cow."

"You're kidding. You didn't take those Lariam pills, right? I told you that doctor here said they were dangerous."

"No pills. I figured malaria was the least of my concerns at this point." I swatted at the mosquito buzzing near my ear, which was no doubt trying to make me eat my words. "Seriously. I never thought I'd say this, but I'm really glad to be here."

"You don't mean that. It's just the jet lag talking. You'll be back to hating it again in the morning," Jay said. He rubbed my thigh, scraping his fingernail across the seam of my jeans. "It's OK. You don't have to be glad to be here. I'm happy anyway."

But I was glad. I was thrilled to see Venkat again, with his serious dark eyes and his mischievous smile, beanie pulled low across his smooth brow. He wore a puffy nylon parka, shiny and black, with an oversized hood that covered his entire head, hair and all.

"Venkat, it's still pretty warm outside. Why are you wearing that huge jacket?"

"Winter, Madam," Venkat replied solemnly.

The air was as pungent as I remembered it, but the harsh unfamiliarity was gone. The bad smells and the good were woven together. Through the less pleasing scents, I could smell things I loved:

sandalwood and wood smoke and hot *chai*. I was looking forward to our next meal at Ginger Court, to catching up with Jena and enjoying an order of chili-fried American corn. I was glad to be safe inside the Scorpio, watching the half-demolished buildings rush by as we drove down Madhapur Road, past a dark and quiet Shilparamam, beneath the gleaming HITEC City arch toward home.

"You're not giving me any credit at all. I'm a changed person, remember?"

"No one changes that fast."

"Thanks for the vote of confidence. You could at least give me credit for trying." I swatted at his hand, pleased our banter had returned to teasing, a more familiar state. The anger-laced tension was gone. This kind of back-and-forth teasing was a throwback to happier times.

"I give you more credit than you know," Jay said. "Why are your suitcases all wet?"

"I had to wipe down the outside of them with wipes. To get the Xs off."

"The Xs? You mean the customs marks?"

"Yep. Luckily Peter tipped me off before I left for the airport. I wouldn't have known to stick baby wipes in my carry-on."

"What does Peter have to do with anything?"

"I called him while I was home. I needed a few pointers. On packing."

"Packing? How could Peter help you with packing?"

"You told me to bring back what I needed, right?"

"So?"

"Well, as it happens, some of what I needed wasn't exactly legal to bring into the country."

Jay raised his eyebrows. "Why don't I like the sound of that?"

"You will when you're eating turkey lasagna for dinner tomorrow."

"Since when can you cook lasagna?"

"There's a first time for everything," I replied, flashing him my best Mona Lisa smile.

ℰ

I curled, C-shaped, around the toilet bowl, taking small comfort in the fact that, at least prior to us moving in, it had been brand new. At least we had sole proprietorship of all the germs. Tucker wove around my ankles, sensing something was wrong, urging me to get up.

"No one dies from Delhi belly," Jay observed, brushing his teeth, unsympathetic to my moans. He used the tap water now, yet another sign of his success in the third world. *Teeth brushing like a local? Check.* He put a bottle of Himalaya on the floor next to me. "You'll be fine in a minute."

"I will *not* be *fine in a minute*," I croaked, retching for effect. "I don't have 'Delhi belly.' I've been poisoned. I'm never eating Indian food again. Don't even think about making me."

"You love Ginger Court. You couldn't wait to go back. I was perfectly happy staying home and eating this turkey lasagna you keep talking about."

"Don't talk about food. It's making me sicker. I'm very, very ill."

"I'm very, very late for a meeting," Jay said, inspecting himself in the cracked mirror. He turned to leave. "I have a work dinner at Peshwari tonight anyway. You can skip it if you want. If you're not better."

"Gee, thanks. That's so nice of you."

"Have a good day," Jay called. He was already halfway down the stairs.

So much for husbandly TLC. Considering the delicate balance of our rekindled tenderness for each other, I'd been expecting him to react with more…*concern*. I was going to murder him. Just as soon as I got up off the bathroom floor.

It was definitely going to be a sweatpants kind of a day. I texted Venkat and told him to stay at the office.

After several mugs of weak Tetley tea with lemon, my stomach settled. I curled up on the couch with a bag of Cape Cod potato chips and a stack of brand new *Us Weekly* magazines, more creature comforts I'd brought along in my luggage. Technically I was supposed to be embarking on my newly revised Indian journey. But surely starting such a huge undertaking with food poisoning would be a terrible idea, right? There was plenty of time to start working on my new bucket list. One more day of moping around the house wouldn't hurt anyone.

The doorbell rang. Tucker went berserk. I ignored it, figuring the porch people would deal with whoever it was. They were still hanging around, overseeing the garbage man who came around on his bicycle, shooing away the stray dogs that tried to hop the gate and sleep on our lawn. Before I left, I was giving each of them fifty rupees a day, just so they'd be able to buy food at the grocery stand outside the tent city. It was twice India's standard daily wage for migrant workers. I knew I'd have to stop soon, but I couldn't help it. They kept me company, made the house feel less empty.

But today they seemed to have disappeared. Their sleeping pallets and *tiffin* pails were gone. The doorbell rang again, now accompanied by knocking.

"Madam! Is Sundar! I see you in there! Let me inside, please!"

We really needed curtains on the front windows. Why today, of all days, had the porch people decided to go AWOL? I needed backup.

Sundar was a cook. Short and stocky, he had four children, two wives, wore a black leather jacket, and drove everywhere on a motorcycle that made him look more Hell's Angel than Hyderabad. He'd been working for expats for years, with the inflated asking price to prove it. The family he'd been cooking for had moved back to Switzerland right around the time Jay and I arrived. He'd been bugging us to hire him ever since.

I opened the door.

"Hi, Sundar."

"Good morning, Madam! Today is the day you will hire me!"

I admired his optimism.

"Thanks for coming by, Sundar, but we're still not hiring a cook."

He pushed past me with a bag of vegetables. One of his wives followed meekly behind, shooting me an apologetic look as she slipped off her shoes.

"I am making food for you. Free of charge, with all fresh and delicious ingredients. Step aside. When the food is ready, you will be tasting and hiring me."

"What makes you so sure we need you to cook for us?"

Sundar lined things up on the kitchen counter. "Are you having a pressure cooker? Where do you keep your *chaat*? And your *garam masala*?"

"I told you, we don't eat much Indian food. It doesn't agree with my stomach. We eat at Ginger Court only." My Indian phrasing seemed to encourage him.

"Ah, already you are speaking more like India. Soon you will be eating like India too. But not Ginger Court. That is fancy restaurant food, too rich. No good for your health. And no more Hyderabadi food, all grease and spice. No wonder you are being ill. Sundar will make you the cuisine of the north. Now go, relax. Your kitchen is my kitchen. You are looking unwell. Perhaps you should drink *chai*."

"I just brought back a lot of American food. I'm going to learn to cook the kinds of things we're used to eating. So the timing probably isn't great. Thanks anyway, Sundar." I raised my eyebrows meaningfully toward the door.

"Ah, Madam, here is where you are wrong. Sundar is wanting to learn to cook American foods too! So you will eat healthy Indian food on some nights, and I will be teaching you to make for when you take leave of Hyderabad. And on other nights you will show Sundar about your American foods, and then I will be cooking those too. So Madam won't have to trouble herself in the kitchen at all. It is, as American say, win-win!"

I sighed. "Just once, Sundar. You can cook me dinner just this once and that's it. And if I don't like it, I'm not paying you."

He shooed me away with a pair of salad tongs we'd gotten for our wedding. "Finding somewhere to rest. Sundar is here."

Jay came home after midnight. I was still awake, downstairs on the couch in my pajamas, eating Sundar's leftover *chana masala* with a piece of stuffed onion *paratha* for a late-night snack.

"How was your day?"

"Why are you still awake? I figured you would have gone to bed hours ago."

"Just thinking."

"I missed you at dinner tonight. It's not the same without you there." He lay on the couch next to me, putting his head in my lap and pointing to the *paratha* in my hand. "You must be feeling better; you're eating. Is that Indian food?"

"Stuffed onion *paratha*. Homemade."

"Bite?" Jay opened his mouth.

I fed him. "I hired Sundar today."

"I thought you swore you'd never hire a cook. What's next, servants?"

"Maybe. It's the Indian way."

"You hate the Indian way."

"That hasn't been working out so well." I wove my fingers through his hair, tracing the strands of silver. "I missed you tonight too. Now that we have Sundar, I was thinking we could eat dinner at home a few nights a week. You can have people over if you want. But it would be nice to get into a routine, stop eating out so much."

"If the new you is going to be like this all the time, I vote we hire a whole staff."

"Don't push your luck." I sat up and looked at him, studying his face for the truth. "Seriously. Do you think this makes me a failure? I'm supposed to be taking care of the house, not turning into one of those ladies of leisure who eats bonbons all day."

"No, I think you're learning." He kissed me on the forehead. "And you're not going to eat bonbons. You're going to start writing again. Come on, let's go to bed."

In the morning, I started interviewing housekeepers. Venkat put the word out in his sister's neighborhood; by noon, I had candidates lined up at the door. Expat households were the most desirable of all: higher salaries, fewer people to tend to. But the first five women who came wouldn't even cross the porch. They were terrified of Tucker. Finally Sundar arrived, another bag of groceries under his arm, and a young girl by his side. Mary, a Catholic and a member of the lowest caste, was desperate for work—no Hindu household would allow her inside. For the longest time, she stood staring in the doorway. I held Tucker in my lap and stroked his fur, willing him to behave. Something about Mary's quiet demeanor made me feel calm. I wanted her to stay.

Finally she slipped off her shoes and crossed the threshold, head held high. I was surprised at how delicate she was, one long braid falling over her shoulder as she demonstrated her skills with a broom and a mop.

Venkat hissed from the doorway, watching. He was Hindu and a Reddy. To him, the presence of a low-caste Christian in our house was offensive. I adored Venkat and hated to make him angry, but Mary felt right to me. Like Venkat, with his hip-hop swagger, was different from the average Hyderabadi driver, Mary was just a little bit different from the typical housekeeper. Her quiet grace set her apart. When I offered to pay her double what she'd asked for, she flushed with pleasure and pressed my hand tightly.

"I be good for you, Madam. I not make you trouble. God bless you." Venkat, watching from the window, stomped back to the car in disgust. But I was certain I'd made the right choice. The Indian way was working out OK after all, at least so far. And those impossible marble floors? Were officially someone else's responsibility.

CHAPTER 20

Now that I was back, Venkat had a million questions to ask about America: what kind of plane I'd flown home on, what foods we'd eaten, what it felt like when snow came down from the sky. I tried to imagine what it would be like to grow up without television and Internet and textbooks, with no window to the world other than the one in your own home. Venkat was as fascinated by the country I'd left behind as I'd been as a child hearing stories about Neverland and the Emerald City. Through his eyes, I could see the magic of a world I'd taken for granted almost all my life.

While Jay and I were gone, Venkat had gone home to his village and received his hero's welcome, regaling his family with stories of working for us. I imagined their reactions, as shocked and amused as my own family had been at my tales of life in India. Our electric bug-killing tennis rackets were as foreign and bizarre to Venkat's village Reddys as their orange-garlanded farm goats were to us.

"Did you see Swapna, Venkat?"

Venkat blushed so hard the tips of his ears turned red. He ignored me and grabbed his comb, swiping it over his already perfect hair.

"OK. I won't ask. You tell me if you feel like it."

Venkat heaved a huge, resigned sigh and reached into the glove compartment. He pulled out a small brown jewelry box etched with gold and handed it to me over his shoulder without turning around.

"What's this?"

"Open and looking, Madam."

Inside were delicate earrings, gold filigree curlicues dangling from posts studded with a single ruby each.

"Wow, Venkat."

He hunched his shoulders, embarrassed. "For Swapna. For when she has fifteen years. I giving these to her. For when asking be my wife."

My throat clenched. Venkat was still just a kid. It was so hard to imagine him as someone's husband, starting a family, shouldering the responsibilities of a man in his tiny, struggling village with a child bride on his arm. "They're beautiful."

He snatched the box out of my hands, snapping it closed like the earrings would disappear if I admired them too long. "No yet. First bike. I ride home on bike and am asking. Then she will being say yes surely."

"Oh, right. We need to talk about the bike."

"Buying bike today, Madam?" Venkat straightened his shoulders and grinned broadly. "Is time? Wanting Yamaha. I told Sir which."

I laughed. His enthusiasm was contagious.

"Not today, OK? Soon. We need to talk about it and figure it out."

"Look, Madam. No safety," Venkat cackled, changing the subject. Ahead of us, a dhoti-clad man dangled from a length of rope, trying to regain his footing on a twenty-foot-high billboard featuring a gorgeous Bollywood actress holding up a tube of Garnier whitening cream.

"Who is that, Venkat?"

"Aish. Bollywood star, much famous. All women want be like her. Much fair skin. Green eyes also."

"Does Swapna look like her?" I teased.

He refused to take the bait. "Music, Madam?"

"Put on Wilco, please."

"*Dhoom*, Madam?"

"Madonna."

"*Garam Masala?*"

Venkat won, as usual. His debate skills, even in his third language, were far superior to mine. Also, I knew if I tried to force the issue, he'd deliberately make my CD skip until he could announce "CD no working, Madam" and replace it with his own. So it was a jubilant, 150 BPM Bollywood soundtrack playing in the background as the Scorpio crept along in traffic, two hours into a "quick" trip to the vegetable stand.

Usually this drove me crazy. But with my new plan in place to embrace all (or at least some) things Indian, Bollywood didn't seem like a bad place to start. I'd always loved those old Hollywood musicals, jazz hands and dancing umbrellas, melodic happy endings. From what I'd glimpsed on the billboards, Bollywood didn't seem so different from bedazzled versions of *My Fair Lady* or *Singing in the Rain*.

"Venkat, let's go to the movies."

"Movies, Madam?"

"Yes. I want to see a movie. Something Bollywood. What's playing?"

"At Prasads is *Dhoom 2*, Madam. IMAX. Much big."

"Perfect." I leaned forward, urging him ahead.

"But vegetables, Madam?" Venkat asked, trying to figure out if I was serious.

"They can wait. Let's go."

Outside the giant Prasads complex, Venkat idled the Scorpio, waiting for me to get out.

"Go ahead and park, Venkat. I want you to come with me."

"Mine coming? No, Madam." Venkat managed to look simultaneously horrified and elated, which meant I'd no doubt broken Rule #387 of the Driver/Drivee Code by asking him to park the car and go to the movies with me. I didn't want to make him uncomfortable, but the theater was huge and intimidating and teeming with Indian teenagers, and I wanted to avoid having to navigate buying a ticket and finding a seat all on my own. Plus, I knew how much Venkat loved his Bollywood movies…even if it was some crazy breach of etiquette, he should still jump at the chance to see one, for free, in the middle of his work day.

"Come on. It will be fun. You've been listening to the soundtrack for weeks." He still hesitated. I decided to sweeten the deal. "I'll buy you McDonald's if you come." The very first McDonald's in Andhra Pradesh had opened in the Prasads entertainment complex a few weeks earlier. The restaurant offered a heavily edited Indian menu (no cow meat, milkshakes, or Chicken McNuggets) for customers willing to brave the two-hour lines. Venkat, who'd never eaten french fries before, was obsessed.

"Chicken Maharaja Burger?"

"And fries."

Venkat pulled out with a screech and headed for the parking garage.

❧

The final credits of *Dhoom 2* rolled, and I stood up, wiping a tear away with the back of my hand. I'd loved it. Well, loved it…but didn't really *get* it. Why was everyone so happy and dance-y when life in India could be so unspeakably hard? Why were the costumes barely there risqué in a country that frowned when my ankles showed beneath the hem of my skirt? Still, Bollywood made me feel happy and dance-y too…nothing short of a miracle considering how miserable I'd made myself in the past few months. Here was something Indian I could get on board with: glitz and glamour and fairy-tale romance. Under the bright lights of Bollywood, everything seemed more exciting and less tragic.

I made Venkat stop at the movie rental place on Road #1. Jay and I had been in before, balancing our *Prison Break* marathons with their small selection of American titles from the '80s and '90s. But this time, I had a different agenda. I carried out as many Bollywood DVDs as the confused clerk would allow, promising to have them back by the end of the week so I could rent a new batch. The movies were the perfect hybrid of action and intrigue and romance, set against the dazzling backdrop of the magical, colorful India I'd always imagined. Maybe I'd been going at this India thing all wrong—instead of learning to be a housewife, I should have been training to be a Bollywood star.

"Venkat, do they take white people in movies? I want to be in one."

He cackled. "No, Madam. No white peoples. Only Indians. You no speaking Hindi. Bollywood only Hindi."

"Well, then I'll learn to speak Hindi."

Venkat laughed harder.

"Thanks for the vote of confidence, Venkat."

"Vote, Madam?"

"Never mind."

❧

Sundar and both his wives were arranged around the kitchen in a *chapatti*-making assembly line. One wife mixed flour and water together in a giant bowl. The other wife kneaded the dough by hand, then used a tiny wooden rolling pin to form perfect saucer-sized discs. Sundar was at the stove, flipping *chapattis* like pancakes with an orange spatula I had bought at the dollar store in college.

"Is much good, this tool," Sundar said as I walked into the kitchen. "We are not having this here."

"It's called a spatula."

"Spah-choo-la," Sundar repeated, testing the English word out loud. His wives looked on, bemused but uncomprehending. Neither spoke a word of English. His first wife, who, like Sundar, was from Kolkata, spoke Urdu. His second wife, from Hyderabad, spoke Telugu. Sundar told me they used Hindi as a common language, though their four children spoke primarily Telugu and English.

I'd never asked Sundar why he had two wives, and he'd never volunteered the information. Their arrangement was highly unusual, especially in Hindu culture. Watching the three of them interact was fascinating. There didn't seem to be any animosity or tension between them. They each performed within the boundaries of their individual roles: the first wife, Amita, was older, more maternal. She seemed like the caregiver, the glue that was holding their eclectic family together. Devika, the second wife was younger, pretty but shy. Sundar flirted with her, catching her eye over the sticky bowl of dough and nodding slightly, like they shared a secret. But it was Amita he deferred to, letting her order him around and treating her with humble, understated respect. Sundar and Amita seemed more comfortable with each other, worn in the same places like a perfectly faded pair of jeans. I wondered, if I had to choose, which wife I'd want to be.

I sat on the kitchen counter and watched them, my legs dangling over the edge. Sundar, always thrilled to have an audience, started to tell me about his latest motorcycle adventure.

"We are driving one hundred kilometers per hour, maybe more. The road to the village is much rocks. Soon I am passing the train, the farms, everything, when there is a dog asleep and I am not seeing. I am saying to Amita and Devika, 'Holding on!' And we are in air, like flying. Then safe." Sundar laughed. "They are much angry for many days after."

"Sundar, do you think I should learn Hindi?" I stuck my finger in the bowl of *chapatti* dough and tasted it. I never understood how mere flour and water could transform itself into golden-warm, delicious Indian bread with a couple of kneads and a few minutes in a frying pan.

"You are wanting to learn? I am teaching. Say, '*Ap kaise he.*'"

"*Ap kaise hay.*"

"Yes! Now again. Longer sounding. *Aaaap kayyyysssSUH hayyyy.*"

"*Aaaap kayyyysssSUH hayyyy.* What does that mean?"

"Meaning, how you are."

"How are you?"

Sundar smiled. "Very well, Madam. Thank you for asking."

That night, I dug out the slip of paper I'd stashed in my nightstand months ago and called Simrahn, the Hindi tutor who'd advertised on the bulletin board at Coffee Day. The phone rang dozens of times before she answered.

"Is this Simrahn?"

"Yes?" She sounded furtive, like she was speaking from a closet. I could hear children shouting in the background.

"My name is Jenny. I found your ad in Coffee Day? About a Hindi tutor?"

"Ah. Very well. You are expat?"

"Yes. I don't know any of the language, but I really want to learn."

"I can teach you."

She named her fee. It was exorbitant. My true function in India seemed to be as a walking ATM machine: handing out coins to street urchins, buying touristy souvenirs, employing "expat-friendly" staff that charged us triple because they knew they could. Still, it seemed worth it. The Australian's words still rang in my ears: *Sometimes the words only come when you teach yourself new ways to think about them.*

Maybe my impromptu coffee date had served a higher karmic purpose. I wanted to communicate better: with Indians, with Jay, with myself. I wanted to write and think and feel creative again. If learning Hindi would bring me closer to the feeling of home I'd been searching for, then that's what I needed to do.

And if someone *happened* to discover me sitting in Coffee Day one day, practicing my newly acquired but highly advanced Hindi skills, and begged me to take a small role in, say, *Dhoom 3*? Well, that would just be icing on the cake.

⠀⠀⠀⠀⠀⠀⠀⠀⠀⠀⠀⠀⠀⠀⠀⠀⠀⠀⠀⠀⠀⠀⠀⠀⠀⠀*ௐ*

Sundar, accompanied only by Devika today, was sopping up lentil juice from a pressure cooker incident. The electricity had gone off, then surged, while he was preparing his "much secret recipe" black *dal*. The results were all over the kitchen ceiling. Sundar swore up and down that a pressure cooker was the "only way to achieve perfect food preparing, Indian and all other kinds," but today's fiasco was only strengthening my resolve to toss the cursed appliance in Lake Hussain Sagar at the earliest opportunity. Tomorrow, I was going to use some of my precious frozen turkey and teach him to make chili the old-fashioned way: On the stove. In a plain old pot.

Tucker, who had been asleep in his dog bed far away from the chaos in the kitchen, leapt to his feet and started barking and wagging his tail like crazy. Jay walked in and dumped his briefcase by the door. He grabbed a fresh *paratha* from a stack Sundar was arranging near the stove. "Mm. Onion. My favorite."

Simrahn and I were sitting at the table. She was glaring at me. I'd been tracing Hindi characters in a Mickey Mouse workbook for over an hour. I'd yet to get a single one right. I didn't appreciate Mickey, such a beloved, *American* character, taunting me from the cover of the book. Wasn't he supposed to be on my side? Didn't Indians have their own anthropomorphized mascot to endear their language to newcomers? A Hindi version of *See Spot Run*? A buffalo would be good. A garland-wearing buffalo, pointing to the hieroglyphic characters of the Hindi alphabet with a dainty hoof. *See Buffalo Sleep in Road.*

"Hi! You're home!" I jumped up to greet Jay. Tucker was thrilled to see him too. He barked with joy and wove circles around Jay's ankles.

"Decided to cut out early. I had an errand to run." He kissed me. "How's the Hindi coming?"

Simrahn rolled her eyes.

"It's coming. It's just that everything is so…backward," I said, shooting Simrahn a look. "Simrahn keeps telling me I'm saying everything the wrong way. But why would it be 'sleeping you are' instead of 'are you sleeping' and 'name what yours is' instead of 'what is your name'? I feel like I'm learning to speak Yoda, not Hindi."

Simrahn patted my empty seat and pushed my pencil across the table. "Madam, please. We are having thirty minutes more. Let's finish writing 'ka,' at least." She drew yet another capital T with an ampersand through it. "Try again, please."

Jay smirked at me and shoved more *paratha* in his mouth.

"I'm going to the gym before dinner, OK? Looks like you're not quite done here anyway." After months of claiming he was too busy at work to make time for the gym, Jay was finally getting back into his fitness routine. In New York, he'd spent every weekday morning working out at Equinox. The exercise was lightening his mood, making him smile more—lately he'd been more affectionate and playful than he'd been in forever. I knew going back to yoga would yield similar results for me, but I still hadn't managed to find a class.

"Don't leave me here. I need moral support."

"You're doing great."

I pouted.

"Seriously. I'm proud of you." He kissed my forehead. "Love you. See you later."

"I love you too."

Simrahn coughed.

"Um. I mean…*tumse pyaar kartaa hoon*."

"*Tumse pyaar kartEE hoon*," Simrahn corrected gently.

"Right. That."

Jay was smiling as he walked out the door.

"You are very fortunate," Simrahn said when he was gone. "My husband, he is not so nice. My children and I, sometimes we are afraid. I am Muslim and he is not, so my family has cast me out. It is only he and I now." She wrung her hands in her lap, toying with the ends of the long *dupatta* shawl she wore over a pale green *salwar* suit.

"Your family cast you out? That's awful. Have you tried talking to them?"

"I have disgraced them. It is as if I did not exist. I miss them very much, my mother mostly, and my baby brothers and sisters. I am the oldest. I used to care for them. But if I went back, they would merely cast me out again. Such shame has no forgiveness." Simrahn shook her head, like she was trying to force the sentiment back down where it came from. "One more row, and then our lesson is concluded."

I focused on the letter I was tracing, pressing my pencil hard into the paper. When I finished the row, I held the paper up for her approval. She nodded and gathered her things. At the door, I paid her for the lesson and watched, silent, as she slipped worn leather shoes back on her feet and wound a *dupatta* around her head. In Hindi or English, I just didn't have the right words to say.

CHAPTER 21

Sundar's daughter Anusha sat cross-legged on the kitchen floor in jeans and a *kurti*, doing her homework. She flipped her textbook's pages aimlessly, scribbling out math problems in a worn black-and-white composition notebook. Every so often, she'd crane her neck to peek at the television screen. The electricity had made a late afternoon cameo. I was watching *Sangam*, with Raj Kapoor, for the third time. It was old-fashioned and Technicolor and epic. I liked vintage Bollywood almost as much as I liked the motorcycle races and flashy dance numbers of modern Indian cinema.

"Anusha," Sundar barked, waving his spatula. She slumped forward over her book with a hassled sigh. I shot her a sympathetic look. She smiled back.

"This is being the reason good Indian girls will be wearing blue jeans," Sundar muttered into the bowl of mashed potatoes he was fighting with. He knew cooking Western foods would increase his marketability with the expat crowd once Jay and I were gone, but taking instructions from a semi-clueless American (me) and a book called *How to Cook Everything* seemed to be damaging his pride.

"What, *Sangam*? This movie is, like, a hundred years old," I said.

"Bollywood is not real India," Sundar sniffed. He licked a blob of potato off his index finger and grimaced. "Just like this recipe is no real use for *aloo*."

"Mashed potatoes are delicious," I countered. "They're comfort food. My mom makes them all the time."

"No comfort for me. No spice. Much too plain." Sundar's hand hovered near the shaker of *garam masala*. "Maybe if we are adding just a portion of spice…"

"No way," I said firmly. "Add more butter if it needs something."

Sundar sighed his long-suffering, *why must I take orders from this crazy American woman* sigh. "If you are wanting to learn true Indian culture, you should stop watching so much this garbage," he said stubbornly.

"Well, where should I go, then?"

"Charminar," Sundar said firmly. "There you will find the true spirit of old Hyderabad. Just wrap your head and keep firm hand on your possessions." He pounded an emphatic fist directly into the bowl of potatoes. "And while are you visiting, bring me home please some saffron. The best spices in the world are in the bazaar at Charminar. This American mashed *aloo* is needing of more help than Sundar can give."

ॐ

I called my mom on the way to the bazaar.

"Sounds great. I can't wait to get there and do some exploring with you. A spice market sounds like my kind of place. Think you can bring me back some saffron? It's so expensive here."

"Sundar asked for some too. I'll see what I can find."

"I like that cook already. Can he teach me how to make *biryani*?"

"I'm sure he'd be delighted. I'm not turning out to be the world's greatest student of Indian cuisine. He'll be much happier with you as long as you let him use all the spice he wants." I made a face. I could hear my mother laughing as I hung up the phone.

The Charminar itself was an enormous marble and granite monument, with four ornately carved minarets reaching twenty feet into the sky. The Laad Bazaar just outside was so crowded that Venkat couldn't get the Scorpio through the masses of people. He agreed, not happily, to let me out so I could walk.

"Meeting here one hour, Madam. No more. Muslim peoples no good people. You remember."

I sighed. Venkat's hatred of Muslims ran deeper than I could penetrate with my preachy talks about equality, most of which I was certain he was merely pretending not to understand. In the West, the Muslim-related conflicts we heard about usually had to do with Israel and the Middle East. Being Jewish in a Muslim city made me nervous at first; I wasn't sure if our heritage would make us stand out even more or cause us to be targets for discrimination. But in Hyderabad, Muslims weren't fighting with Jews. In fact, no one seemed to be clear on what "Jewish" even was—most Indians assumed because we were white, we were also Christian, which earned us rousing choruses of "Happy Merry Christmas, Ma'am and Sir!" nearly everywhere we went from early December until long past the new year. Most of the time, we just said "thank you." It was too confusing to try and explain.

There were occasional reports of religious violence between Muslims and Hindus, but mainly the unrest in India lay between the Sunni and Shia denominations of Islam. There were whispers about militant groups, rumors of terrorist attacks that happened in other parts of the country. In Hyderabad, we'd never felt unsafe, but a ripple of tension was always present. It wasn't surprising that Venkat blamed Muslims for the threat of violence in his city. Hinduism was one of the most peaceful religions; any religious violence in Hyderabad was always attributed to the Muslims. Still, how he could call all Muslim people "no good people" when Younus was one of his best friends, I simply couldn't fathom.

Venkat stared at the giant mosque looming before us with suspicious eyes.

"No safety here, Madam. I coming?"

"No, thanks. I'll be fine." I climbed out of the car and wound a tasseled *dupatta* shawl around my head and shoulders. My white face still stood out, telltale pale against the sea of dark faces. But as little anonymity as it offered, I wanted a layer of fabric between myself and the teeming crowds.

Tourists were everywhere, jostling each other on the narrow staircases that climbed to an open observation deck. But I reached the top, and the atmosphere changed from charged and chaotic to serene and near-silent. All of Hyderabad was laid out before me, cars and buildings and people transformed to tiny dots on winding streets, a whole intricate, moving world I could fit into the palm of my hand. From up here, it was easier to see the beauty in the chaos, all those moving parts woven together to create a whole.

Along the upper walls were dozens of prayer spaces. Charminar opened into a mosque on the western side. On Fridays, the tolling bells that announced morning prayer rang through the vast bazaar, calling the male worshippers to prayer. Today, the bells were quiet. Only a few men knelt at the prayer spaces, facing west toward Mecca.

A few dips and turns through the narrow streets that led away from the main bazaar and suddenly the crowds disappeared. It reminded me of the tiny village road Younus brought us to when Jay was sick so many months ago. The street, too narrow for cars, was filled with wooden-wheeled pushcarts. Grains and fruit spilled from overstuffed baskets. I found the saffron easily, the crown jewel in tall stacks of spices. The bundles of fragile crimson threads were tied into scraps of canvas, filling the air with their delicate scent.

I followed the lilting sound of a sitar down a slender alley. Cross-legged on a stack of wooden crates was an old, bearded man in a long embroidered coat, a worn white turban wound around his head. He played his instrument with hypnotic skill, drawing out elegant notes that lingered in the air above us, three-dimensional in a way only he and I could see.

"*Bathiye*," he said, pointing to a crate beside him.

I sat. The old man began a different song, swaying in time to the melody, transported by his own music. When he finished, I stood back up and bowed, my hands to my heart in *namaskar*. He bowed back. But when I tried to hand him a crumpled fifty-rupee note, he frowned and turned away. I sighed. I hadn't meant to offend him, just to show my gratitude for his talent and the small moment of harmony he'd provided.

"Sorry," I said, stepping away. "Your music is beautiful. *Sundar musica?*"

He stared at me for a moment. Then his papery face, creased with sun and years, broke into a toothless grin. He cradled the sitar and played again, serenading me as I continued down the alley.

It was so different here, this old-world India, away from the honking horns and gangs of child beggars, the endless smog and traffic and construction of HITEC City. Yet the two parts of the city were inextricably linked, two halves of an unlikely whole. The tent camps next to the guarded, palatial mansions, the IMAX theater just minutes from the ancient bazaar. Could one world exist without the other? I wondered if all the technology and American industry forcing its way into the city was taking something from Hyderabad that could never be replaced. Would paved roads and high-rise buildings eventually take over everything, ruining these centuries-old back alleys, forever altering what was authentic and elegant and real?

I'd spent so much time being frustrated with India, wishing it would catch up to the West, complaining about the electricity and the infrastructure and the livestock in the road. Now I was starting to realize some of the things I'd been wishing for didn't really belong here at all. The heat and the dust, the spices and the jewels and the colorful, mystical gods and goddesses—that was what India was really about. As foreigners, we came in and tried to transform it all into something more familiar, more orderly, more modern. But why? Sundar had been right. The secret to India's magic wasn't in the overcrowded, traffic-clogged cities or in the Technicolor fantasies spun by Bollywood. It was here, in these alleys, untouched by the values of the first world. A place where chaos and beauty came together to form a perfect balance.

I wandered further, lost in my thoughts and the hypnotic rhythm of the activities around me—people cooking, polishing their wares, bartering and buying and laughing together in a haze of *beedi* cigarette smoke. Soon the spice carts disappeared, and metal pots and vases replaced spilling bins of produce. Ahead of me, there were stalls filled with piles of hand-crafted bangles. They were stacked high, dozens and dozens of them, in watercolor hues so vibrant they looked like candy.

I admired the bangles wistfully, knowing they would never fit over my oversized American wrist bones. I felt giant and awkward, hesitating even to touch the bracelets with my fingers for fear of breaking them to pieces.

A young girl sitting behind one of the stalls beckoned me closer. "Ma'am?"

"*Shukriya, nahi*," I said, shaking my head sadly. "*Bahut bara.*" I pointed to my wrist, then made an exaggerated circle with my thumbs and index fingers, hoping I was getting the Hindi words right.

She smiled and shook her head, long black pigtails tied with red yarn swinging merrily as she moved. Her plaid school uniform was covered in metal filings, which she swept carefully off her pleated skirt as she stood and grabbed my hand, leading me behind the counter. From beneath the display cases she pulled out plastic bags crammed tight with bracelets. She opened her eyes wide and shoved them toward me, motioning for me to try them on. I shrugged and gave in, choosing one at random to prove my point.

The first bracelet I tried was delicate navy blue painted with intricate scrolls of gold. It slipped over my knuckles, circling my wrist like it had been made just for me. The salesgirl grinned, triumphant, and stacked more bangles on my arms until I was covered from wrist to elbow. The tinkling metal circles glittered like magic in the sunlight.

"*Beautiful,*" she said, watching me carefully.

"Yes," I agreed, admiring the kaleidoscope of color. "Beautiful."

❧

Sundar knocking at my door at the exact moment I needed him most. Finding old-world beauty in the last place I'd thought of looking. Suddenly, karma felt real again. The idea of the universe spinning with intention was something I'd abandoned months ago, but I was beginning to believe in the sense of higher purpose that had guided me so firmly in my old life. New signs appeared every day to show me I was finally on the right path. Even the water buffalo and I seemed to have formed an understanding. The white, long-legged birds that perched on top of them in the daytime made the buffalo seem friend-lier somehow. When they weren't charging the car or sleeping in the middle of Road #2 during rush hour, the stocky black beasts were even sort of...cute.

"I *knew* you liking city buffalo, Madam!" Venkat crowed when he caught me smiling out the window at a particularly benevolent-looking one chewing grass near the Jasmine Heights gates. There was something peaceful about all that rhythmic chewing.

"Not *liking*, Venkat," I corrected. "More like 'tolerating.'"

"I no knowing what is 'tolerating,'" Venkat said with a grin. "But I knowing you smile at buffalo. Smiling buffalo much good fortune."

In the name of much good fortune, I looked out the window and smiled grudgingly at the buffalo. I swear it smiled back.

Back at Plot 39, I took an extra-long shower, using up all the water in the tank. Then I turned my attention to my wardrobe. Half an hour later—three outfit changes, two applications of makeup, and both arms stacked high with my Indian bracelets—I stared at myself in the mirror and tried to decide if I looked like someone a total stranger would want to be friends with.

Karma was at work again, literally this time. Thanks to my blog, retitled *Karma in the (Indian) City* once we'd moved to Hyderabad, I had a date. A blind date. With an Indian person. Who I was hoping beyond hope was not some sort of crazy Internet stalker/ax murderer who would kill me and then dump my body in Lake Hussain Sagar.

Considering how little electricity—and therefore wireless access—I'd grown accustomed to having, I never thought the friend I desperately needed would come to me via the Internet. With Peter and Alexis gone and Jay, Kyle, and Diana consumed with work, I'd resigned myself to just the household staff for company until we moved back to the States. And while I was especially fond of all of them, I longed to have a real friend again.

In those early days before Twitter and Facebook, the web wasn't really about reaching people or making connections—it was still just an information dumping ground, an uneasy digital hybrid between the encyclopedia and the yellow pages. I'd never intended my blog to be a means to connect with people in my situation. It was just a way to keep myself sane, to remind myself how to get words and emotions down on a page. But I opened up the blog site one day, and there it was: a comment, from a real, live, flesh-and-blood Hyderabadi female, on the ranting post about how much I hated my Indian haircut.

Ummm, I hear you about the hair. I look like I have my finger stuck in an electric socket…forever, the comment said, floating there in cyberspace. *I hate getting my hair cut in Hyderabad too. And I was born here. Maybe we could grab a* chai *sometime.*

So I did the unthinkable. I emailed her, a total stranger who may or may not have been an Internet-stalking, serial-killing ax murderer, and left my mobile number. Anjali called the next day. Over the phone, her honey-smooth voice blended American slang into a lilting Indian accent with unlikely harmony.

"I've been reading your blog long enough to know how you feel about coffee," Anjali said. "I can't guarantee their lattes are any good, but there's a place in Jubilee Hills near my parents' house that does a decent chai. Shall we try it?

Mocha, a hookah bar on Road #1, was crowded with the hippest-looking Hyderabadis I'd ever seen. Forget Coffee Day…clearly, this was the place to be. Silk patterned lounge pillows were scattered around private alcoves. Low tables set with flickering candles. I waited, anxiously, just inside the entrance.

A tall man in a business suit appeared in the doorway, with a young woman gliding gracefully behind him. Anjali had warned me that her father, traditional and strict, would need to see me with his own eyes before he'd leave her in the company of a Western stranger. I smoothed my hair down one last time. This had to be them.

Stern and forbidding, the man raked his eyes over me before offering me a solemn hand. I couldn't tell if he was relieved or disappointed to find me as his daughter had described. As his car pulled away, Anjali flung her *dupatta* off her head and adjusted her *kurti* over her bell-bottom jeans. "Thought he'd never leave," she said with a wink. "I'm Anjali. Nice to meet you."

I checked for hidden weapons, sneaky and fast so she wouldn't catch on. Then I shook her hand and smiled.

Being with Anjali made me feel like I'd known her forever. She laughed at my jokes. We liked the same American music and the same Bollywood movies. Her effervescent energy reminded me of a younger, more carefree version of myself. A recent college grad, she had single girl stories to tell, about nightclubs and beach holidays and bad-boy boyfriends gone wrong. I laughed so hard my stomach hurt. Our conversation stretched for hours. The part of my soul that had been starving for companionship felt nourished again.

"So…what about you?" Anjali asked, stirring the dredges of her tea. "I mean, I read the blog and everything. It just seems like there's more to the story than you're sharing online."

"I'm trying to figure things out," I admitted. I broke the remnants of my veg samosa into tiny crumbs. "It hasn't really been going like I'd planned." And then, ignoring the fact that she was a total stranger, that I'd known her for all of five minutes and she *might still be an ax murderer*, I spilled. Every detail, every worry and failure and heartache. Anjali listened and nodded and laughed at the right places.

Finally, when the tea was freezing cold and my tears had run out and the restaurant was loud with new crowds of hookah-smoking hipsters, she signaled the waiter and ordered a new pot.

"You can do this two ways," Anjali said, pouring more *chai* in my cup. She was one of the most beautiful women I'd ever seen. Her long dark lashes cast shadows across delicate cheekbones. Even doing something as simple as pouring tea from a teapot made her seem mysterious and ethereal.

"Stop, I'm being serious," she said, catching my faraway stare and assuming I'd stopped paying attention. "I'm giving you the benefit of *years* trying to blend these two lives together. You can come here and fight back against all the things that aren't the same, all the things you can't get and can't wear and can't do. You can try to force it to be like New York and it won't be, and you'll keep making yourself miserable in the process.

"Or you can love it for the things that it is. Love it for the mangos. Love it for the *chai* and the sunshine and the festivals. It will never be New York, but it *will* be India…and if you can learn to live with that, you'll be fine."

My eyes burned and I gulped my tea, trying to rein in my emotions. Regret. Shame. But most of all, hope. *Love it for what it is.* A single sentence that would become the mantra for the rest of my journey—and the rest of my life.

"You know, we've been here all this time…and I haven't eaten a single mango. Pathetic, right?"

"Very," Anjali agreed.

"You know I forgot to ask you in my email, but how did you find my blog, anyway?"

"I was searching for ashtanga yoga classes in Hyderabad. It popped up in a Google search, and I just kept reading."

"But I haven't been to a single yoga class since I've been here," I said, confused.

"I know. But you've sure been complaining about it a lot. Enough for *ashtanga yoga Hyderabad* to bring up your blog first in the search engines, anyway." Anjali winked. "Don't worry, I found one for us. We can go this week. Right after we feed you your first mango."

That night, Jay and I ate with Anish and Sunita at Ginger Court. For the first time, being in their company felt like eating dinner with friends, not strangers. My heart-to-heart with Anjali had smoothed my rough edges. Better still, my recent activities left me brimming over with things to talk about—Bollywood, Charminar, the hipsters at Mocha. I even tried my best to chat with Sunita in Hindi, which she endured bravely without so much as a raised eyebrow. Across the table, Anish covered his laughter with a fist.

"You might remember," he suggested gently, "that the national language of India is English. We much admire your attempts at learning Hindi, but we are equally happy to speak to you in your native tongue as well."

I stuck my native tongue out at him. "Just wait. Soon I'll be speaking Hindi better than you do."

This time Anish didn't bother to squash his laughter. "I believe you just might. First Hindi, then Indian cooking…what's next, Indian dress? Shall we see you in a sari on our next occasion?"

"Don't push your luck," I said. "I'm just trying to blur the edges, not totally reinvent myself."

"You would look very well in blue," Sunita mused, looking me up and down. "Perhaps we should visit the master at my clothing shop. He would…"

"One thing at a time," I laughed, scooping up *chana masala* with a piece of *tandoori roti*, leaving my fork untouched beside my plate.

Jena buzzed around us, pleased to see such a lively conversation between his favorite customers. He too was bursting with news to celebrate.

"My wife and I will be having a baby," he exclaimed, bouncing on his toes so high it looked like he might actually launch himself into the air.

"Jena, that's wonderful news! Congratulations," I said, getting out of my seat to give him an exuberant hug. For a split second, he looked shocked—yet another breach of Indian etiquette, it seemed—but he recovered, returning my embrace with grateful intensity.

"To new beginnings, Sir and Ma'am!" Jena cried, toasting us with custom cucumber mango drinks he'd delivered on the house. A single, thick slice of mango was proudly displayed on the edge of each glass. Almost like Jena had known about my conversation that day. Almost like karma.

I took a bite. The fruit swirled into my mouth like butter. Creamy sweet and floral, like edible perfume...unexpected and heavenly. *Love it for the mangos.* Under the table, I reached for Jay's hand and squeezed hard.

CHAPTER 22

I sat on the kitchen counter, dangling my bare legs against the cabinets and sipping smuggled-in Starbucks House Blend. I was making a grocery list. Anjali was coming to dinner tomorrow and I was eager to show off my developing culinary skills. I wanted everything to be perfect. Below me, Tucker was curled into a ball on the cool marble floor, gnawing on a smuggled-in beef treat. It was amazing how the smallest luxuries from home made life in India easier for both of us. Outside, I could hear Venkat humming as he applied yet another coat of wax to the Scorpio's already shiny exterior. Recognizing the song from *Dhoom 2*, I hummed along. It was going to be a good day.

"I may be dying," Jay announced from the stairs. "Or someone might need to come kill me." He was paused for effect on the landing, clutching his briefcase and looking greenish-pale beneath his collared shirt.

As usual, I'd spoken too soon.

"Oh, no…is it your stomach?" I ran a mental checklist of the things we'd eaten yesterday: Captain Crunch and yogurt for break-fast, *aloo palak* at Ginger Court for lunch, Sundar's black lentil *dal* with onion-stuffed *parathas* for dinner. Nothing especially out of the ordinary, but maybe the samosas were bad? Or perhaps I'd been just a little too optimistic about buying that expired yogurt at Q-Mart?

"It's not my stomach. I have a cold. A bad one."

I jumped off the counter and felt his forehead.

"Should I take your temperature? Or do you want DayQuil? There's some in that box of drugstore stuff Peter and Alexis left." I tried to pry the briefcase from his grasp. "Go back upstairs and go to bed. You shouldn't go to the office like this. Plus Anjali's coming tomorrow night after we visit the orphanage I was telling you about. I'm excited for you to meet her. I need you to be healthy."

"No, I need to be at work," Jay said, shrugging into his jacket with his best martyr expression. "I'll survive. I guess." He kissed me good-bye without touching my lips. "If only I had…"

"What? I'll get it. Tea? Cough drops? That shack behind the *halal* butcher sells them, I think."

"Chicken soup," Jay said, his brown eyes big and sad. He sneezed. "I wish I had some chicken soup. Like my mom used to make."

Chicken soup? Like, from scratch? In a country where edible chicken was as rare as Bigfoot? Um, OK. I could do this. No problem.

"With *celery*," Jay called over his shoulder as he slunk into the car. "My mom always uses celery." The man could handle third-world corporate politics with ease, contemplate hiking Mount Everest without batting an eyelash, but a common cold had him calling for Kevorkian and his mom's chicken soup? Unbelievable. I felt a stir of excitement as I watched him go. Finally, he wasn't the strong one. He needed me. After so many months of him having to care of me, I was getting another chance to prove I could take care of him too.

The Scorpio pulled around the bend and out of sight. The electricity clicked off, right on schedule. The air conditioner whined to a halt. Tucker growled in disappointment, abandoning his treat to nuzzle my ankles. Adjusting my eyes to the now-dim light, I sighed and went back to my grocery list. Apparently, I needed some extra ingredients. I crossed my fingers and prayed a bag of noodles would be waiting for me at Q-Mart.

Forget his mom—my mom made the best chicken noodle soup in the world. Like most Jewish mothers, she believed wholeheartedly in its medicinal powers. Served with fresh, thick slices of challah or homemade whole wheat bread, just a whiff of that soup's fragrant steam made me feel safe and cherished. The soup wasn't just for sick times, either—it was for sad times, crisis times, and celebrations. The day I was elected sixth-grade class president? Chicken soup. When my best friend stopped speaking to me over a boy we both liked in my sophomore year of high school? Chicken soup, with extra noodles. When my grandfather died, there were fresh pots of chicken soup simmering on the stove for a week straight, even when no one felt like eating.

Chicken noodle soup was the cornerstone of my mother's nurturing strategy. She filled that pot with a complex assortment of herbs, vegetables, and good intentions that, when combined, formed the perfect alchemic expression of maternal love. The South Indian wives wove their communities together with iron pots of *biryani*. My ancestors had their own version of nourishment that embodied an entire culture, and it started with a simple broth.

I looked at the VOIP phone with longing, knowing it was useless until the power went back on. I missed being able to "reach out and touch someone," like the old AT&T commercials used to say. I wished I could call my mom to get the specifics of the recipe. I vaguely remembered her chopping a pile of this and tossing a handful of that into her giant fire-orange Le Creuset stockpot. She'd be here in just a few more weeks, but I couldn't wait that long. Worse yet, no electricity meant no Internet—even Google couldn't help me now. I was on my own.

Venkat beeped the horn from the driveway. He was back from the office and ready to go. I ran upstairs to change out of my cutoffs and into jeans and a sky-blue *kurti* with delicate gold embroidery. I'd been making a careful study of Anjali's East-meets-West style of dressing. And while it would never be the same as an afternoon at Barneys, I was learning to love shopping Hyderabadi-style too, now that she'd shown me some trendy, insider-only places to go. A personal introduction from Anjali went a long way.

Look the part, my dad used to remind me when I got ready for interviews or presentations. He'd meant neat fingernails and properly ironed cuffs and collars, but the working principle was the same. If I *looked* like I belonged, the challenges of actually belonging were easier to manage. Alexis had tried to teach me that lesson long ago. I just hadn't been ready to listen. I accessorized with a few bright bangles and smiled at myself in the cracked mirror. Not so bad.

The vegetable stand was crowded—not a good sign. I needed to make this quick if I was going to hit Q-Mart for noodles and still make it home in time to start cooking. I grabbed a shopping basket. The woman next to me, exquisite in a red and gold sari, delicate arms covered with bangles, examined a fresh crate of mangos.

"Are they any good?" I asked, reaching for one and offering a tentative smile. I'd never been good at choosing fruit; they all looked the same to me. Jay always complained that I wouldn't recognize a decent pear if it fell off the shelf and hit me on the head.

"You need them like this," she answered, holding out a smooth, thick-skinned green mango. Her bracelets slid together with a melodic chime. "It should feel firm but flexible in your palm." She skimmed her fingertips through the pile with practiced efficiency, tossing a few into my basket. "*Dhanyavad,*" I said, grateful. They'd be perfect for breakfast tomorrow morning.

"You're welcome," she replied, moving toward the cash register.

The stand was jam-packed with customers rifling through bins of produce, gossiping to each other in Telugu or haggling with the cashiers. I shut my eyes tight and tried to visualize the exact ingredients my mother tossed in her chicken soup pot. Butter—we still had some Amul in the fridge. Carrots, of course, and onions. Those two were easy. I'd need to make a trip to Q-Mart for ever-elusive chicken, and some pasta to sub for the Manischewitz egg noodles my mom always used. There was something leafy and dark green in there... parsley, maybe. And then Jay's celery.

A hand tugged at my basket, interrupting my thoughts. Instinctively I clung to the plastic handles, protecting my mangos from the would-be thief. A little boy, no more than seven, with a shaggy bowl haircut and impossibly long black eyelashes tugged back. The basket was almost as big as he was. He shuffled his feet, bare and filthy, along the dirt floor.

"I carry, please," he said. He wore a blue collared polo shirt like the ones the cashiers wore. Could he work here? He was so little.

"Vimal," he said, pointing to his shirt with pride. "I work." I let go of the basket. Vimal pointed to my list. "I finding."

"Oh, OK." I'd never had a shopping helper before. "Umm...carrots. And I need some onions. And do you have celery?" I struggled to find a Hindi or Telugu word that would convey the essence of celery and came up blank. "Green, pale, with stalks? And leaves?" I pantomimed with my hands. "I also need parsley. And garlic."

Vimal dashed off, grabbing handfuls of things from hidden places in the jam-packed aisles. He returned with a selection for my approval. Since he clearly knew more about produce than I did, I thumbs-upped his picks and smiled my appreciation as he dashed off for round two. Within minutes, I had everything on my list, plus a crate of fresh dates, several gorgeous pomegranates, and an unidentifiable melon Vimal assured me, via body language, would be delicious. The only thing missing was the celery.

Damn celery. My soup was shaping up nicely, at least in raw material form, but how could I fail to include the *one ingredient* he'd specified? With my luck, celery was the only vegetable in the mix that actually contained magical medicinal properties and my whole *chicken-soup-will-heal-you* mission would fail.

"Celery," I told Vimal. "My husband really wants it." Again, I pantomimed the long stalks with my hands. I'd always been terrible at charades. Vimal nodded in concentration and disappeared into the back of the store. I waited, impressed with his tenacity. He returned moments later, clutching a damp cluster of greens in his triumphant fist.

"Finding, Ma'am!" His enthusiasm was terrible to squash, but what he was holding wasn't celery. I swallowed a sigh of disappointment.

"No, Vimal. It's OK. It's probably not something you grow here."

"Celery, Ma'am," Vimal replied, thrusting the bunch toward me. "Is yours."

"But celery has stalks, you know…long. Like sticks."

"Celery," he insisted.

I didn't want to hurt his feelings. He'd made my shopping trip so much fun so far. I took the greens. I'd use them for something.

Vimal wasn't buying my submission. "Smell," he demanded, setting my basket down behind him and crossing his arms. "Celery."

I smelled.

He was right. It was celery. But not the long, ribbed stalks I'd been so patiently describing. The leafy, green top part. His vegetable was my vegetable, just turned upside down.

There had been so many moments when I'd expected things to be one way, and had been bitterly disappointed when they weren't. Every collision between what I wanted and what I got was another reason to lash out at my surroundings, to mark the experience a failure instead of opening my heart to something new.

In that moment, a seven-year-old boy working at a vegetable stand drove home a lesson I'd been struggling to learn for months. I came to India with a whole lifetime of expectations and assumptions about the way the world should work, the way life was supposed to be. Before we left, I'd have been bitterly insulted to be called close-minded—that was a word for bigots and racists, not for a liberal, city girl me. But when you can only accept life the way you've always known it, when you fight back against every deviation from "normal," your mind is closed. It took nine months, a hundred tiny failures, and a shaggy-haired Indian boy holding a bunch of celery to open my eyes to a bigger picture.

Chicken soup for a cold, Indian celery for the soul. I reached down and shook Vimal's hand. He beamed back at me, pleased with his victory. Wisdom and innocence blended together in his calm brown gaze. It was like he could see straight into my heart, like he knew he'd helped me cross over into a place I'd been longing to be.

"Thank you, Vimal," I said, bowing my head.

"Welcome, Ma'am," he replied. "Now friend?"

"Yes, friend. Definitely friend." Vimal flushed with pleasure and made a silly face that reminded me how little he was. I laughed. He grabbed my overflowing basket and headed for the cashier. A tiny spiritual guide with long eyelashes, a blue polo shirt, and dirty bare feet.

≈

At home, Mary was straightening the bedroom. I watched, fascinated, as she arranged flower petals in complicated patterns on the dresser and in front of the doorway. A yellow sun with triangular beams of pink and green took shape on the black marble floor.

"Is for good fortune, Ma'am," Mary said.

"It looks so pretty. Will you show me how?"

Mary smiled and beckoned for me to join her with a flick of an impossibly thin wrist. "This way." Together we huddled over the basket of petals. Beneath her smile, her eyes looked sad.

"Mary, are you feeling well?" I asked, concerned. I'd grown so accustomed to her quiet, cheerful presence. The sudden melancholy made me concerned.

"Yes, Ma'am," Mary said. But her forehead was creased with worry.

I sensed whatever troubled her ran deeper than she'd ever reveal. "Are you sure? If you're sick, you should take a couple of days off and rest."

"Mine family poor. If I no work, much anger," she said. But when I pressed her further, she refused to speak.

"You can't get too involved," Anjali told me later when I described the moment over the phone. "You're treating her like family."

"But she *is* family, practically."

"She's not, though. Not really," Anjali replied gently.

≈

My ingredients were lined up and ready on the kitchen counter. Butter, carrots, onions, the celery greens, a couple of chopped-up chicken breasts. No Manischewitz, of course, but there had been a package of fettuccine I'd crunched up into little pieces to create the same effect. An exhausting citywide search had yielded no whole chickens to make the soup part from scratch, so I was cheating with a packet of Knorr bouillon cubes I'd found buried in the tea section at Q-Mart. My Jewish ancestors—the ones who boiled chicken feet for days to make the broth exactly right—were probably rolling in their graves, but it couldn't be helped. When in Rome, you do like the Romans. And when in India...you do what you can with what you have.

Everything was ready. All I had to do was light the stove.

Except I was still deathly afraid of lighting the stove.

I held the box of matches in my trembling hands and, for the tenth time, turned the knob on the orange rubber hose that led from the gas tank to the range. I lit a match, tossed it on the front burner, and ran to the other side of the room with my hands over my face. For the tenth time, there was no explosion...but the stove didn't light either. I crept back to the gas tank and turned the knob back to closed.

Sigh.

I needed to do this. I needed to do this because my husband was sick and he wanted me to make him feel better. I needed to do this because I had to prove to both my Jewish ancestors and my Indian neighbors that, like millions of women before me, I was capable of nurturing my family. I needed to do this because Anjali was coming for a home-cooked dinner and I wanted to impress her.

But mostly, I needed to do this because not being able to light a stove with a match was *pathetic* and I was tired of being a hostage in my own kitchen. If Jay came home and found me with yet another empty book of matches in my hand and another pile of uncooked ingredients, he would laugh himself silly and I would be tempted to make good on his request for a visit from Dr. Kevorkian. I took a deep breath and fanned the remaining gas fumes from the air. I turned the knob, lit the match, threw it in the range, covered my face, and ran.

There was no explosion.

When I peeked out between my fingers, the front right burner was lit with a tiny, sturdy blue flame.

My soup was saved.

Jay walked in just as the electricity went back on. I was a little disappointed; the dining table had looked so warm and romantic by candlelight. I met him at the door and he pulled me into a hug, burying his face into my neck. I smiled into his thick, dark hair, soaking up the feeling of being cherished again.

"How are you feeling?" I asked, taking his briefcase in one hand and dragging him toward the table with the other. "Your chicken soup is ready."

"OK. Not great. I'm going to eat and go to bed. I've got another big day of meetings tomorrow. Hey, did you light the stove? Yourself?"

"Yup." I beamed with pride.

"No way. Venkat helped you. Or Mary?"

"Nope. Just me."

"Nice work, Wife."

"Thank you."

"You found celery," Jay said, smelling the bowl in front of him with pleasure. "How on earth did you manage that?"

"I had a little help from a new friend," I replied, passing him a piece of buttered *nan*, the closest challah-substitute I could manage. "Drink up. Let's see if this stuff really can work magic."

The soup worked. Jay, looking much more human and much less gray, was adjusting his tie at the front door when Anjali's car pulled up outside the gate. She waved.

"Is it OK if Anjali's driver takes you to the office this morning? We're going to the orphanage and I want Venkat to drive."

"Sure," Jay said, looking dubiously at the black Honda out front. "You're sure he's safe to drive with, right?"

"Having met her father, I'm pretty sure her family only hires the best," I replied, kissing him good-bye.

"I'm so excited. I've always wanted to visit the Township," Anjali said as she climbed in the backseat next to me. "Thanks for inviting me along."

"Don't thank me...I needed the moral support."

"No, you didn't," Anjali chided. "But I'm happy to be here to give it."

The Scorpio jolted sharply to one side as we left the smooth surface of Road #2 and started down a barren dirt path. A few prairie dogs hopped up from their holes to see what was causing the commotion, then disappeared back beneath the earth again.

"Are you sure it's this way, Venkat?" I asked, squinting into the harsh morning sun. Ahead there was nothing but an endless stretch of scorched earth.

"Yes, Madam," he replied, pulling his beanie lower onto his forehead. "Much far still."

Even the tent cities were far behind us. I wondered who'd chosen to build the orphanage so far from the city. Was land cheaper out here? Or was the isolation by design, to keep the children safe?

With my feet back on firmer ground, I was ready to start moving forward, to give my time in Hyderabad some real meaning. Alexis had emailed an introduction to the director of a local children's orphanage where she'd spent time volunteering. The director agreed to let Anjali and I visit for the day.

A non-profit organization originally formed to rescue a group of children who'd been kidnapped by criminals hoping to make money on adoptions, the Hyderabad Children's Township officially opened two years earlier. Now, the facility consisted of twelve bungalows that housed more than two hundred orphaned or abandoned children. The Township was dedicated to providing nutrition, health care, and education to both its own residents and the community at large, enabling at-risk families on the brink of abandoning their own children to stay together. During our visit, we would meet kids who had been rescued from unimaginable fates—abandonment, illness, sex-trade trafficking, or slavery. For many of the children here, the organization had saved them from certain death.

After so much time wasted feeling sorry for myself, I was more than ready to start making a real difference in the community. I couldn't just stand by and watch anymore. I wanted to find a way to help, even if it was the tiniest ripple across an ocean of need.

The Township was almost an hour out of HITEC City. A stone archway and a security guard blocked the parking lot from the rest of the compound. The barren landscape suddenly exploded with life—banyan and mango trees, stone pathways and meticulously maintained lawns. We'd stepped into a different world.

"Ma'ams? Right this way, please." A slight woman in a denim jumper approached us and bowed her head, gesturing for us to follow. "The director is waiting for you." She ushered us into a glass-walled office and pointed to two folding chairs in front of a massive metal desk. "Wait here, please. He will be with you in a moment. I'll be needing to take a copy of your identification."

We handed over our passports and sat. Anjali studied the awards and degrees hanging on the wall. I fidgeted with my mobile phone, crossing and uncrossing my legs beneath the floor-length *ghagra* skirt I'd chosen in an effort to look as modest as possible. The office windows were open wide; the strains of a guitar and the sound of dozens of voices singing came from beyond the courtyard.

"It is assembly," the director said as he entered the room. "We sing traditional Indian melodies as part of our morning program. It gives the children a sense of the history they come from." He shook our hands, solemn and businesslike. He wore a red polo shirt and crisp Dockers khakis. "I am Srinivas," he said. "I'll be giving you the tour."

We followed him through the courtyard down a narrow path shaded by vine-covered trellises. Classrooms flanked the sides of the path, looking surprisingly similar to the rooms I remembered from my own childhood—blackboards stacked with boxes of chalk, construction paper art projects dangling from the ceiling, the letters of the English alphabet marching across walls. It felt ten degrees cooler within the compound walls than it had in the scorching desert just beyond the gates. The flagstone path rounded a corner and we found ourselves in a bigger courtyard in the center of a dozen small bungalows arranged in a circle. A group of kids playing soccer stopped mid-game and stared at us as we passed.

More staring. I waited, primed to hold back the usual flare of defensive self-consciousness. It didn't come. These stares felt different. Partly, I realized, because I was different; changing, slowly, from the inside out. But also because these eyes belonged to children. Kids who were just being kids—innocent, friendly, curious.

"These are the children's houses," Srinivas explained. "Up to twelve children will live in each one with one house 'mother.' They will stay in their house for the duration of their time here; for some of them, that will be until they are eighteen years of age. We like to think of them as small families of their very own. Often the children will come visit their housemothers and siblings for many years after they have moved on from here and begun their new lives."

We entered the first bungalow and a group of children burst into excited applause. They'd been expecting us, and clearly, we were honored guests. Some of them lined up to shake our hands. Each child was clad in a worn but clean blue uniform, short-sleeved jumpers for the girls, shirts and short trousers for the boys. The youngest, still in diapers, clung to her housemother's legs, peering at us through tiny fingers that covered her face.

"Welcome," they sang out in English. A girl with an immaculate dark brown bob grabbed my hand, pulling me toward the back of the house. "Please, Ma'am, come see my room first," she said, eyes shining with excitement. A boy with a scarred, shaved head pulled Anjali into the backyard. "This way, this way to the garden," he shouted, grinning.

"They speak English?" I asked Srinivas, surprised.

"We teach them English as soon as they arrive here," he confirmed. "Some are stronger in the language than others, but we try to converse in English at least 50 percent of the time to enhance their skills. Starting with the first grade, their school lessons will be taught entirely in English." The hand in mine tugged impatiently. "Go ahead," Srinivas laughed. "They are excited to show you around."

The girl pulled me into a small chamber containing three neat bunk beds and a chest of drawers. Grinning, she gestured around the room with a proud sweep of her arm. Six drawers, one for each inhabitant of this tiny, bare space. I thought of the four-thousand-square-foot marble house I used to think of as a cage—an absolute palace compared to the room I stood in now. The little girl's love for her simple home was equal parts pride and gratitude. Like watching the tent city from my window, witnessing that love humbled me. I still had so much to let go of, so much still to learn.

"I am Kamala," the girl whispered. "I have nine years. What's your name?" She stared up at me, her caramel brown eyes framed beneath impossibly long black lashes. They reminded me of Vimal's.

"Jenny," I said. She kept my fingers wrapped firmly in her small palm.

"Je-nny," Kamala repeated, sounding it out. "Do you have child-rens, Ma'am? A daughter?"

"No, I don't. I'd like to have some, though. Someday." *I'd like a daughter just like you, with big brown eyes like Jay's and a sweet, tinkling voice.*

"My real mother wore long skirts like you." Kamala's eyes clouded. I wondered how long she'd been here, what kind of life she'd led before. Without thinking, I knelt down and folded her into my arms. She stiffened in surprise, then relaxed, leaning her head into my shoulder. I reached across her forehead and brushed the hair out of her eyes. She felt fragile and unreal, like hugging a tiny, quivering butterfly. Abruptly, she pulled away, remembering her duties as tour guide.

"Will you look at my drawings? I keep them here in my journal, in my own drawer. Here we have our own drawers and two sets of clothings. And one of shoes. And these are our beds, where we will be sleeping." Her words came out in an excited gleeful rush, but her gestures were graceful and deliberate. A circle of younger children clustered around her, silent but brimming with excitement to be part of the scene.

The walls next to each bed were decorated with drawings. It reminded me of my bunk at summer camp, where I'd pinned photographs and letters from home to comfort me when I felt homesick. But this was the only home these children knew—and how very lucky they were to have it. So many children in India could not imagine this kind of luxury in their wildest dreams. I thought of the starving, disease-ridden urchins begging for coins on the sides of the road in HITEC City and wondered which of these children had been rescued from similar circumstances.

Kamala pulled a worn black canvas journal from the top drawer, standing on tiptoes to open and close it with gentle reverence. We sat down on a lower bunk together. Kamala watched the way I smoothed my skirt over my legs and imitated the gesture with her faded navy jumper. She opened the book and began turning pages, explaining each carefully rendered pencil drawing as she went. Anjali, back from the garden, poked her head in the door.

"It's wonderful here. They eat everything they grow," she said, munching a sprig of mint.

I stepped onto the back porch, where clotheslines full of tiny kid clothes swayed in the breeze. A few feet away, a little boy scrubbed industriously at a pair of brown trousers, his expression a mixture of concentration and pride.

"They love doing the wash," said the housemother from behind me, dusting *roti* flour from her hands. "We teach them early to participate in the tasks of the household. It makes them feel useful and teaches them skills for life on their own."

"That's so important," I said. "I'm almost twenty-nine and I just started figuring it out." The housemother laughed. "I wish I were kidding," I said with a rueful smile. From the garden, Anjali giggled too. Insulted, I leaned over the porch railing and made a face at her. She stuck her tongue out. The two little boys with her imitated the expression, hooting with delight. They grabbed Anjali's hands and pulled her away, eager to demonstrate the expression to the rest of their siblings.

"Would you like to see the kitchen?" the housemother asked,

shaking her head with weary amusement. "Some of the children are helping make a broth for their little brother, who is feeling unwell with fever today."

"I'd love to."

The broth was a fragrant, herb-flecked tomato soup that simmered in an aluminum pot on a makeshift stove. Jostling each other for a turn with the spoon, four of the siblings bickered over which ingredient to add next. "It has to be exactly right or Vishnu won't get better," cried a girl, waving a handful of spices.

I thought of Jay and the chicken soup, and how indescribably blessed we'd been to have mothers who made us better with recipes handed down from generation to generation. If we were lucky enough to have children of our own, I needed to make sure they understood what a miracle family was, biological or otherwise. In this small bungalow, people with no blood ties were bonded together forever. I watched the housemother settle their arguments, laugh at their antics, brush hair out of their eyes, and knew she would love these children as her own for the rest of her life.

Compared to the huddled camps of urchin gangs I'd grown accustomed to seeing alongside Hyderabad's crowded streets, this was paradise. A house and a mother to call their very own, a close-knit "family" of other kids to play with. But a closer look revealed that these children bore the same haunted expressions, the same scars and marks that whispered of cruelties in a past too painful to fathom. A handful of them had grown up here at the Township, safe in the arms of their foster mother, protected from what would have been by the compound walls and the kindness of strangers. But others, older and wiser, remembered all too well an existence of pain, hardship, and sorrow. The Township orphans were the lucky ones. Gratitude was not a lesson to be taught here. It was a way of life.

"I'd like to come back," I told Srinivas as Anjali and I started back to the gates. "To volunteer. I could help the kids with their lessons or do art projects or play games with them…or just be an extra pair of hands…" My voice trailed off. I wasn't sure how to read his expression.

Kamala trailed a step behind me, her tiny fingers clinging to the hem of my skirt. She slipped something into my palm and closed my fingers around it. "I made you a gift, Jenny Ma'am."

It was a pencil drawing, a woman in a skirt with long hair surrounded by a group of shorter people with clasped hands and open mouths. "It's a picture of you and all of us singing."

I knelt down and gave her a hug.

"I love it."

Kamala beamed, hugging me back with a force that made my eyes sting.

"Please, Ma'am, will you come back? You could be coming with us to assembly next time, to hear the singing. It is making a lovely sound."

I looked at Srinivas. "Can I come back? I'd really like to spend more time here."

"We need to follow the proper protocol," he said, handing me a handful of papers. "Fill these out and we will notify you." His voice softened as he held his hand out for Kamala, gently pulling her from my side. "But it would be our pleasure to see you here again."

As we pulled down the driveway, I looked back at the cluster of children still waving from the gates as the Scorpio disappeared down the dirt road. I was deeply moved by their trusting faces, their breathless excitement in sharing joys and secrets with someone who would listen. Those children saw me in a light more gracious than I'd ever seen myself. On the front porch of an orphanage bungalow, I'd seen strength and beauty reflected back to me in the caramel-colored eyes of a little girl.

CHAPTER 23

"Inhale and feel your chest rise. Exhale and let it fall. Surrender yourself to this moment. You are nothing more than your breath as it passes through your nostrils and into the air above you."

I lay on my ancient blue yoga mat, eyes closed, palms open, trying to calm my mind and surrender to the universe. Or at the very least to the soothing alto of the teacher's voice and the flickering leaves of the mango tree outside the window. *I am not getting* chikungunya, I told myself sternly. *I am not annoyed at how slow this class is moving. I am not distracted by all that whispering coming from the back corner.*

In New York, learning to let go and rise above my environment had always been my biggest challenge in yoga class. The tiniest distractions upset my balance: a buzzing fly, a too-hot room, the heavy breathing of the person next to me. But I'd made progress over the years. Finding peace by letting go of everything was the Zen state I'd been crawling toward since my very first class. Then India happened. I'd let the distractions and the discomforts become all that there was.

Now, finally, I was finding my way back to the more enlightened path I'd set out to find in the first place.

Anjali woke me bright and early to attend a vinyasa class at Satya's Global Yoga studio, a sunny space with shiny, faux-wood linoleum floors on the top floor of a house in Banjara Hills, about twenty-five minutes away from Madhapur. None of my Internet searches had turned up so much as a whisper about the studio; as usual, Anjali's network of friends and family yielded far better results. Despite being the technology capital of India, Hyderabad still functioned better on word of mouth than computers. As a consolation prize for the ungodly hour, Anjali brought me a croissant from the Ofen bakery across the street.

"Only place in Hyderabad to get halfway decent European pastry," she had said, daintily wiping croissant flakes from her fingers. "Sometimes they roast chickens. Those aren't bad, either."

Now I snuck a peek in Anjali's direction. Not surprisingly, she was the picture of serenity: fully relaxed against her black Nike yoga mat, eyes closed, tips of her thumbs and index fingers pressed gently together, palms open in devoted meditation.

I had a terrible itch on my right big toe.

"Separate yourself from the natural world," Satya intoned. "Separate yourself from the physical world. Leave your earthly concerns behind. Let your unconscious mind take over, emptying all unnecessary thoughts. Absolve yourself of all mental, emotional, and physical discomforts and challenges."

I will separate myself from physical discomfort. I will ignore the fact that my right big toe is so itchy it might be gangrene or worse. I will lie here and let my unconscious take over. I will surrender to the universe.

Breathe in, breathe out, focus. My mat was worn thin at the top and still smelled like sweat and lavender from hundreds of Bikram classes in New York. The ceiling fans stirred the air ever so slightly, creating an illusion of coolness. I felt my body relax and my mind begin to let go.

Then the woman next to me, struggling to remove her burka, stumbled backward and tripped over my outstretched feet, falling on top of me in an awkward heap. I popped upright and stared at her, startled. Underneath the swathes of black fabric, she was wearing Mickey Mouse pajamas.

She followed my gaze and blushed. "I love Mickey Mouse."

"So do I."

We both laughed.

In the weeks that followed, I became a regular at Satya's yoga studio. Anjali, who had a full-time job at a consulting company, came with me whenever her work schedule allowed her to get away, but mostly I went alone. The studio—worn but gleaming floors, dust particles swimming lazily in beams of sunlight that streamed in from the windows, the smell of sweat and dust and incense—was starting to feel more like home than I'd imagined anywhere in India ever could. Satya applauded my progress and encouraged me to take my practice deeper.

Despite Satya's best efforts at maintaining, as she described, a "Western style" level of decorum, the yoga sessions were filled with conversation, complaints, and interjections, women coming and going or moving through different postures than the rest of the class.

"Yoga in the West is different than it is here," Satya explained. "In the West, you choose yoga as a hobby, like a sport or a musical instrument. In India, yoga is ancient, part of the fabric of our daily life without needing to try. But for that, people are messy, undisciplined in their studies. We do not assign the same value or reverence as you do in the West."

"So you're saying in the West, yoga is actually *better?*"

"Not better. Different, yes. But even though India is the birthplace of yoga, there are things we can learn from those who have carried our disciplines into the modern world. Your respect for orderliness, for mindful attention, is a lesson all Indian people should learn to achieve, not just in the quiet of their own minds, but in a group, like this." She gestured to a trio of women, swathed in black burkas, lounging and gossiping on their mats, ignoring the flow of sun salutations around them.

"We all have our struggles and our darker days, you know," Satya said. "Forgiveness is the greatest gift one can give to the self. Healing starts there. Sometimes I see you fighting with yourself in *asanas,* trying too hard to make your body achieve what you believe is perfection within your mind."

I stared into the leaves of the mango tree outside the window. "There's a lot I'm trying to make up for. I used to be better at this. I used to be better at a lot of things."

"Free your mind from the prison of 'better,'" Satya said, gently pressing me to my knees and motioning for me to take child's pose. She adjusted my body with practiced movements, pressing her fists between my shoulder blades, kneeling on my hips and forcing them to release into the ground. She crouched behind me and rested both palms on the small of my back. "Let go and receive. That is what they teach us at Mysore. You will come with us some day, and you will see."

Yoga began to heal my body, to bring back the strength and flexibility that so many months of misery and moping had taken away. If the studio was beginning to feel like home, then my body—for so long a foreign vessel I'd felt trapped inside—began to feel like a familiar place too.

One weekend, Satya planned a retreat for her regular students. We piled into buses and drove through dusty back roads until we reached a secluded resort and spa tucked away in the hills. After a rigorous session of vinyasa in a jam-packed ballroom, we changed into bathing suits and headed to the pool.

I wore a bikini, the only bathing suit I owned. Most of the other women wore 1920s style bathing costumes, long-sleeved with pants that came down past their knees. Feeling conspicuous and indecent, I clutched my towel around me and dangled my legs in the hot tub, which was filled with freezing-cold water.

Fahmida came to sit beside me. She arrived at the yoga studio every day wrapped in a black burka edged with bright, elaborate embroidery. Only her stunning hazel eyes were visible among its folds. Her yoga clothes, like many of the other Muslim women's, were loose-fitting nylon pajamas—a far cry from the curve-hugging Lululemon pants and sports bras I wore to class. Today, perhaps in honor of the vacation-like retreat, Fahmida's burka was pale blue, stamped with violet flowers and embroidered in gold.

"Cold," Fahmida said, sliding into the water beneath me. Her burka floated to the top of the water, swirling around my ankles with gentle caress. "Are you feeling chilled?"

"I don't have another bathing suit," I said, pulling the towel around me tighter still. "I guess I should have figured something else out."

"I meant the temperature of the water. Your bathing costume doesn't offend me," Fahmida said with a laugh, leaning her head back against the tiles so her face was tilted toward the sun. "Just because you are not wearing *habib* doesn't mean you and I cannot still be friends."

"I didn't mean…"

"I know," she said, holding up a lined brown palm in defense. "You are Western, and Jewish also, no? You and I are enemies only in certain worlds. Here it is not so complicated. Just women and bathing and yoga. Friendship."

"Much easier than real life, I guess."

"We are the lucky ones. We get to choose whether it is easy or not. That's what yoga has taught me. To choose ease over struggle. Not everyone is so fortunate to be making such a choice."

Warm now in the sun, I shrugged out of my towel and slipped down into the cool water. I leaned my head back beside hers and closed my eyes against the bright light in the sky above me. Laughter and shouts and the sound of splashing water rained down around us. I closed my eyes and chose ease.

"Did you hear they're building a new airport? With a *Coffee Bean* in it." Diana raised her eyebrows and sighed. "I might need to fly somewhere every single day just to get a Vanilla Ice Blended."

"There's other stuff coming too," Kyle said. "I heard a rumor they're putting in a T.G.I. Friday's."

"No way," I said. "With potato skins and everything?"

"Pretty soon we won't recognize this place. We're such pioneers. One day we'll tell the new expats we used to ride buffalo to work. Uphill both ways," Kyle said.

The waiter appeared.

"I'll have a martini," Diana said, placing her menu down on the table.

Jay looked at me. "Want to try a martini?"

"With vodka that freezes? No, thanks. With my luck, I'll get sick again. Fake vodka parasites or something."

We'd bought a bottle of Indian-manufactured Smirnoff from the liquor shack on the side of Road #1 last week. I'd been hoping to make a batch of vodka-infused lemonade to kick off what would have been Memorial Day weekend back in the States. Sundar had finally mastered the art of barbecued chicken, which he cooked for our small expat crowd. Three hours in the freezer and the contents of the vodka bottle had frozen solid. My science skills weren't great, but even I knew that wasn't a good sign.

"You have a weak American constitution," Kyle said smugly, tossing a handful of anise seeds into his mouth from the bowl in the middle of the table.

"I do not! Look how much progress I've made. Sundar says my Indian palate is greatly improving."

"Sundar just wants you to stop trying to teach him how to make macaroni and cheese."

"All he has to do is open the box. I don't know why he gets so bent out of shape about it. And look, I'm expanding my horizons," I said, pointing to the menu open in front of me. "Tonight's specialty menu is Malaysian food."

"Sorry if she doesn't expose herself to flesh-eating bacteria for fun," Jay retorted, pointing accusingly at the bowl of seeds. "Do you *know* how many people have stuck their dirty hands in that bowl before you?"

"My stomach is primed to handle any situation," Kyle said, unmoved. "It's because I'm Chinese. We were born to eat street food and survive."

"You were born in Memphis," I pointed out.

"Hardly relevant. It's in my blood. Like knowing how to make perfect wontons."

"We've been married two years and you've never made me a wonton," Diana said. Behind her, a loud splash signaled yet another unsuspecting patron's descent into Laguna's moat. "God, I can't believe that's still happening. Why don't they do something about those moats already? Someone needs to talk to management about it."

Kyle and I exchanged glances.

"Why do you think we come here? It's not because of the food," Kyle said.

"I can't believe you guys. And Jenny, you get upset when Indian people are always staring at you."

"This isn't a racial thing. I think it's funny no matter who it happens to. That huge German guy fell in ten minutes ago and it was the best one yet. He yelled at the waiter to go find him new pants. Besides, I'm learning to take joy in the small things. It's all part of the yoga."

"I'm pretty sure making fun of innocent victims doesn't fall under the umbrella of 'taking joy in the small things,'" Diana said. Her martini arrived, suspiciously murky-looking. She took a sip and made a face.

"It tastes sort of like apple." She sipped again. "With some olive mixed in."

Diana called the waiter over, grabbed his pad, and wrote down instructions in careful block letters. "Take this to your bartender," she said with a sweet, *do-as-I-say-and-you'll-get-a-big-tip* smile. "Vodka. A little bit of vermouth. One olive. Nothing else."

The waiter bobbled his head and disappeared. A minute later, he returned to the table. "Your previous martini did have those ingredients, Ma'am," he said, handing the glass back to her. "But we are of adding mix, Ma'am, because Ma'am shouldn't be having drink too strong."

Jay and Kyle smirked. I sipped my wine. Diana thanked the waiter for his consideration.

"That's awfully nice of you. But I'd like a regular martini, just the same."

He brought out another martini. This one was clear-ish. Diana, eternally the optimist, took a small, brave sip and smiled.

"At least this one doesn't taste like apple." Which meant, of course, that it must still be terrible.

The guy at the next table stared at me throughout an otherwise unremarkable meal. Strangely, I didn't feel even the slightest urge to run over and strangle him. Maybe all the yoga really was translating into Zen inner peace that made me immune to the petty workings of my insecure American mind. Or else I was just getting used to the unwanted attention. Either way, it was progress.

After dinner, stepping carefully over the moats on our way out, Jay suggested we grab a drink at the nightclub that had just opened next door.

It was late. The old me would have demanded to go home.

"Sure," I said.

Amid throbbing techno and a layer of cigarette smoke three inches thick, we made our way to the bar and settled ourselves on stools shaped like animal heads. Kyle and Diana ordered Kingfishers. Jay asked for vodka.

"We don't have, sir."

"Really?" Jay said. "It's on the menu."

"How about a mixed cocktail?" the bartender asked, holding up a carafe of something electric magenta and thick as tar.

"No, thanks. I want vodka. Do you have Smirnoff?"

"Ah, yes, sir. Smirnoff we have. India Smirnoff. But we are not having vodka."

A collective eye roll went around the table. I was beginning to think this impromptu nightclub visit was bad karma for my path to enlightenment.

"But Smirnoff *is* vodka," Jay said, voice calm but emphatic.

"No, sir," the bartender said. "Is no vodka, sir."

"Well, then, what is it?"

"Is alcohol, sir."

Kyle laughed out loud, but Jay's patience was waning. He was still smiling, but a few more minutes and I was afraid something might happen. Like my dad, Jay's fuse was extra, extra long. But when he reached the end of it, the results could be disastrous.

"Let's just go, Jay." I climbed off my barstool. Jay pulled me back down and held up one finger. *Wait.*

"Sir!" The bartender exclaimed, suddenly excited, like he'd just remembered his locker combination or found a five hundred rupee note in the pocket of his apron. "We have Flin, the American vodka!"

Jay sighed. "So you DO have vodka!"

The bartender heaved a mournful sigh in return. "No, sir. I am sorry, sir. We are having no vodka."

"But you just said…"

"Yes, sir, but I am remembering that Flin, the American vodka, is actually being gin."

"Bring me the bottle of Smirnoff," Jay snapped.

The bartender dipped low, disappearing behind the polished mahogany bar. Clanking sounds ensued, the sound of glass shattering, then some Hindi curses. A moment later, he returned with a bottle of Indian Smirnoff and a bleeding finger wrapped in a towel. Jay snatched the bottle from his grasp, turning it so the label faced the bartender, and ran his finger over the word VODKA.

"See? This here? This says *VODKA.*"

The bartender grinned. "Ah, yes, sir. Vodka we are having. Shall I get you a vodka drink?"

It took Jay one and a half vodka drinks to stop scowling at the bartender, who bobbled his head in delight every time we looked in his direction, pleased he'd found the perfect solution to our situation.

"I'm just glad it's not always me," I said, stirring the ice in my glass with a plastic toothpick.

"What, getting frustrated with the Indian way of communicating?" Diana asked, laughing. "Jay does this all the time at work. You should see him in line for lunch at the cafeteria. 'NON-veg! NON-VEG, I said!'" She imitated him with surprising accuracy.

I turned to Jay. "Maybe you need to start coming to yoga with me."

"Probably not. I'll stick to the gym. I like to find my inner peace in the weight room."

"Ugh."

"Speaking of yoga, are you going to stop at that ashram in Kerala when you visit with your mom next month?" Diana asked. "Someone at work told me about it. It's supposed to be amazing."

"I think so. Anjali's been before and she said I shouldn't miss it. It will just be me and my mom, so I think we'll have time to stop for a few days."

"I've heard those places are like cults," Kyle said. "Is it one of those silent ones where you can't say a word the whole time you're there?"

"Just don't sign anything or give them any money," Jay said. "Your new attitude might make you easier to live with, but I'm afraid you might sell our first-born child if you go too far overboard."

"I'll do my best," I said primly. "The path to enlightenment is often invisible but for the first few steps."

Jay rolled his eyes and kissed me on the forehead. "I might miss the mean, nasty you after all. That one was a little more realistic."

"I'm trying to find a balance."

"Keep working."

I glared at him.

"That's more like it."

CHAPTER 24

Six months after my desperate flight back to the United States, Hyderabad felt like a totally different place…less like someplace we'd stumbled into and more like where we lived. Jay spent his mornings at Latitudes, a brand-new Western-style fitness center, and raved about his workouts with a new personal trainer. I went to yoga class and spent a few afternoons a week hanging out with Kamala and the other children at the Township. I started writing again, finally able to give words to the emotions of our journey. When the power was on, I blogged like crazy, catching up on all the anecdotes I was now eager to share. The carved wooden idol Venkat had given me on Ganesh Chaturthi became my good-luck charm, an elephant-shaped champion of my creative aspirations.

Lunches with Anjali, Hindi lessons, hanging up the laundry I'd finally figured out how to do on my own. Cooking with Sundar. Walks with the dog around the neighborhood, quiet afternoons with a *chai* and my journal beneath the banyan tree. I ate mangos by the basket and watched Mary play fetch with Tucker, her tinkling laugh echoing through the hallways as she threw his ball again and again. When her duties were finished, she'd teach me things, like how to braid my hair and wrap the blue sari I'd bought to wear to the Township's year-end assembly. Watching me wrestle with the complicated mess of fabric, pins sticking out everywhere, made both of us laugh.

Jay and I were back in rhythm with each other again. The sparks that used to ignite our arguments died before we let them catch fire. Instead of forcing us apart, life in India began to draw us closer together. It may not have been the journey we planned for, but it was still the experience of a lifetime. Both of us were forever changed. I realized that the unthinkable had finally happened—life in India had become some kind of normal.

Maybe even the good kind.

෨

We were sitting around the table at Ginger Court after an early dinner, sipping one last round of Jena's now-legendary mango cucumber cocktails, when a chorus of beeps and vibrations erupted from everyone's cell phone at once.

"That's weird," Diana said. "It's Saturday. Usually they try to keep work emergencies out of my hands until at least Sunday morning."

But my phone was ringing frantically too.

Where are you? Are you OK? Answer now please! said an SMS message from Anjali. I had three missed calls from my mom and a dozen unread emails. Jay scrolled through his BlackBerry messages, confused, then looked up at us with an odd expression.

"There were bombings," he said. Around us, the restaurant was awash in sudden panic. Everyone was shouting into their cell phones. A woman was crying. Jena rushed past us, calling out his wife's name.

"There were two, one at Lumbini Amusement Park and another one at a *chat* restaurant three miles away. A bunch of people are dead. They think it was terrorists." He paused to scan the report again. "It's already been picked up by the international wires. Front page of CNN. That's why everyone is calling."

The panic in the air was a living thing, choking us all. The city went on lockdown. We called our families to let them know we were safe, but Airtel was already succumbing to the crushing influx of calls and texts; we could barely get a few words out before the signal disappeared and our mobiles went silent. In the parking lot, Venkat was stoic and calm. He'd already spoken to his sister, who was safe with her husband at home. The rest of his family was far away from the dangers of the city. Jay and I climbed into the car, stricken and silent.

Madhapur Road was teeming with riots; police were everywhere, trying to control the mobs. On the radio, early reports of the death toll came in: at least forty people had been killed. Two more bombs were detonated in other parts of the city as the Scorpio inched its way through the frenzied streets toward home. Barricades and security checkpoints were everywhere. Venkat pressed our U.S. passports against the windshield. A quick pass of the flashlight and the officers waved us through.

When we finally made it back to Jasmine Heights, my initial numbness turned to panic. I tossed things in suitcases, then took them out again. Jay called BKC's SOS International hotline to try and get more information. Were we safe here, as expatriates? Were the attacks targeting Westerners? Should we stay put in Hyderabad or try to catch the next flight home? With the city on lockdown, an eerie quiet settled over the night. The absence of commotion was deafening.

Later, we'd learn that police discovered nineteen more bombs planted around the city, in popular areas like movie theaters, restaurants, and pedestrian bridges. Most were homemade explosives devices fitted with timers. The victims of the terror attacks were all ages and from all backgrounds: women, children, businessmen. A group of engineering students and faculty visiting Hyderabad on holiday from a college in Maharashtra had been watching a laser show at Lumbini Park when the first bomb went off. Seven of them were killed. Early reports implicated a militant Islamic group from Bangladesh.

"Muslim peoples no good peoples," Venkat spat when he arrived the next morning. "Much killing. Much bad. No more Muslims meaning no more problem." He shook his fist at the sky, like he was demanding something from his gods.

Things were just starting to feel normal. And now, for the first time, living in India made me feel truly afraid. But beneath the fear and doubt were other emotions. Ones I'd never felt about this place before. Empathy. Loyalty. I felt protective of Hyderabad and angry at its attackers. The Indian city suddenly felt like *my* city; a country I'd thought I'd never understand had finally found its way into my heart. For the first time, I wasn't jumping at the chance to leave 'Bad for good.

ॐ

1. RIDE AN ELEPHANT.
2. SLEEP IN A PALACE.
3. VISIT THE TAJ MAHAL.
4. HOUSEBOAT IN KERALA.
5. ASHRAM IN MYSORE.
6. EAT AT LEOPOLD'S CAFÉ.
7. MAKE A BABY.

"You can't put getting pregnant on your India bucket list," Jay said, snooping over my shoulder. "I don't even think that belongs on a list at all. Shouldn't we just keep quiet about it and do our thing?"

"I'm trying to get organized," I said. "There's so much more I want to do."

"We have plenty of time, and you've got trips planned all over the place. If you spend every minute trekking all over India, you might as well forget about that last entry entirely. It takes two of us sleeping in the same bed to make a baby, you know."

"Very funny. I won't be gone too long. I promised the kids at the Township I'd be back for the assembly. They're performing a dance routine and we've been practicing for weeks. Bollywood-inspired, of course." I smiled at the memory of them shimmying their hips in time with the music, trying so hard to get every move right. "You're not going to miss it, right?"

"And lose out on my one chance to see you in a sari? No way."

"We have our Golden Triangle trip, and my mom and I will head down to Kerala. Then there's just Diana's birthday trip to Mumbai."

In exchange for babysitting Tucker, we finally agreed to buy Venkat the "bike" he'd been dreaming about, a second-hand Yamaha motorcycle he'd picked out himself. Swapna's fifteenth birthday was this weekend, and Venkat planned to ride his new bike all the way to his village to see her and, I imagined, ask her to marry him. I was dying to know if she'd say yes.

The terror attacks made me jumpy and nervous for weeks. We were steadfast in our decision to stay in Hyderabad, but every loud sound made me duck for cover and wonder if I'd been crazy not to pack my bags and go. But gradually, the fear faded and the "normal" quality to our daily lives resumed. For the first time in ages, I wiped a layer of dust off my *Lonely Planet: India* and began dog-earing the pages of all the places I wanted to go, from the north tip of Delhi to the black-sand beaches in Goa. It had taken so long to make peace with my life in Hyderabad. Now I was eager to roam through the exotic locales of my current "home" country.

Armed with my camera, the travel guide, and a pocketful of rupees, being a tourist gave me the freedom to ask questions and make my foolish American mistakes without feeling like a failure. An expat needed to blend into a society, but a tourist was only there to marvel and observe. And what better place to marvel than at the seventh wonder of the world itself, the Taj Mahal?

My parents were arriving soon for their long-anticipated Indian vacation. After much coaxing, I'd convinced Jay to take some time off work and come along for a weeklong sightseeing trip in the Golden Triangle. Working with a travel agent, I'd planned the trip so that we'd arrive at the Taj Mahal on the morning of my parents' thirtieth wedding anniversary—it was the perfect place to celebrate lasting love.

Secretly, I was hoping our Taj trip might inspire a little extra romance between Jay and me too. The ground beneath our marriage was finally solid enough to try for the next milestone we both wanted desperately: parenthood. Conceiving new life in the shadow of the Taj Mahal would be the perfect metaphor for a love we'd rebuilt from the ground up.

Now if only I could stop him from sneaking peeks at my bucket list. For, in black magic marker, he'd scribbled in a few items of his own.

1. ROAST A CHICKEN.
2. LEARN HOW TO IRON HUSBAND'S SHIRT.
3. BALANCE THE CHECKBOOK.

4. MAKE ME SOME BREAKFAST. I'M STARVING/LATE FOR WORK.
5. LOOK IN THE MIRROR. YOU'RE BEAUTIFUL.

I looked up, expecting a big sentimental moment, but he was in the kitchen, staring into the refrigerator and tapping one foot impatiently against the marble floor. I threw my arms around him anyway.

"Really?"

"Come make me breakfast," he replied. He handed me the container of eggs, gathered fresh yesterday from the chickens that lived across the road. "I'll make the toast."

CHAPTER 25

All four of us were temporarily speechless as we stood at the entrance and stared at the Taj Mahal, impossibly huge and perfect and real. Sun glittered off white marble, making a thousand tiny rainbows dance in the air. In the reflecting pool, a perfect mirror image of the stunning mausoleum shimmered back at us. It was surreal, like walking straight into a history book.

"I can't believe we're actually here," I whispered to Jay.

"I can't believe we made it here alive," he replied.

I laughed. The ride had been harrowing, it was true, but I would have spent *another* eight hours with the same gasping, hacking bus driver who may or may not have had tuberculosis, another eight hours riding through an endless landscape of cow-patty-covered huts, just to see my parents as they were now, arms wrapped around each other while they took in the view. Celebrating thirty years of hardships and joys, tears and laughter, and still, somehow, standing together and ready to face thirty more.

Jay stood behind me and rested his chin in my hair.

"We should come here on our thirtieth anniversary," he said, looking out over the horizon. "What a cool way to celebrate."

"Does that mean you're not trying to divorce me anymore?"

Jay pretended to think. "Well, let's see. You did make me chicken soup. And my shirts are clean. You learned how to stand on your head, which is pretty cool. You haven't written a bestseller, though, or figured out how to roast a chicken, and your taste in movies has gone a little crazy."

I turned my head and glared at him.

"Yes, I'm keeping you," he whispered, sending a shiver down the back of my neck. "Did you think I wouldn't?"

"Maybe."

"Good thing one of us stays rational in times of crisis."

I jabbed him in the stomach. Some things would never change.

"It's so romantic," I sighed as we climbed the marble stairs toward the Taj's inner chambers.

"You do know this is a tomb, right? Somebody's grave?"

"Not a bad place to spend all of eternity."

"I thought you believed in reincarnation now."

"Yeah, maybe not. I think my Eastern philosophies are just about hitting their maximum. I'm ready to go back to the Upper West Side."

"We've got some time left. Think we'll be bringing a little something extra back with us?" Jay asked, patting my stomach affectionately. "Six whole months of trying sounds kind of fun."

"I hope so. I feel ready to be a mom. I think I might be good at it. I hope so, at least."

"I never thought you were going to be anything but great," Jay said. "But…"

We reached the top and paused, taking in the stunning view of the gardens far below.

"But?"

"I think now you'll be better."

A flurry of clicks interrupted the moment. We turned to see a rogue photographer beaming at us, immensely proud of his paparazzi-worthy sneak attack. He held out his digital camera so we could admire his work. In the photograph, Jay and I were wrapped together, relaxed and laughing, gazing out at the horizon from the balcony of the Taj. It looked like something out of a movie or a complicated daydream, an all's-well-that-ends-well episode in someone else's life.

"Did you ever think we'd be those people?" I said, pointing to the young, happy couple captured forever in an impossibly perfect moment.

"No. Not really. But I'm glad we are."

"Sir and Ma'am, you are being those people forever! For the bargain price of two thousand rupees only!" He snatched his camera back and held out his palm. "Isn't love being wonderful thing?"

୧♡

We returned to Hyderabad a few days later, still buzzing with energy and laughter from our adventures in the Golden Triangle. Being an actual tourist in India was more fun than I'd ever imagined. I didn't have to be an expat trying to fit in or a spoiled American princess getting a harsh dose of reality. I was just me, wide-eyed and appreciative. For once, I wasn't trying to figure out how to *live* in a foreign world—my only concern was taking it all in.

My dad spent a couple of days with us in Hyderabad, fixing things as he'd done in every apartment I'd ever lived in—reinstalling faulty toilets, fixing the broken lock on the front door, teaching Venkat how to vacuum, wash, wax, and service the engine on the Scorpio.

"Do you want me to take care of that broken glass upstairs?" he asked, scrubbing at his grease-stained hands with a dishtowel and taking a deep swig from a can of soda. "Blech, what's wrong with this Diet Coke? It tastes terrible." He reached to grab another one, but I stopped him.

"They're all like that. Manufactured in India. It's an acquired taste."

"Just like Indian food."

"Exactly. Speaking of which, we're taking you guys to Ginger Court to meet Jena tonight. He's been taking very good care of us."

"Won't Sundar be offended?"

"It's his night off. Someone has to go home and feed all those wives, right?"

My dad laughed. "That's right; I knew there was one thing left on my souvenir shopping list! I wanted to bring home another wife. Think Mom would be mad?"

"Depends on how good her Indian cooking is."

"That, and I want one of those metal lunch pails the construction workers use. And a turban! A gray one, so it looks like my real hair and no one will know I'm bald."

"Dad?"

"No turban?"

"I love you."

"I love you too, little peanut." He pulled me into his arms for a hug. I took a deep breath, inhaling his scent—shaving soap, breath mints, Tide laundry detergent—and felt home.

"So, do you want me to fix that broken mirror or not?"

"No, you can leave it. I'm used to it."

"I'm your father. I'm supposed to fix everything, remember?"

"You do fix everything, Dad. Always. But this one thing, I think, was meant to stay broken."

"If you say so."

"*Dhanyavad.*"

"God bless you."

❧

My dad had to fly home and go back to work, but I'd convinced my mother to stay on in India so we could explore more of the country together. After one last night all together, reminiscing and feasting on Jena's "especially for Sir and Ma'am's wonderful family" specialties, Venkat escorted my father to the airport for his trip back to Boston. The next morning, my mom and I hopped on a SpiceJet flight and headed south to Kerala.

My mother's spirit of adventure was huge. She embraced other places and cultures in a way I'd sometimes teased her about but secretly envied. Her unconscious habit of mirroring an accent within minutes of conversing with a foreigner was a standing family joke. She'd read extensively on Indian customs to prepare for this trip. Now she was happily identifying local flowers and addressing every man wearing a turban as "Mr. Singh."

If being at the Taj Mahal had felt like walking into a history book, Kerala felt like walking straight into an episode of *National Geographic*. The backwaters were quiet and still, lush with flowers and fruits that grew along narrow channels sheltered from the sun by low hanging vines. Hidden among the riverways were entire villages; craftsmen absorbed in their art, women hanging laundry in the whisper-like breeze, children diving naked from cliff tops into the gentle waters below.

Together, my mom and I paddled through quiet canals that shimmered in the sunlight. We whispered in elaborately painted churches and browsed endlessly through craft stalls along the fisherman's wharf.

"Do you have these in a size medium?" she asked the woman

behind a cart of brightly-dyed cotton fisherman's pants. Her speech was tinged with the slightest trace of an Indian accent.

"Mom. You're doing it again."

"Oops. Sorry." She paid for the pants with an exaggerated eye roll in my direction. The woman laughed as she handed my mom back her change.

"You won't think I'm so crazy when you have kids of your own," she said, watching me haggle with a vendor over a strand of sandal-wood prayer beads.

"I don't think you're crazy. Not anymore, anyway."

"Very funny."

"Remember when I'd get mad because you'd park the car outside the lines when we went to the grocery store?"

"You still do that."

It was sort of true. Mystified, I'd watch her wiggle over the white painted lines, oblivious and unconcerned. A couple inches off on one side or the other just never seemed to bother her. *How*, I wondered to myself, *can she just get out of the car and walk away knowing that she hadn't paid attention to the simple guidelines on the pavement?*

It was the same with her chocolate chip cookies, which despite my best efforts I'd never come close to replicating. But when I made my (subpar) versions, I carefully measured and molded each ball of dough before placing it on the baking sheet, ensuring that the cookies would be evenly baked and perfectly round when they came out of the oven. My mom's cookies were misshapen and oddly sized. Sometimes she forgot to set a timer and the cookies stayed in the oven too long, turning deep brown on top. But her cookies always tasted amazing, no matter what they looked like.

Life in India was one big browned, misshapen cookie—delicious in spite of its imperfections. Or maybe because of them. Nothing here was ever the way I thought it was supposed to be. My mother knew how to let go of the "supposed to's" and live life outside the lines. Years after she'd taught me to read and draw and tie my shoe-laces, I was still learning about life from her example.

"Motherhood isn't about being perfect," she said, winding the necklace of prayer beads I gave her around her neck, running her fingers over the carved wooden spheres. "Life isn't either. You can try as hard as you possibly can and it still won't be enough. If you can't keep learning, keep evolving, you might as well stop living. It's like my wedding vows with your father. I've probably told you a hundred times. We took them from a Wiccan wedding ceremony."

"*To the evolution of each other,*" we said together. She laughed. "So I've told you before."

"Just a couple of times."

"Are you and Jay doing OK?" my mother asked. I could tell she was trying not to pry too deeply. "It seemed like you were having a rough go for a while."

I fingered the *japa mala* strand around my own neck. "It was hard. I thought for a while we might not make it. I never knew you could be with someone and still feel so alone."

My mother put her arm around my shoulders. "You both have such strong personalities. Neither of you can stand to be wrong. But from watching the two of you the past few days, I think the worst is over. In marriage, you can do it two ways: you can get through it or you can get over it. From what I've seen you and Jay are getting through it."

"I think so too."

"Which," she continued, looking mischievous, "is a good thing. I've always thought the two of you would make gorgeous babies."

"I hope so." I looked at my watch. "Speaking of gorgeous, I've got a surprise for you. We've got appointments at the Ayurvedic spa in an hour. Kerala is the birthplace of Ayurveda. It would practically be sacrilegious if we left here without at least one treatment, right?"

Shockingly, my mother—a lifetime poo-poo-er of all things girly, especially frivolous "time wasters" like manicures and facials—grinned with pleasure. "I guess I could stand to learn a thing or two about Ayurveda," she said. "Isn't that where they pour oil all over your head?"

"Yep. And cucumber slices, and a neck massage…sounds relaxing, right? We've done enough exploring for one day. Let's go get pampered."

CHAPTER 26

M a'am? Are you OK? You have stopped reading."

Kamala's caramel eyes, wide with worry, stared into mine. I looked around, startled. I must have zoned out for a minute.

"Sorry, sweetheart. I just...spaced out for a second. Everything's fine." I lifted the copy of *Peter Pan* I'd been reading from. "Can you show me where we left off?"

"'Spaced out?'" Kamala repeated, wrinkling her forehead in confusion. "What is the meaning of that?"

I laughed. Coming from her mouth, the American expression did sound strange.

"It just means I got distracted for a second and forgot what I was doing. It's nothing to worry about. I'm OK. I promise."

But the truth was, I wasn't OK. For weeks now, I'd felt awful. My head hurt, I was exhausted all the time, and my body ached in strange, inexplicable ways. My skin was extra sensitive, breaking out in acne on my face and hives on my body. Even showers were unpleasant—the weak stream of water felt like tiny razors on my irritated skin.

Worst of all, India had become intolerable again. I couldn't stand the dirt or the heat or the traffic. The staring I'd finally gotten used to now made me as bitter and resentful as it had the day I got off the plane. And the noise—the constant, cacophonous riot of car horns and livestock and construction workers banging on cement. My head throbbed with the assault from morning till night. My battle with food poisoning was back in full force. For weeks, Sundar had been making me pots of boiled rice I ate morning, noon, and night. Leaving the house was a major production; I'd been skipping yoga and sending Venkat to the office to play poker all day. All I wanted to do was lie in bed or watch movies on the couch with Tucker curled up next to me. It was like I'd gotten caught in a time warp, transported backward and trapped inside my first few months in Hyderabad instead of enjoying my last.

"I just don't get it," I told my mother on our VOIP call that night. "It's like my body is going totally haywire." It was the middle of the night for me, but despite my chronic exhaustion, I couldn't sleep. For her, the day was just beginning. Over the staticky crackle of the phone, I could hear the sounds of her morning: the gravelly whir of the coffee grinder, the clink of her cereal spoon against a ceramic bowl, the rustle of the newspaper she'd have read cover to cover by the time breakfast was done.

"Maybe you're pregnant," she suggested. "I was exhausted all the time before I found out I was having you. Also, I had the hiccups. With your brothers too. Do you have the hiccups?"

A frisson of excitement started in my toes and coursed through my entire body. It would be early…but it was possible.

"I don't have the hiccups. But I have been burping. Do you think that might be the same thing?"

"I don't know. Couldn't hurt to take a test."

"What was the date of your last menstrual cycle?"

"August 26."

"And what does your husband do for work?"

"Consulting." I fidgeted, nervous and queasy, in a metal folding chair, my hands resting protectively on my stomach.

"Your husband's father? What is he doing for work?"

"He's an engineer. A civil engineer."

The OB-GYN scrawled a note on her pad. "And your father? What does he do for work?"

"He's a doctor. But I don't see how that's relevant. Aren't you going to examine me or something?"

Dr. Rao peered at me above her wire-rimmed glasses. "Do you want me to?"

Prenatal vitamins, thermometers, ovulation calculators. For some reason, it had all seemed like a silly science experiment...right up until the moment we saw two tiny blue lines on a pregnancy test. And then another, and another. My mom had been right. My body wasn't going haywire after all—it had just been taken over by one last, very special, made-in-India souvenir.

Jay and I had been dreaming of a baby since before we got married. We'd had maybe-names picked out for ages and talked about moving to Brooklyn once we started a family, where there were grassy parks and fleets of rainbow-colored Bugaboos ambling down the sidewalks. With our departure from India just a few months away, the possibility of a future together, not just as the two of us plus Tucker, but as a real, full-fledged family, was finally beginning to feel real.

Dr. Rao took out a cardboard calendar wheel. "You have, I assume, taken a home pregnancy test."

"Yes. Three, actually." I let out a nervous laugh. The tiny room smelled like formaldehyde, reminding me unpleasantly of my sixth-grade science classroom where we'd been forced to dissect frogs. I gagged a little behind a polite fist. There was a reason I hadn't pursued a career in biology, and it wasn't my poor math skills.

"And they were coming out positive?"

"Yes. That's why I'm here. To make sure I'm really pregnant and everything."

"You are due twenty-sixth of May, next year. You may call your husband in, if you wish."

I opened the slim metal door and crashed into Jay, who'd been pacing on the other side. "She says you can come in."

"Congratulations, Sir. We have confirmed the pregnancy," Dr. Rao told him as he sat in a metal folding chair next to mine.

"That's great!"

"No," I whispered. "She means *we* have. You and me. All she's done is ask me a bunch of questions about what our fathers do for a living."

Dr. Rao cleared her throat. "We have tested you for HIV, malaria, hepatitis A and B, and a variety of other sexually transmitted diseases. You have passed all tests. You are very fortunate for your American vaccines, you know. Many Indian mothers come to us with no such protection for themselves or their babies."

"What about a pregnancy test?"

"No, Ma'am. You are telling you already performed one, true?"

"Oh. Right." So far, I had no more information than I'd walked in with, and that was from spending half the night on BabyCenter.com.

"You will be having the baby in India? Or in U.S.?"

"U.S.," Jay and I said simultaneously. Earlier, I'd collected a urine sample over a hole in the ground in a unisex bathroom. There had been no sink to wash my hands. From there, I'd gone for a blood test, waiting over an hour for the nurses to produce a hypodermic needle that was still wrapped in manufacturer's plastic. Across from me, a man in an orange dhoti with filthy feet and bloodshot eyes scooped handfuls of curried rice into his mouth from a Styrofoam bowl, staring at me with every bite. We were at the best hospital in Hyderabad.

"That is good," Dr. Rao declared. We looked up at her, surprised. "I do the best I can here," she said, meeting my eyes for the first time. "I'm proud of my education and my training, my staff here. But there is only so much we can do, so much care we can provide. In U.S., you will get better care. And, if you are choosing, you will be allowed to know the sex of your baby."

"Allowed? You can't find out the sex here? Don't you have ultrasound machines?" Jay asked.

"We are having ultrasound, yes," she answered. "But it is illegal in India to know the gender of an unborn child."

"Why?" I blurted out, even though I was sick to my stomach imagining the answer.

"Sometimes the baby girls, they don't make it," Dr. Rao said, polishing her glasses with an edge of the lab coat she wore over her charcoal-colored sari. "Accidents happen. This is the only way we have of protecting them."

Outside in the sunlight, I blinked a few times, readjusting myself to a world that suddenly felt upside down. I looked down at my stomach, flatter now than it had ever been thanks to all the yoga. I couldn't believe there was life somewhere in there, a tiny being that might survive to see a brilliant blue sky just like the one above us now. Jay put his arms around me and held tight, wrapping me up in his arms like I was a child myself.

"Are you happy?"

"Yes. Are you?"

"Very."

"Should we go meet everyone for brunch? We'll only be a little bit late if we leave now."

"Yes. Let's go."

ℰↄ

Our sea container was packed and ready, waiting to begin its voyage back to the United States. All that was left was our clothing and the essentials we'd need for our remaining weeks in India—dishes, cooking pots, sheets, and towels. The house looked strange without the furniture and artwork we'd collected. I wandered from room to room, looking into empty cubbies and rubbing at the marks our belongings had left on the black marble floors. One day, these faded imprints would be all that was left of us in Hyderabad. Another family would move in and fill the rooms with beds and clothing, the smells of their cooking and the sound of their laughter. The *puja* room would be filled, as it should be, with idols and altars. The servants' quarters in the yard, instead of being stuffed with old issues of *Us Weekly* and *Elle*, extra dog toys, and spare parts for the Scorpio, might become home to someone's cook or housekeeper. Our crazy American habits would disappear along with us into the Hyderabad night, and the house would be returned to its Indian roots. I traced my finger along the crack in the bathroom mirror. I hoped whoever's face it reflected next would learn to appreciate the imperfection as much as I had.

Soon I would be headed back to the States to spend a few months with my parents in Boston while I organized the details of our repatriation. Jay would stay on in Hyderabad, bunking at the Novotel hotel until the transition out of his Region 10 role was complete. We would spend our last weekend together in Mumbai, celebrating

Diana's birthday and doing some eleventh-hour sightseeing. Then we would head back to Hyderabad, where I'd planned a bon voyage feast for our friends, Indians and expats alike. We had a few cases of wine left to finish, and a lot of good-byes to linger over. Never, when we began this journey, would I have imagined that saying good-bye to 'Bad would be so bittersweet.

Mumbai was crowded and messy and exciting. We feasted on seafood at Trishna and had drinks at the Intercontinental on a balcony that overlooked the entire city and beyond it, the Arabian Sea. Here, there were lights—twinkling and bright and spread out for miles. In the distance, the Gateway to India rose out of the glistening water, majestic against the foggy night sky.

In the morning, I left the others behind and took a rickshaw to the Mumbadevi temple. In the early hours, the streets were still quiet. The driver whistled. We passed the Dhobi Ghat laundry, where hundreds of men and women were already deeply ensconced with the day's work, and the slow stirrings of the Zaveri Bazaar, where peddlers were just beginning to set out the day's wares of copper bangles, incense and spices, woven carpets, and hand-tooled leather slippers.

At the entrance of the temple, I paid the driver and told him, in Hindi, not to wait. I stowed my shoes under a carved marble bench and scanned the sign of visiting rules posted just before the gates. I wondered if being pregnant, like having my period, would prevent me from visiting the temple's interior. But the sign said nothing about expecting mothers, and I slipped through the turnstile into the dim inner chambers.

I wanted a few moments alone in the quiet. I needed a place to say thank you to the universe—for bringing me here, for allowing me to find a path that led to acceptance and understanding. My sandalwood prayer beads wove between my fingers as I focused my thoughts on

gratitude for what I'd been given and prayers for what was to come—
for me, for Jay, and for our unborn child. Karma had given me the
greatest gifts anyone could ask for. Now it would be up to me to live
life with my eyes and heart open to everything I'd learned.

"Done praying to Lord Krishna?" Jay joked when they arrived to
get me. "You told him you're Jewish, right?"

"It's Ganesh I was talking to," I countered. "And I don't think
he cares."

"So is the baby going to be raised Hindu?" Jay asked.

"Probably not. But she'll know about it. Or he. And one day
we'll come back so they can see where they came from, where their
story began."

We rode the ferry out to Elephanta Island to roam through the
caves. I was walking slowly up the giant hill, sipping a lukewarm
Sprite to calm my still-churning stomach, when a monkey leapt onto
me and snatched it from my fingertips, chugging it down in one
noisy gulp before I even had time to react.

"Hey," I protested. "NO! That's my Sprite!"

"Here, have mine," Jay said, handing me his can. But the monkey
was faster. He grabbed that one too, snatching it and running to a
pile of rocks nearby, sipping it greedily and watching us with a mocking expression.

"You should have said no in Hindi," Diana said. "Maybe they
don't speak English."

"Simrahn would love that. All these months of lessons and the
best I can do is tell a monkey not to steal my drink."

"I think these monkeys are smarter than we are," Kyle said, watching the monkey rub his stomach in satisfaction. "And your Hindi is
actually pretty good."

"For sure they're better at adapting to their environment than I ever was," I muttered, mourning the loss of my soda. "Talk about survival of the fittest."

We took the ferry back to the city. Diana and I browsed sidewalk stalls for souvenirs. She picked out *om* key chains for both of us.

"So we'll always have the universe at our fingertips." Diana smiled as she handed me the carved wooden symbol that dangled from a smudged brass chain.

Kyle and I ducked into our favorite bookstore, which was packed floor to ceiling with uneven towers of dusty paperbacks. I browsed the classics sections, hoping to add a few more titles to my collection before we left India for good. Kyle came up behind me and handed me a giant tome wrapped in paper.

"What's this?"

"It's a going-away present. *Shantaram*. If you really want to love and hate India at the same time, this will do it. It's incredible. You'll have a totally new appreciation for Leopold's too. Plus they say '*yar*' all the time, which I'm going to adopt as my own personal catchphrase."

"Thanks, *yar*. This is awesome." I wanted to thank him for more, to find the words to tell him how much I appreciated so many things—the guidance, the comic relief, the companionship that kept me from being lonely when Jay and Diana got wrapped up in their BKC world. His comment about my Grace Kelly Indian haircut was one of the nicest things anyone had ever said to me. I tried to tell him all of it, but the words just stuck in my throat.

"Come on, let's go get a Kingfisher at Leopold's and watch the tourists try to haggle with the street guys. It'll be almost as good as moat watching."

"Nothing could ever be that good."

CHAPTER 27

We returned to Hyderabad in the late afternoon. Venkat seemed unusually jumpy on the ride home from the airport. His black brows were knit down across his forehead and he tapped his fingers furiously against the dashboard. Something was bothering him, big time.

"What's wrong, Venkat?" I asked. It wasn't like him to be so anxious. He was barely speaking to us, hunched down over the wheel and driving more slowly, it seemed, than usual.

"I no say," he muttered, under his breath, like he was admonishing himself. "I no say."

When Jay unlocked the front door, we knew immediately what was causing Venkat's distress. Everything we'd left in the house was gone. Our dishes and clothing, the linens and the bedding, pots and pans, and even the spices that had been left in the kitchen cabinets. Tucker was frantic, darting back and forth between the empty rooms. Only my laptop was left behind, alone in a pile of dust on the marble floor.

"Venkat, what happened?" Jay shouted, shocked and furious.

Venkat crossed his arms and refused to speak. His face was a mask of frustration and anger.

"Venkat, you must know who did that. What happened?"

"Is Mary," he burst out, anguished. "She coming here with brothers. Many rickshaws. Taking everything. I sorry, Sir! I no doing!"

Jay and I stared at each other in stunned silence. Mary, who I'd treated like family, who I'd given food and money and clothing. Half of the things Mary had stolen had been destined for her anyway, once we'd officially moved out. But she'd had no way of knowing that. She had worked with us for months, diligent and true, so honest she'd leave a stack of coins from Jay's pocket lined up on his nightstand, carefully arranged in plain view as if to prove she'd never dream of taking so much as a single rupee. Mary had taken care of me when I was sick, played with Tucker while we were gone. She'd been part of our family, part of our lives. Now she'd taken everything, leaving behind piles of cobwebs, forever altering the memories of the time we'd spent together, of a person I thought I knew.

Venkat cowered in the doorway, angry and distraught. "I tried stopping, Sir," he said, his brown eyes wounded.

"Take me there," Jay said, his face hard.

"Sir?"

"To Mary's. You know where she lives. Take me there."

❧

Jay pounded on the door of the crumbling concrete shack. A man, presumably Mary's brother, answered the door lazily, wearing an undershirt and a pair of plaid pants. He saw it was Jay and tried to slam the door shut again, but Jay forced his way past him into the dim interior.

"You stole from us," Jay said, his voice level. "I want my stuff back."

"Get out of my home," the man shouted. "We no stealing from you. Stealing nothing. Get out now!"

"Oh really?" Jay replied, his voice rising. "You stole nothing? Then how come you're WEARING MY SHOES?"

The man looked down in spite of himself, where his hairy toes stuck out of Jay's favorite pair of Adidas flip-flops. Jay gave him a look of disgust and pushed past him into a room no bigger than a closet. Cockroaches scurried beneath his feet. A single burnt pot smoked on a hot plate, a watery rice mixture cooking inside. The smell inside the shack was rank and sour, the smell of illness and filth and desperation.

Mary lay huddled in the corner, eyes swollen, protecting her body with her arms like Jay was going to start beating her any second. All around her were our belongings: jeans and shirts, the plastic Q-mart cups with fruit on them, my orange and yellow towels from college.

Jay looked at her for a long moment. Then he turned and walked out without a word.

"Go home, Venkat," he said wearily, climbing back into the Scorpio. "Take us home."

"But, Sir, you things? Mary having?"

"Just drive."

Driving through the rioting crowds in the aftermath of the terrorist attacks had felt like the lowest possible moment on our journey. It made me question the lessons I was learning and challenged my resolve to stay in India until I got things right. But the betrayal I felt now made the fear and uncertainty of that night seem mild in comparison. I'd wanted to cancel the bon voyage party, too confused and heavy-hearted about Mary to feel like celebrating anything. But Jay had insisted we continue as planned.

"You're the one who believes in karma," Jay said, gesturing to the crates of wine still hidden beneath the stairs. "Don't you think there was a reason the wine was one of the only things she left behind? That, and your laptop? She didn't want to take away your writing. She knew it's what meant the most to you."

"That's not karma," I said. "Mary's Christian. She doesn't believe in drinking alcohol. And she probably didn't know what to do with the laptop."

"The point is, who cares? She needed all of it way more than we did. It's the way it is. I'm just glad she's OK, that those thug brothers of hers didn't hurt her or anything."

"Do you think they might have?"

"At least they'll have a little money to get by for a while. I know it's not the best note to go out on, but…let's just forget about it and have a party. We've got plenty to celebrate."

"I didn't get to tell her good-bye," I whispered. I imagined her slim chocolate face peeking over my shoulder in the mirror while she wrapped me, laughing, in my bright blue sari. One long braid falling down her back, white even teeth, spine held straight and proud despite the hardships of the life she lived. Which Mary was the real one? The cowering thief, or the honest, good-hearted version I thought I'd known? I never wanted to find out.

☙

"Madam? I am having something good instead. Bad Mary. But for mine is good news."

"What is it, Venkat?" I pressed a palm against my forehead. I'd had about enough news for one day.

"Swapna being my wife, Madam!" Venkat announced, bursting at the seams with joy. I jumped up in my seat, headache forgotten.

"Venkat, that's awesome! She liked the earrings? She said yes?"

"Yes, earrings much liking." He grinned. "But Swapna even more liking mine new bike."

We pulled up outside of the store. "Does that mean we get to come to the wedding?" I asked.

"Yes please, Madam." Venkat nodded vigorously. "You and Sir are being mine much honored guests."

୧୬

My shopping cart was stacked sky-high, loaded with imported luxuries for this, our final expat bash. Dented boxes of Duncan Hines brownie mix; plastic tubs of deli turkey, cheese, and crackers; and jars of Old El Paso salsa. I shielded my eyes as the cash register cranked out a total. It was more than an Indian family would spend on groceries in a year, more than Venkat's monthly salary. But if we were going out, we were going out in true expat style. I dug in my pockets for a credit card and came up empty-handed. No cash, no plastic, nothing. I'd been so distraught over Mary that I'd run out of the house without my wallet or my bag.

A manager rushed over and took in the scene: the mounds of groceries, bagged and ready to go, me red-faced and mortified, mumbling apologies and calculating how long it would take to go all the way home and come back again. If they'd be willing to put all the ice cream back in the freezer. If this was really karma telling us to cancel the party after all. The manager put a hand on my shoulder. Unexpected, unorthodox, reassuring.

"It's OK, Ma'am. Take your items. Be bringing your payment later. We trust you."

In that moment, everything came full circle in the oddest of ways. We had trusted Mary, and she had betrayed us. But already, in our hearts, we'd forgiven her. What choice did we have but to look beyond ourselves and our sense of righteousness? We had everything, and she had nothing. The world kept spinning, whether we understood it or not. Whether we fought back or let go.

And now, India trusted me. After all my transgressions, India had forgiven me. Or at least, Q-mart had. Which is more than I'd expected. And, maybe, more than I deserved. If India could forgive me—for every misunderstanding, for every judgment, for every minute I wasted with expectations that set us both up to fail—then maybe it was time to forgive myself. To smile at that girl in the broken mirror and tell her everything was going to be OK.

I'd learned to survive. More importantly, I'd learned to let go. I'd learned to live.

"*Dhanyavad*," I said to the manager, bringing my hands to my heart in *namaskar*. "Thank you so much. Your kindness means more than you could ever know."

⟡

Jay and I stood together on the empty balcony. The last of our guests had straggled home. Now it was just the two of us, staring out over the tent camps and the vast empty fields the way we'd once gazed at the Manhattan skyline from our balcony on the twenty-second floor. I held his hand tight in my palm, needing the strength of his fingers to keep my own steady.

"I'm sorry this wasn't everything we wanted it to be," Jay said. "I guess we really didn't know what we were in for."

"Don't be," I answered. And meant it. "I wouldn't change a thing."

Because, really, what was there to change? There had only been one path to this day, this feeling, this moment. Karma had brought us here, and now karma was taking us home again.

Home. The space I moved and breathed in, the one where I woke up every morning and tried my absolute hardest to live like the day was beautiful and amazing and my very last. I'd learned to love India for what it was, and to let go of my frustrations for all the things it wasn't. I'd learned that embracing a new culture didn't have to mean abandoning the one I'd left behind. Home and happiness had always been right in front of me. I'd just needed to open my eyes to what the universe had been trying to show me all along.

I rested my head on Jay's shoulder just as an explosion of fireworks lit up the dusty night sky.

"Think those are for us?" I asked, only half-kidding. I scooped Tucker into my arms, completing the circle of my own perfect family.

"Hyderabad is celebrating the fact that we're finally going back to where we came from, you mean?"

"Exactly. A bon voyage present. Or an early baby gift," I said, patting my stomach, willing the tiny life form within it to stay strong and grow.

"More likely it's some festival we didn't know about. India always has something to celebrate." Jay ran a hand down my back and pulled me closer.

"Always," I said. We stood there, our faces lit up red and green and blue in the darkness, and looked west over the horizon toward home.

ACKNOWLEDGMENTS

To my agent, Lauren Galit, who earns the adjective "amazing" ten times over, for inspiring me, believing in me, and seeing straight through to the heart of this story in a way no else could have (me included).

To my editor, Shana Drehs, for her unparalleled expertise and enthusiasm, and for her insightful feedback, along with Anna Klenke's, that made this book a hundred times better. To Connie Gabbert, for the beautiful cover design I love more every day, and to Nicole Villeneuve for being the perfect ambassador to bring this book into the world. And to everyone at Sourcebooks, for making the journey incredible and giving my book the perfect home.

To the teachers, editors, and mentors I've leaned on more times than I can count who have offered wisdom and encouragement: Sasha Emmons, David Gates, Vivian Gornick, Daphne Kalotay, Scott Leibs, and Linda Roghaar. And most especially to Helen Smith, who informed me I was a writer and then, with her fierce red pen, taught me to be a better one, and to Helen Schulman, for reminding me to take deep breaths and good notes.

To the dear friends and family members who served as beta readers and champions for this book every step of the way: Jon Feldon, Kent Liu, Robert Mockler, Nancy Molesworth, Jason and Amanda Tracey, and my "other half" Katie Hurley, who is living proof that karma is everywhere…even on the Internet. And to the incomparable Ed., who catches my typos before I've even made them.

To the entire 'Bad crew, for the adventure of a lifetime.

To Soleil Moon Frye, for the exciting journeys we've taken together and the ones still to come. There's no one I'd rather make dreams come true with.

To Katie Donohue, Alexina Vick, and Laura Dine Million, for every cup of coffee at the kitchen table and every glass of wine on the living room floor—I am so grateful for your friendship.

To Milcy Palacios, for taking care of my children and loving them like crazy during the hours I spent lost in my world of words, for taking equally good care of me in the moments I was running on empty, and for the strong Guatemalan coffee that fueled me through the longest of nights.

To Dorothy Cohen, for the artistry in her soul she passed on to me.

To Sylvia Feldman, for her limitless supply of love, wisdom, kisses, and matzo balls, and for believing in me and inspiring me every single day.

To my parents, Nan and Paul Feldon, for teaching me to dream big, and for a lifetime of unconditional love and steadfast support, plus lots of Krazy Glue and chicken noodle soup. And to Jon and Jess Feldon for being the best partners in crime a big sister could ask for.

To my husband Jay, for supporting my dreams in every imaginable way, and for the beautiful life we've built that turned out to be so much better than all those dreams put together. (And, of course, for dragging me to India in the first place.)

To my children Eva and Noah: You light up my world; you are my everything. I love you fifty-five million gazillion a hundred infinity… plus one.

And to Tucker: my first "child," my third-world sidekick, and my furry muse…I couldn't have done any of it without you.

ABOUT THE AUTHOR

Jenny Feldon was born in California and grew up in Newton, Massachusetts. She completed her bachelor's degree in English literature at Boston University and earned her MFA in creative writing from the New School University in New York City. Her work has appeared in nonfiction anthologies, as well as many online and print publications. She writes the popular blog Karma (continued…) and was named one of BlogHer's Voices of the Year in 2012.

Jenny lives in Los Angeles with her family, where she balances writing, motherhood, and giant cups of coffee…mostly all at once. *Karma Gone Bad* is her first book. Visit her website at www.jennyfeldon.com.